The MMPI-2
in Psychological
Treatment

The MMPI-2
in Psychological
Treatment

The MMPI-2 in Psychological Treatment

JAMES NEAL BUTCHER

University of Minnesota

New York   Oxford
OXFORD UNIVERSITY PRESS
1990

Oxford University Press

Oxford New York Toronto
Delhi Bombay Calcutta Madras Karachi
Petaling Jaya Singapore Hong Kong Tokyo
Nairobi Dar es Salaam Cape Town
Melbourne Auckland

and associated companies in
Berlin Ibadan

Published by Oxford University Press, Inc.,
198 Madison Avenue, New York, New York 10016-4314

Oxford is a registered trademark of Oxford University Press

Library of Congress Cataloging-in-Publication Data
Butcher, James Neal, 1933–
MMPI-2 in psychological treatment / James Neal Butcher.
p. cm. Includes bibliographical references.
ISBN 0-19-506344-9
1. Minnesota Multiphasic Personality Inventory. I. Title.
RC473.M5B87 1990
616.89′075—dc20 89-78535 CIP

5 6 7 8 9

Printed in the United States of America
on acid-free paper

Foreword

Over the past 50 years, the Minnesota Multiphasic Personality Inventory (MMPI) has become the most widely used clinical testing instrument in the United States. Its utility and practical value have gone unchallenged and, as thousands of studies document, it has been subjected to critical research unlike any other test. Its popularity among practicing clinicians and researchers has remained high, which is surely eloquent testimony to its value. The revised version, MMPI-2, is intended to update the original by bringing it in line with various developments in psychological assessment and treatment. The present volume, devoted entirely to treatment planning, represents a particularly welcome addition to the clinical literature.

Why has treatment planning come to assume such prominence in recent years? Among important and interrelated reasons, one should mention concerted efforts to make psychotherapy more efficient and cost effective, the growing influence of "third parties" (insurance companies and the federal government) that are called upon to foot the bill for psychological as well as medical treatments, and society's disenchantment with open-ended forms of psychotherapy without clearly defined goals. This statement should not be interpreted to mean that psychotherapy should always be brief or limited—in certain cases long-term therapy remains the realistic and rational choice—but the thrust is certainly in the former direction. Research has also led to the realization that many patients are more or less unsuited for therapies predicated on the formation of an interpersonal relationship between patient and therapist. Today, there are other treatment options whose potential value must be studied in greater detail and depth. The search for the "right" therapy for the "right" patient continues unabated, and there is also greater recognition that the therapist's personality and skill must be factored into the equation. In addition, psychopharmacological agents can often be of great help.

For these reasons, and others, careful assessment of a patient's personality resources and liabilities is of inestimable importance. It will predictably save money and avoid misplaced therapeutic effort; it can also enhance the likelihood of favorable treatment outcomes for suitable patients. In these endeavors the MMPI will play an important role—even greater than has been true in the past.

As Dr. Butcher discusses in clear and understandable language, there are, of course, many other uses for diagnostic information obtained from the MMPI and its computerized printout. In the psychotherapy process and outcome studies conducted by my research group, the MMPI has been used as a valuable instrument for tracking change and evaluating treatment outcomes.

For practicing therapists, particularly those in private practice who have no access to a diagnostic team, the MMPI can provide an economical overview of the patient's potential for a particular form of psychotherapy. Giving the patient useful feedback is another important application.

Obviously, no diagnostic instrument can be a panacea, and while information derived from an MMPI profile can be of great value, it must be viewed in the context of the particular treatment situation and the emerging patient–therapist relationship. In my experience, the MMPI is more useful in identifying obstacles and limitations in a patient's suitability for psychodynamic therapy than in highlighting his or her strengths. The perceptive therapist, however, can make appropriate allowances as therapy gets under way. In the hands of a skilled clinician, the MMPI yields even more valuable data.

Among the great virtues of the MMPI are its foundation in empirical data, the meaningfulness of its scales and profiles, and the straightforwardness of its ability to translate complex clinical phenomena into readily understandable language irrespective of the clinician's theoretical preferences. Dr. Butcher's book is in the best MMPI tradition and will undoubtedly take its place as a valuable contribution to the literature. I wish it godspeed!

Nashville, Tennessee   Hans H. Strupp

Preface

The first major revision of the MMPI in 50 years has been completed. The MMPI-2, as it is called, is now available and will likely become an even more widely used instrument over the next few years than the original version. It provides a broadened set of personality and clinical measures in addition to the traditional scales that have worked so well for so long.

Given the broad application of the original MMPI in clinical practice and research, the expanded MMPI-2 will likely be quickly incorporated into contemporary clinical settings since it provides clear continuity with the original instrument through the validity and clinical scales. MMPI-2 incorporates new and expanded ways of viewing personality characteristics and clinical problems through measures that address the major content dimensions reported by the client.

Practitioners are finding more and more that careful psychological assessment of individuals in pretreatment planning is an important clinical function. Of major importance is the goal of arriving at an acceptable, workable treatment plan consistent with the client's personality features and environmental resources. Several new measures in the MMPI-2, specifically the Work Interference scale and Negative Treatment Indicators scale, focus on issues that are particularly relevant to treatment decisions. My hope is that practitioners will find the discussion of the new content scales valuable in framing sound personality descriptions and in formulating realistic treatment plans.

Another important goal in clinical assessment for treatment planning is the need to provide the client with valid, useful personality information. In my own clinical practice, I have found that the self-report information available through the MMPI-2 provides considerable information for the client. The MMPI-2 descriptions, particularly the content scales, are "direct quotes" by the patient about his or her own problems. Introduced properly, this information can be usefully viewed by clients as a friendly "outside opinion" in their search for information about themselves.

Finally, an important side effect of using the MMPI-2 in treatment planning is the fact that it promotes better communication between clinician and client. The MMPI-2 provides clues to problems that therapy will address and issues with which patients will need to come to terms if changes are to be incorporated into their lives. I believe that the procedures and interpretive material described in this book will help promote more open communication and facilitate more direct interaction between client and clinician.

My purpose in writing this book was to provide diagnosticians who are using the MMPI-2 in clinical settings an effective guide to assessing the client's problems and viewing the clinical assessment. The procedures used in interpreting MMPIs for clients, as discussed in this book, have been developed over a number of years of treatment planning in clinical practice. I hope the procedures for integrating personality assessment study into the treatment process will enhance your clinical interactions as I believe they have mine.

PLAN OF THE BOOK

This book is devoted to an exploration of how the MMPI-2 can be used in psychological treatment planning to provide the client with relevant information and to help the clinician develop an external frame of reference for the patient's problem. To begin, a descriptive overview of the MMPI-2, with a summary of the empirical correlates of the MMPI-2 validity and clinical scales, is given in Chapter 2. Chapter 3 presents a summary of available treatment-related information that can be obtained from the clinical scales and provides many of the MMPI-2 code types. In using the summary format I have tried to bring together in a single chapter what is known about the use of the traditional MMPI scales in treatment evaluation. Most of the descriptive material was culled from the empirical literature on the MMPI in treatment contexts. Chapter 4 contains information on the content-interpretation approach to the MMPI-2. Several MMPI-2 content scales have been found useful for treatment evaluation, and these are described in some detail. Chapter 5 is devoted to a discussion of several MMPI-2 "special scales," like the Ego strength (Es) scale and the MacAndrew addiction scale—revised (MAC-R), which have been found to provide specific treatment-related information about the client's present self-orientation. The use of computerized psychological interpretation in treatment planning is included in Chapter 6. Chapter 7 discusses a procedure with which to provide test feedback to clients, which is illustrated with several clinical examples. Finally, Chapter 8 provides a summary and overview of the issues covered in this book.

ACKNOWLEDGMENTS

I would like to express my appreciation to Yossef S. Ben-Porath, Ted Henrichs, and Jack Graham, who provided valuable feedback on an earlier version of the manuscript.

I am also grateful to my medical colleagues, Drs. David Zanick, Alex Webb, Dean Erickson, and Charles Hipp of the Airport Medical Clinic in Minneapolis, Minnesota, and to Thomas Jetzer, formerly of the Airport Medical Clinic, for their support and ample diagnostic and treatment referrals over the years.

Minneapolis, Minnesota   J. N. B.
September 1, 1989

Contents

1

Importance of Psychological Assessment in Treatment Planning

Psychological treatment—whether psychodynamic, behavioral, or based on some other theoretical viewpoint—proceeds best when both the therapist and the client understand the client's problems and weaknesses, resources and strengths. The task of assessment may precede the initiation of treatment or it may be ongoing throughout therapy. Therapists of different theoretical views approach the task of assessing and evaluating the client from different avenues. Assessment can involve providing a "normative framework" within which the therapist can compare the patient's problem with others, or it may be more "idiographic," with the therapist seeking to understand the patient on his or her own terms.

This book is devoted to appraising and understanding self-reported problems and personality factors of clients by bringing to them the objective perspective of the Minnesota Multiphasic Personality Inventory (MMPI-2), the most widely researched and most frequently used clinical assessment instrument. Before delving into the applications of the MMPI-2 in treatment planning, let us explore some general issues related to the use of psychological tests in mental health evaluation.

WHY USE PSYCHOLOGICAL TESTS?

What benefit can a client derive from a therapist who uses psychological tests in pretreatment evaluation? A person facing the difficult task of gaining self-knowledge through therapy with an eye toward making or consolidating important changes into his or her life is committed to the task of self-scrutiny. The therapy setting itself, particularly in relationship-oriented treatment, provides an arena for personal discovery of behaviors, attitudes, and motivations that might evoke painful emotions. In the course of therapy a skillful therapist and a willing, motivated client can uncover many of the sources of difficulties that plague the patient, and they may have considerable opportunity to explore them in depth. Not all therapies, however, have the luxury of time or involve an insight-

3

ful, verbally fluent patient. Psychological assessment can provide a short-cut and, at times, a clearly defined path on the way to revealing a client's problems. Psychological assessment through the use of objective tests can offer an "outside" opinion about personality maladjustment and symptomatic behavior. The descriptive and predictive information obtained through a psychological measure like the MMPI-2 can provide both therapist and patient with invaluable clues to the nature and source of problems. In addition, such information may forewarn of possibly dangerous psychological "minefields," as well as reveal areas of potential growth.

In most cases, psychological assessment is undertaken as a means of obtaining information that will be helpful to the client in therapy. Foremost among the benefits of pretherapy assessment is that psychological testing can provide information about motivation, fears, attitudes, defensive styles, and symptoms of which the client may be unaware. As we will see, psychological test results can provide both client and therapist with a normative framework from which such problems can be viewed. All clients need to be evaluated, understood, and at times confronted by information outside their personal awareness. They need to know how severe their problems are in comparison to those of other people. Patients seek and deserve to have personal feedback from their therapists about the nature and extent of their problems. Psychological testing provides an excellent framework within which *initial* feedback may be provided.

Test-based descriptions and predictions, even though they may only reaffirm a person's expectations or beliefs, nevertheless serve an important function: they bring into focus important material needed for the therapeutic exchange. Moreover, through the use of the MMPI-2 validity indicators, the individual's openness to treatment can be discerned. It is usually assumed that patients who enter therapy are motivated to seek help and to become engaged in the task of describing and relating their problems to the therapist. It is further assumed that patients, because they want to be understood, are accessible to the therapist's inquiries and will disclose problems appropriately. Unfortunately, the assumption that patients are ready to engage in the treatment process is not always well founded. The MMPI-2 validity indicators provide a direct test of a patient's readiness for treatment. By directly assessing response attitudes, the therapist can evaluate the patient's level of cooperativeness and encourage or reinforce the willingness to engage in the task of self-disclosure. For example, patients who produce defensive, uncooperative test patterns, as reflected in the test validity scores, may likewise be relatively inaccessible to the therapist during sessions. When the therapist has this knowledge early in the treatment process, problems of lack of trust or hesitancy to disclose personal information can be confronted.

Personality assessment instruments have three major applications in treatment planning: in pretreatment planning, in assessing progress dur-

ing therapy, and in posttreatment evaluation. The functions of these assessments differ somewhat and so need to be addressed separately.

PRETREATMENT PLANNING: OBTAINING AN "OUTSIDE OPINION"

It may seem obvious that people in treatment need to have pertinent,
objective information about themselves if they are to know what behaviors need to be changed. Thus, providing patients with objective information about themselves and their problems becomes one of the most
important tasks the therapist undertakes. Psychological test results provide a valuable framework from which clients can obtain information
about themselves. For example, the symptoms and problems a person is
reporting can be viewed in an objective framework in comparison with
thousands of other troubled individuals; clues to a person's coping strategies are also obtainable in the MMPI-2; and the client's need for treatment is reflected in the profile. Normative psychological testing can provide a valuable perspective that allows a person to view personal
problems from a different vantage point and to obtain an objective measure of the extent of such problems.

Moreover, people who are seeking professional help to remedy psychological or interpersonal problems are usually motivated to learn all
they can about themselves. Test feedback sessions can involve patients in
the clinical process. And yet psychological treatment can be a difficult
undertaking for the client. It is a path that may be filled with countless
obstacles and deep emotional chasms; however, it promises the client
help through a time of trouble. The client is faced with the task of disclosing to a stranger a great deal of personal information that may be
painful to recall. It may at times seem to the client to be a hopeless
mess—too difficult to sort through and even more difficult to formulate
into words and sentences that can be relayed to another person.

A client's problems or beliefs may have been stored away for a long
time and may only be selectively remembered. The self-expression of
troubled individuals is frequently hampered by bits and pieces of mem-
ories that enter into consciousness in a random fashion. It is difficult for
the therapist to know what to focus on and what to ignore. And, certainly, some of these pieces of information are believed by the client to
be too dangerous to report to anyone—even to a professional who pro-
poses to help. Therefore, early treatment sessions are frequently filled
with gaps and "untold secrets," either because the client cannot accurately remember, cannot articulate well, or consciously chooses not to
report.

Furthermore, many people entering treatment for the first time have
an unclear or confused picture of their problems and may actually be

unaware of the presence or extent of their psychological distress. Thus, it is usually valuable to provide feedback to patients early in the treatment to determine if there is any recognized or unspoken problem that requires attention. And confronting problems can be an important motivational element in the early stages of psychotherapy.

Another important benefit of using psychological tests in pretreatment evaluation is that they identify problems that are not apparent from the clinical interview. In fact, psychological test results might reveal issues or problems that the therapist and patient did not discuss in initial interviews. For example, in one case a patient failed to disclose the extent of his substance abuse and the impact it was having on his life. His MacAndrew Addiction (MAC-R) score on the MMPI-2 (an addiction proneness scale; see Chapter 5) was in the range (raw score 28) that is highly suggestive of alcohol abuse. When the therapist discussed this score with the patient as an indicator of possible problems, the patient acknowledged, after an initial denial, that alcohol addiction was likely to be a factor.

As we will discuss in more detail later, people who seek help feel the need to be understood by the therapist; they usually appreciate the therapist's efforts to know them. Consequently, when a therapist communicates the need for pretreatment testing to gain a better understanding of a client, the client will generally recognize the therapist's purpose and will respond positively.

The therapist should recognize, however, that clients who have undergone pretreatment testing feel that they have disclosed a great deal of personal information and will seek some acknowledgment of the risk they have taken. Most patients want to know their test results and would like the therapist to provide detailed feedback of what it all means.

TREATMENT PROGRESS: EVALUATION OF ONGOING TREATMENT CASES

There may be more than a grain of truth in the humorously intended comment that therapy is a process by which an emotionally disturbed person gradually convinces the therapist that his or her unswerving view of the world, though bizarre, is in fact real. Therapists are notorious for their efforts to understand and accept individual idiosyncrasies and pathology. Indeed, one of the highly desirable qualities of a therapist is the ability to provide "unconditional positive regard" to an individual whose behavior is seemingly unacceptable to others. But in addition to providing much needed support for the patient, acceptance of patient pathology can also lead to a loss of perspective on the part of the therapist. Thus, periodic psychological assessment during therapy or at its completion is an important facet of psychological treatment. Retest evaluation in the course of therapy can promote accountability and further encourage the patient's self-examination.

The use of an objective instrument like the MMPI-2 to monitor progress in therapy can provide an external view of the patient's pathology and the progress being made in treatment. For example, a 29-year-old man (see MMPI-2 profile in Figure 1-1) sought treatment because he was so fearful that he was going to be fired from his job and so sure that things were out of his control that he was unable to go to work. In the initial therapeutic interview he appeared fearful, ruminative, tense, and anxious, and he was self-critical about being unable to perform his job. He had worked for his present company for about 5 years and had recently been promoted to a new position that required more interpersonal skill and assertiveness. He felt that he was not performing well (although his supervisors were pleased with his work) and believed that he was going to be fired because of his ineffectiveness. His high level of distress is shown in Figure 1-1 in the marked elevation on scales 2 and 7.

He was referred to a female therapist with the recommendation that the initial treatment goals might be to reduce the high levels of anxiety and to help him become effective in dealing with his immediate concerns over his job. The therapist, employing a cognitive–behavioral treatment approach, initiated efforts to reduce the work-related stress and then "inoculated" the client against a return to the level of distress he had experienced. The first eight therapeutic sessions were supportive efforts to assist him in reducing his tensions while getting him to return to work. The therapist assisted him in problem solving while providing the appropriate feedback. The client showed marked improvement at work and became confident that he would be able to perform the job satisfactorily. He was retested on the MMPI-2 after eight sessions and produced the MMPI-2 profile shown in Figure 1-2. Inspection of the profile indicates a considerable reduction in tension and anxiety, as apparent in the reduction in scale 7.

Both the client and therapist were confident that his initial goal of dealing with work stress had been met. The MMPI-2 profile, however, revealed other significant clinical problems, particularly depression, withdrawal, and social isolation. In providing test feedback for the patient, the therapist was able to focus on the great success he had had in dealing with his fears and insecurities on the job. She praised him for the gains he had made in overcoming many of his problems and pointed out the need to shift the treatment goals toward reducing his depression and social isolation. In making this shift, the therapist and her client explored his unrealistic expectations and examined how these negatively affected his self-evaluations. In addition, she encouraged her client to deal with his social isolation by becoming more active and assertive in

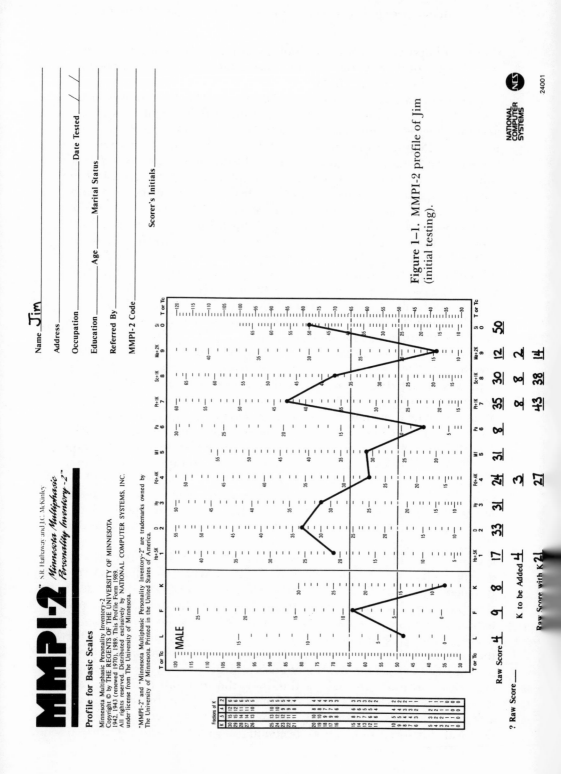

Figure 1–1. MMPI-2 profile of Jim (initial testing).

8

MMPI-2™ S.R. Hathaway and J.C. McKinley
Minnesota Multiphasic Personality Inventory-2™

Profile for Basic Scales

Minnesota Multiphasic Personality Inventory-2
Copyright © by THE REGENTS OF THE UNIVERSITY OF MINNESOTA
1942, 1943 (renewed 1970). 1989. This Profile Form 1989.
All rights reserved. Distributed exclusively by NATIONAL COMPUTER SYSTEMS, INC.
under license from The University of Minnesota.

"MMPI-2" and "Minnesota Multiphasic Personality Inventory-2" are trademarks owned by
The University of Minnesota. Printed in the United States of America.

MALE

Name __Jim [Re-test]__

Address _____

Occupation _____ Date Tested __/__/__

Education _____ Age _____ Marital Status _____

Referred By _____

MMPI-2 Code _____

Scorer's Initials _____

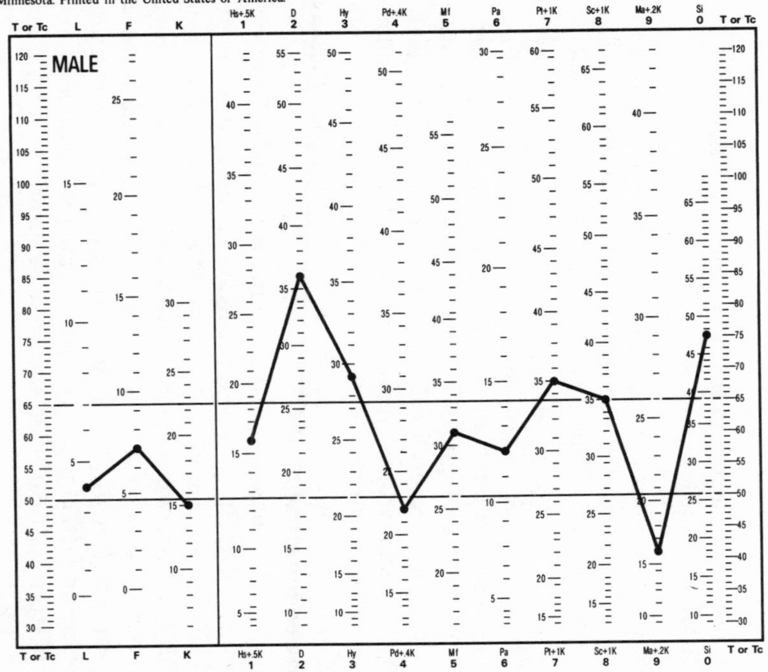

	L	F	K	Hs+5K 1	D 2	Hy 3	Pd+4K 4	Mf 5	Pa 6	Pt+1K 7	Sc+1K 8	Ma+2K 9	Si 0
Raw Score	6	7	15	8	36	29	16	31	12	20	20	13	47
K to be Added	8			8			6			15	15	3	
Raw Score with K	16			16			22			35	35	16	

? Raw Score _____

Figure 1–2. MMPI-2 profile of Jim
(retesting during therapy).

NATIONAL
COMPUTER
SYSTEMS

24001

9

developing social relationships. In this case intermediate testing revealed the progress made and new goals to be met, and was of significant value in the therapeutic outcome.

POSTTREATMENT EVALUATION

Psychological evaluation at the end of treatment can be an important aspect of the therapeutic process. It enables the client and the therapist to appraise the changes made and to gain insight into problems the client may encounter as therapy ends, as well as the resources the client can call on to meet such problems. As a result of end-of-treatment testing, clients can get a sense of their progress and gain the confidence that comes from being more in control of their personal life than when treatment began.

Psychometric Factors in the Assessment of Change in MMPI-2 Profiles

Clinicians and researchers using the MMPI in treatment evaluation have long been aware of the stability of MMPI profiles over time. Test–retest among various groups has been reported to be moderate to high depending on the population studied and the retest interval used (Dahlstrom, Welsh, & Dahlstrom, 1975). Even test–retest correlations over very long retest intervals, 30 years, for example (Leon et al., 1979), have reportedly been high, with some scales (Si) showing correlations as high as .736. One reason for the high test–retest stability is that the original MMPI contained many extreme items that draw similar endorsement, even over long periods. Studies (Goldberg & Jones, 1969; Schofield, 1950) have shown that many MMPI items, about 87 percent, are similarly endorsed when the test is administered on two different occasions. The MMPI-2 has included some items that may be more susceptible to change on retest; however, the heavy "trait saturation" in the item pool is likely to be characteristic of the MMPI-2 item pool as well. Although MMPI responses gravitate toward stability at retest in group studies, it is interesting that an individual, after a major traumatic event or after treatment, can display a dramatic shift from initial testing to retest. Dahlstrom (1972) reported a very dramatic example of an MMPI profile shift from a spike 9 profile to a 42 profile over 7 months following therapy.

Another factor that makes assessment of change in MMPI-2 profiles after treatment difficult is that retest profiles tend to regress toward the mean on the second testing. Profiles, for example in inpatient groups, are in general highly elevated at initial testing. Even without an accompanying behavioral change, profiles tend to be lower in elevation at retest. It may be difficult to know at retest how much scale elevation change to expect on the basis of the regression phenomenon. Interpretation of change in a patient's profile at retest should be made cautiously. It is clear that interpretations should not be made unless the differences exceed the standard error of measurement (SE_m) for the scale (Butcher et al., 1989) and preferably are two times the SE_m for conservative personality appraisal.

Illustration of Posttreatment Change

A posttreatment evaluation can provide valuable information for the therapist because it permits assessment of the effects of the treatment on the client's personality and symptoms. It allows the therapist to determine if, for example, mood changes have occurred or if the client is experiencing problems in controlling anger. An evaluation of the individual's attitudes and behavior at this point, when one hopes that most significant issues have been resolved, can provide the therapist with insight into major unresolved issues or problems that the client is likely to face at the termination of therapy. The case that follows illustrates the use of MMPI-2 in evaluating progress in treatment and in enabling the therapist to understand the client's psychological adjustment as he or she leaves treatment.

▶ Illustration of a Test–Retest MMPI-2 Following Psychotherapy: A Case History

A 23-year-old man named Ed, who had recently moved to the Midwest, was referred for psychological treatment by his therapist in his hometown on the East Coast. Ed had moved to get away from his family, particularly his father, the tyrannical owner of a large manufacturing firm. Ed had been very unhappy working for his father and one day, without telling anyone his plans, left family, job, and Porsche and headed West on his motorcycle. He stopped in St. Paul, got a job as an accounting clerk, and started a new life, but he soon became dissatisfied and, at the suggestion of his previous therapist, sought psychological treatment in St. Paul.

Presenting Symptoms
Ed appeared to be depressed and anxious when he came to his first appointment. He reported that he felt pessimistic about his future and thought he might not be able to accomplish his goal of becoming independent. He was obsessive about being inadequate and unable to think for himself. He felt lonely, isolated, and very unsure of himself socially. He had particular difficulty initiating conversations, and was having trouble making new friends. Ed reported a considerable amount of anger toward his father and a sense of inadequacy and inferiority that resulted from feeling "oppressed" by his

father. He also complained of physical problems—especially headaches, when he worked for his father, and stomachaches. He felt so depressed that he did not venture out of his roominghouse in the evenings. He was inactive and stayed glued to the television because that took no energy. He knew no one in town and felt he would not be a very good friend to anyone now anyway because he "was too self-preoccupied."

Comment on the Initial MMPI-2

Ed approached the testing in a frank and open manner, producing a valid MMPI-2 profile (see Figure 1-3). He related a number of psychological adjustment problems and seemingly was seeking help in overcoming them. The MMPI-2 clinical profile highlights a number of problems and symptoms that Ed was experiencing at the time of his first treatment session. He reported being depressed and anxious about his situation and related feeling tense, lonely, and insecure. He appeared to be having great difficulty concentrating on his work and was indecisive. He had no zest for life and was preoccupied with his inability to accomplish personal goals. The relatively high score on the Psychopathic deviate scale (Pd) reflects rebellious attitudes and family conflict (the Harris–Lingoes Family Problems Scale, Pd1, was T = 69). He appeared to be a somewhat passive young man who reported being shy and isolated.

Psychotherapy

Ed was seen in psychological treatment for 6 months. During the assessment phase, the therapist provided emotional support and listened to his perceptions of his problems and feelings about his family. This therapeutic approach is best described as cognitive–behavioral treatment for depression. The therapeutic goals included helping Ed to see his situation differently by exploring his expectations and providing him positive feedback when he was able to experiment with alternative (more adaptive) approaches to a problem. For example, the therapist provided positive reinforcement by praising Ed when he began to take steps to break his isolation and meet other people. The therapist encouraged him to experiment with and adopt more effective behaviors, and through role-playing, provided Ed with some techniques for meeting other people and for asserting himself in appropriate ways.

Ed used the therapy hours to great advantage and implemented alternative behaviors effectively. Before long, he began developing a circle of friends and became socially active. He played in a soccer league and joined several singles groups. During the first 3 months of therapy, he avoided contact with his parents. (It is interesting that his treatment bills were paid by his father, who mailed payment to Ed's previous therapist, who then forwarded the payment to his present therapist.) During the latter period of treatment, Ed began to view his relationship with his parents in a different light. He no longer saw himself as a "helpless wimp" who had to go along with his father's wishes. He was feeling fairly comfortable with his work, even though it was "pretty boring," and began to feel that he had showed his "old man." At the termination of therapy, Ed thought that he might be able to visit his family but really felt that things were working out

MMPI-2™

S.R. Hathaway and J.C. McKinley
Minnesota Multiphasic Personality Inventory-2™

Name _Ed_

Address _____

Occupation _Clerical_   Date Tested __/__/__

Education _____ Age _____ Marital Status _Single_

Referred By _____

MMPI-2 Code _____

Scorer's Initials _____

Profile for Basic Scales

Minnesota Multiphasic Personality Inventory-2
Copyright © by THE REGENTS OF THE UNIVERSITY OF MINNESOTA
1942, 1943 (renewed 1970), 1989. This Profile Form 1989.
All rights reserved. Distributed exclusively by NATIONAL COMPUTER SYSTEMS, INC.
under license from The University of Minnesota.

"MMPI-2" and "Minnesota Multiphasic Personality Inventory-2" are trademarks owned by
The University of Minnesota. Printed in the United States of America.

MALE

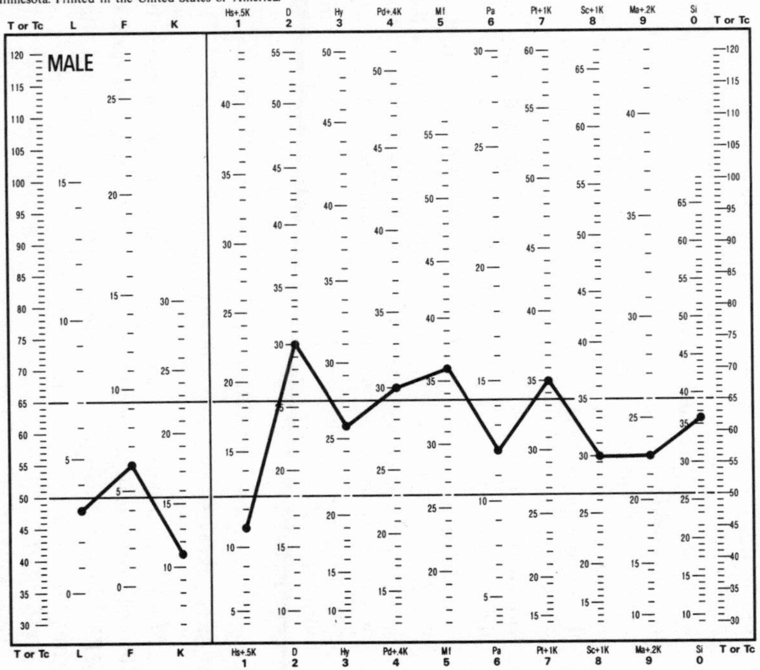

	L	F	K	Hs+.5K 1	D 2	Hy 3	Pd+.4K 4	Mf 5	Pa 6	Pt+1K 7	Sc+1K 8	Ma+.2K 9	Si 0
Raw Score	3	6	11	5	30	26	26	36	12	24	19	21	36
? Raw Score													
K to be Added			6				4			11	11	2	
Raw Score with K			11	6	30		30			35	30	23	

Figure 1-3. Case of Ed: Pretreatment MMPI-2 clinical profile.

NATIONAL COMPUTER SYSTEMS

24001

13

well where he was. He was busy every night and had no time to go home for a visit. He surmised that he might return home someday but certainly not under the old circumstances.

Posttreatment MMPI-2 Profile

Retesting at the end of Ed's treatment showed significant changes in his self-reported symptoms and behavior as reflected by the MMPI-2. His validity scale pattern depicted a clear shift from an essentially problem-oriented presentation of symptoms to one that revealed few psychological problems. As with most people who show improvement in psychological treatment, Ed's K score increased in magnitude over his initial test administration (Barron, 1953), and he reported fewer symptoms, as reflected by the lower F scale elevation.

The most significant change in his posttreatment clinical picture (see Figure 1-4) was the overall lowering of the profile, with all scales below a T-score of 64. Most dramatic was the large drop in the Depression scale. Ed was clearly reporting few symptoms indicative of depression. His mood had improved markedly, and he did not appear to be having the same problems of low self-esteem and depressed mood. Similarly, he produced a lower elevation on the Psychasthenia scale (Pt), revealing that his morale had improved considerably since the first test administration. The anger and irritation directed at his family members, reflected in the Pd scale, were not as pronounced as they were in the initial test. Interesting shifts in two generally stable aspects of the profile occurred as well: Ed showed less elevation on the Masculinity–Femininity (Mf) and the Social Introversion (Si) scales. Both of these profile changes probably resulted, in part, from his having taken a more active approach to his problems. During treatment he made some changes in his day-to-day activities that altered the way he perceived himself; he became more socially active and reached out to other people more effectively. He became a member of a soccer team whose activities, on and off the field, were "macho." In addition, part of his treatment program involved initiating social relationships with women. He began dating and found several new circles of friends, which resulted in a lessening of the social isolation he had been experiencing at initial testing.

Use of the MMPI in Treatment Evaluation Research

The MMPI has been used extensively as a criterion measure in the evaluation of treatment approaches. A detailed discussion of the use of the MMPI-2 in psychological treatment research is beyond the scope of this volume; however, the reader should be aware of the extensive research on the MMPI in treatment evaluation studies. Readers interested in research in MMPI changes following treatment would find the following studies informative: in general psychopathological samples, see Moras and Strupp, 1982; Skoog, Anderson, and Laufer, 1984; and Chodzko-Zajko and Ismail, 1984. In chronic pain treatment, see Brandwin and Kewman, 1982; Long, 1981; Malec, 1983; Moore, Armentrout, Parker, and Kivlahan, 1986; Oostdam, Duivenvoorden, and Pondaas, 1981;

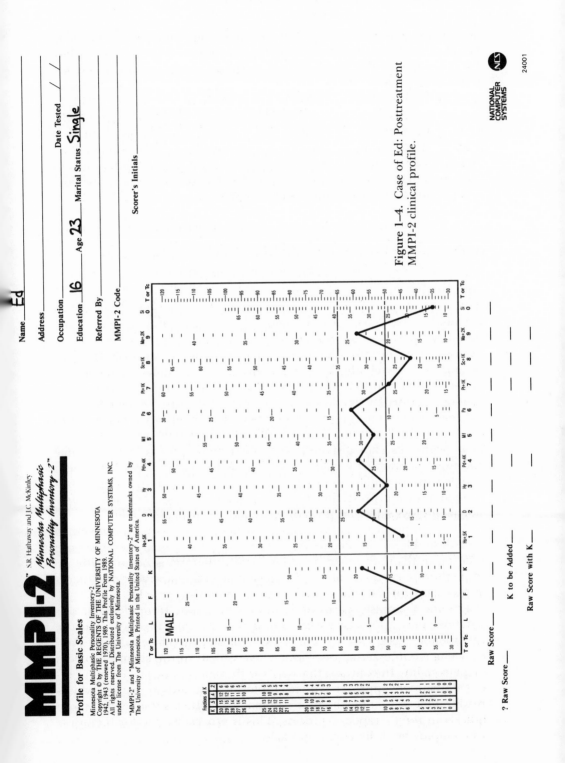

Figure 1-4. Case of Ed: Posttreatment MMPI-2 clinical profile.

Strassberg, Reimherr, Ward, Russell, and Cole, 1981; Sweet, Breuer, Hazelwood, Toye, and Pawl, 1985; Turner, Herron, and Weiner, 1986; Uomoto, Turner, and Herron, 1988. In substance abuse populations, see Cernousky, 1984; Ottomaneli, Wilson, and Whyte, 1978; Pettinati, Sugerman, and Maurer, 1982; Thurstin, Alfano, and Sherer, 1986. In mixed samples, see Archer, Gordon, Zillmer, and McClure, 1985; Walker, Blankenship, Ditty, and Lynch, 1987; Walters, Solomon, and Walker, 1982; Young, Gould, Glick, and Hargreaves, 1980. An excellent comprehensive summary of the use of the MMPI in psychotherapy outcome research, mostly summarizing research on treatment of depression, was provided by Hollon and Mandell (1979).

THE THERAPIST'S ROLE IN TREATMENT EVALUATION

The primary thesis of this book is that there is an accumulated base of knowledge about personality and its maladjustment that is pertinent to making treatment decisions about individuals in therapy. The field of personality assessment provides both methods and substantive information to support treatment-oriented evaluation. My aim is to explore the extensive base of information, particularly from the MMPI-2, that can be applied in psychotherapeutic assessments to facilitate understanding of the patient and to appraise the effectiveness of the treatment intervention. Given that feedback is an important aspect of psychological treatment, it is interesting to consider why some therapists choose not to conduct formal personality assessments of their patients before treatment begins. Psychologists and psychiatrists undergo extensive academic and practical training to gain knowledge and experience needed to help people with psychological problems. Although the training backgrounds of mental health professionals and treatment roles differ, each professional employs skills and procedures to aid problem assessment.

Although pretreatment assessment of personality seems intuitively to be a desirable, if not necessary, task, many professional therapists use little more than an intake interview before therapy is begun. Why do some therapists choose not to do a psychological assessment of patients at pretreatment? Several possible factors can be identified.

1. Some therapists, particularly those with a long-term, dynamic orientation, may approach psychological therapy with the view that the therapeutic process itself is the assessment and therefore may not typically engage in external or objective assessment of the client's problem or personality. In contrast, therapists with a more directive or more focused treatment approach tend to employ outside assessment procedures readily. One reason for the pretreatment evaluation is the need to move quickly in the therapeutic process. This is especially true for therapists who employ brief directive approaches.

2. Another factor that influences pretreatment assessment is the belief of some therapists that tests will *bias* them in their approach to the client. Consequently, they initiate treatment with little or no idea of the nature and extent of the patient's problems. A possible pitfall of this approach is that the therapist cannot determine if major blocks to treatment are likely to occur or if the treatment approach they are planning is the most appropriate one.

Because many treatment effects are specific to a particular treatment rather than general to all treatments, there can be some advantage to the therapist's being aware of benefits that are likely to accrue from treatment efforts with a particular type of problem. For example, through employing objective procedures, therapists can determine if serious relationship or character flaws that would sabotage therapy are present. If so, the therapist may be able to determine more effective ways of initiating treatment. For example, a 37-year-old woman sought therapy after her second divorce. She wanted to enter long-term, dynamic therapy because she viewed her problem as "unique and difficult to understand." She "shopped" for a therapist (without disclosing this wish) by keeping the initial few appointments, during which she put the therapist to a test (which was invariably failed). She then left treatment, only to seek out yet another therapist. Her MMPI-2 profile (a 46 code; see Figure 1-5) revealed the following characteristics:

> rigid, moralistic, vindictive, aggressive, and secretive; given to hasty generalizations; shows suspicious behavior; is unchanging in the face of input; impulsive; prone to rationalize her own actions; and has difficulties in forming relationships.

Two previous therapists who had seen her in treatment, seemingly without assessment information, were apparently impressed in the initial interview with her "tendency to gain sudden insight" and her driven "desire to understand herself." However, they were probably unaware that her well-ingrained oppositional behavior led her to jump to conclusions about the therapists' intentions and competency to understand her, and thus led her to reject them.

In this case use of the MMPI-2 provided the third clinician with information about her negative attitudes toward authority figures (including therapists), her tendency to make and hold firm conclusions on the basis of little information, and her inclination to act impulsively. This information forewarned the therapist, who prepared himself and the patient for a stormy opening treatment session. The patient herself became disarmed by the early but friendly confrontation of her difficulties, particularly in forming relationships, to the point that she was challenged to stick with therapy longer than she had in the past.

3. Some therapists do not employ external assessment strategies to

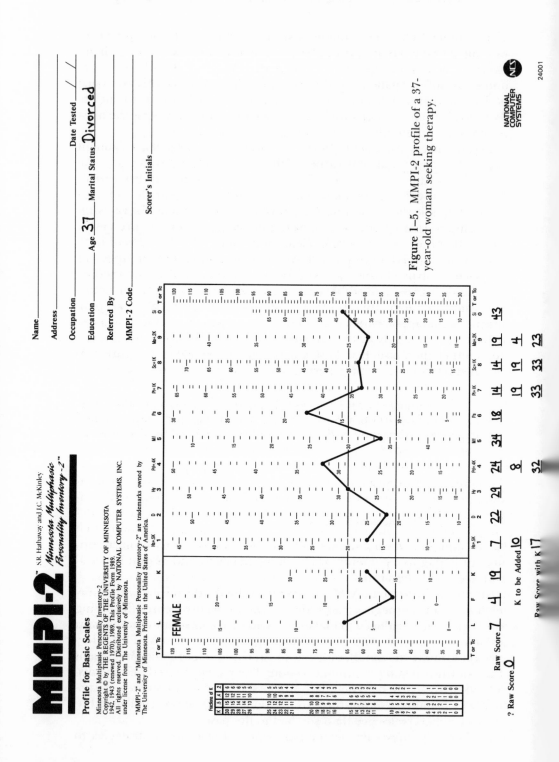

Figure 1–5. MMPI-2 profile of a 37-year-old woman seeking therapy.

plan treatment or to monitor the progress of therapy. Their training in assessment methods may have been incomplete, or their professional training has led them to the view that psychological assessment is unimportant to understanding the client. Professionals trained in or exposed to one treatment model or one training setting will be shaped to do clinical work in a certain way. For most therapists, the familiar becomes "right," and other techniques are excluded from consideration.

Value of Assessment

An important goal for the therapist is to provide appropriate and useful feedback to the client. Approaching this task directly can help promote an atmosphere of openness in therapy that will have later benefits. The establishment of honest communication is one of the most important early goals of treatment. Indeed, the most prominent challenge in the early stages of psychotherapy is to develop a comfortable relationship that allows disclosure. Basic to productive therapeutic communication is the incorporation of a process that facilitates development of a mutually informing and constructive exploration of problems.

Most therapists, whatever their treatment orientation, are faced with a puzzle—the complicated task of understanding an individual's present difficulties in the context of past experiences, current pressures, social network, aspirations, and other life patterns, and to integrate the findings and apply a workable treatment plan. It is important in the early stages of treatment to increase the flow of relevant information between the patient and therapist and to promote communication and understanding between them. Some professionals rely more on interview and observation; others, particularly psychologists, employ standardized assessment procedures.

The Therapist's Assessment Task

Conducting successful psychological treatment involves more than passively listening to a person describe his or her day or their early life experiences. The therapist has the responsibility of first forming a helping relationship, understanding the person's immediate problems, appraising the person's strengths, resources, and potential, and then developing a program of intervention that will assist in alleviating the individual's problems.

Successful psychological treatment is not simply a friendly, social exchange between two people; it demands that the therapist bring the accumulated evidence of the science of psychology into the treatment setting. People who seek therapy usually view their psychotherapists as experts. Most clients expect that the therapist will apply special techniques or knowledge gained from training and experience that will aid them in resolving their problems. As they enter treatment, patients believe that the mental health specialist will use objective methods and established, proven procedures. Once the therapist has established a tolerant, accepting treatment environment for the patient, it is important to assess the patient's problems and provide appropriate feedback.

The patient, however, may or may not be aware that the specific training and academic background of different professionals qualify them to apply some procedures but not others. For example, having the requisite medical background enables a psychiatrist to prescribe medications for a patient, whereas having a background in clinical or counseling psychology may lead a clinician to use different techniques, such as psychological tests, to help understand their patients' problems.

Regardless of the differences we find among various schools of psychotherapy and psychiatry, we find that patients are consistent in their desire to receive direct feedback about their problems. Feedback, which will assist in a client's recovery, thus becomes a key element in the treatment setting—a necessity at appropriate intervals in the therapeutic process.

The necessity of providing feedback, discussed in more detail in Chapter 7, is variously interpreted by different schools of psychotherapy. Some approaches to treatment give extensive and in-depth psychological feedback to the client early in therapy; others may only indirectly address the task of providing personality and interpersonal data for the patient to incorporate into his or her treatment plan. Perhaps the most extreme viewpoint is the psychoanalytic view, which follows the strategy of limited feedback (i.e., limited direction by the therapist) early in therapy. Interpretations often do not enter into treatment directly; when they do, treatment is much farther along. Other treatment orientations, such as the client-centered approach, provide minimal feedback and operate on the assumption that individuals will, under the unconditional positive regard and assurance of the therapist, eventually develop a consistent view of themselves without much directive feedback from the therapist.

As already noted, after sharing personal information about themselves with a stranger through the psychological assessment, patients need and expect to have their self-disclosure acknowledged by the therapist. They usually appreciate that the therapist has taken the time and effort to discuss and try to understand their problems.

An Objective Means of Providing Feedback

Most psychologists and many psychiatrists are trained in techniques of psychological assessment and methods of providing feedback required in therapy. Beginning with a person's responses to MMPI-2 items is an excellent way to provide feedback. The symptoms, attitudes, feelings, and other test responses are the patient's own self-perceptions, and the therapist organizes them into a standard format (profile or computer-based report) that compares the individual's responses with those of other people.

An interesting and valuable "side effect" of the appropriate use of psychological tests in psychotherapy is that it communicates to the patient that the therapist has available an objective means of—a technology for—evaluating the client. Most patients will voluntarily participate in self-study, and many will recognize and appreciate the effort at accountability that the therapist is addressing in using objective assessment methods. One patient, a certified public accountant, was intrigued when the therapist used an "accounting procedure" to evaluate his problems and then summarized them on a chart! He was very cooperative with the posttreatment evaluation, because he wanted to see what the "bottom line" was in terms of treatment gains at the completion of therapy. Most important, his Depression score on the MMPI-2 had dropped well into the normal range after he had experienced both behavioral and mood improvements.

Role of the MMPI-2 in a Test Battery

In using psychological evaluation for treatment planning, many clinicians incorporate information from a broad base of techniques—clinical interview, projective testing, behavioral data, personal history—and do not rely on data from a single source. This book is about use of the MMPI-2 in treatment planning, but not to the exclusion of other measures. Because of space limitations, other procedures, such as the Rorschach, are not covered in any detail. The reader needs to keep in mind the importance of incorporating non-MMPI-2 information into the test battery and assigning relative importance to information from various sources available to the clinician.

Importance of Demographic and Status Characteristics

The interpretation of any psychological test proceeds best in the context of a personal history. Important aspects of the case—for example, ethnic group membership, education level, marital status, and the presence of a precipitating stressor or trauma—are important variables to consider when MMPI-2 profiles are interpreted. Errors of interpretation can occur if MMPI-2 profiles, or other psychological test protocols, are considered apart from nontest parameters. Blind interpretation of test profiles can provide general information about a client's symptoms and behavior. These impressions, however, need to be verified by direct patient contact. A good discussion of this topic can be found in Heinrichs (1987). The clinician also should keep in mind how relevant "backdrop" variables affect psychological test scores and interpretations. Background variables are important to the appraisal of MMPI-2 scores, and the reader should be familiar with a basic text on the MMPI-2, such as Graham's text (1990).

SUMMARY

The therapist and the patient generally come to the first therapeutic session with differing perceptions of the nature and extent of the problems, what needs to be done in therapy, and how long it will take for the problems to be resolved. Patients typically view their problems as requiring a briefer period of time than therapists do. Therapists often consider time as being on their side and may think that, if they listen attentively for a long enough time, they will discover the source of a person's problems and will be able to assist the patient in resolving them. Research, however, has shown that therapy is usually shorter than therapists anticipate (see Koss & Butcher, 1986).

Clear assessment of the nature and extent of the patient's problem is a pressing concern for the competent, responsible therapist. It becomes imperative for the therapist to use effective means to bring understanding to the problem and to communicate to the patient a clear picture.

2

Introduction to the MMPI-2

Hathaway and McKinley (1940, 1943) originally developed the Minnesota Multiphasic Personality Inventory (MMPI) as a diagnostic aid for use in medical and psychiatric screening. In their original work, they used a method of scale construction referred to as the *empirical* scale development, or criterion referenced strategy, to develop the MMPI clinical scales. The items comprising the clinical scales were selected with the assurance that each item on a given scale actually predicted the criterion or membership in a clinical group. For example, in the development of Scale 2, the Depression scale, responses of patients who were clinically depressed were contrasted with those of a group of "normal" individuals, as well as those of normal individuals and clinical subjects who had high scores on a preliminary depression scale, but who were not clinically depressed. The items that empirically differentiated the groups became the Depression scale; and the individuals who had received high scores on this scale displayed symptoms found in the reference group of depressed patients. The test authors provided a set of appropriate norms for the basic MMPI scales to enable test users to compare a particular patient's scores with responses of a large group of "normal" individuals. Thus a high score on the Depression scale indicates that the patient has responded in a manner similar to the criterion group of depressed patients and different from the normal group.

The MMPI can serve as an objective, reliable screening instrument for appraising a person's personality characteristics and symptomatic behavior. The interpretive information available on the MMPI has been widely researched and documented through more than 50 years of clinical use. More than 12,000 books and articles on the MMPI have been published and it has become the most frequently administered clinical psychological test in the United States (Lubin et al., 1984). Furthermore, there are more than 115 translations of the MMPI, and it is used in some 45 countries (Butcher & Pancheri, 1976; Butcher, 1985). A number of factors account for the MMPI's broad acceptance by researchers and practitioners.

1. The MMPI-2 has been validated for a number of clinical and personality applications. The information it provides is relevant in many settings where personality profiles are helpful. The profile provides the clinician with a visual presentation of important personality information, plotted on an easy-to-read graph for each new case, and it supplies extensive normative and clinical data for profile interpretation. A wide range of descriptive information is available on numerous clinical groups in the published literature.

2. The MMPI-2 provides an *objective evaluation* of the subject's personality characteristics, symptom patterns, and personal attitudes that have been shown, by numerous research studies (i.e., Dahlstrom, Welsh, & Dahlstrom, 1975), to be relevant to many aspects of a clinical profile and prognosis.

3. The MMPI-2 is one of the easiest personality assessment instruments to use in a clinical practice, since it requires little professional time to administer and score; however, the interpretation requires the care, skill, and experience of a trained practitioner.

4. The MMPI-2 is cost effective since administration and scoring can be done by clerical staff. The only professional time required involves the interpretation. (For example, in clinical settings, it usually takes a patient only about an hour and a half to answer the items; it takes a clerk about 15 minutes to hand score and draw a profile; and it takes an experienced interpreter about 30 minutes to prepare a profile interpretation.)

5. MMPI-2 administration, scoring, profile plotting, and even some interpretation can be accomplished by computer. Automated MMPI reports can provide a very detailed and accurate clinical evaluation of a profile.

6. The MMPI-2 is one of the easiest clinical personality tests for students and professionals to learn since there is an abundance of published material on MMPI-2 interpretation for the beginning interpreter. Some suggested general interpretation references follow:

Carson, R. C. (1969). Interpretive manual to the MMPI. In J. N. Butcher (ed). *MMPI: Research developments and clinical applications.* New York: McGraw-Hill.

Finn, S. & Butcher, J. N. (in press). Clinical objective personality assessment. In M. Hersen, A. E. Kazdin, and A. S. Bellack (eds.) *The clinical psychology handbook* (second edition). New York: Pergamon Press.

Graham, J. R. (1987). *The MMPI: A practical guide* (second edition). New York: Oxford University Press.

Graham, J. R. (in press). *MMPI-2: Assessing personality and psychopathology.* New York: Oxford University Press.

Greene, R. (1980). *The MMPI: An interpretive manual.* New York: Grune & Stratton.

DEVELOPMENT OF THE MMPI-2

In response to the problems that had been noted with use of the MMPI (Butcher, 1972; Butcher & Owen, 1987; Colligan et al., 1983), the test publisher, The University of Minnesota Press, initiated a program to revise the MMPI and establish new, nationally representative norms for the instrument. A revision team that included James Butcher, John R. Graham, W. Grant Dahlstrom, and Auke Tellegen was appointed to modify the existing item pool, add new items, and collect new normative data on the instrument.

The revision of the MMPI involved several stages (see Butcher, Dahlstrom, Graham, Tellegen, & Kaemmer, 1989). The existing item pool was modified by rewriting obsolete and awkwardly worded items, deleting repetitive ones, and increasing the content coverage of the item pool by including new items that deal with contemporary problems and applications. Once the revision of the MMPI item pool was complete (14 percent of the original items were rewritten and 154 new items were included to measure additional personality dimensions or problems), Form AX, a 704-item experimental version of the MMPI, was produced for the MMPI restandardization project.

MMPI-2 Norms

To make the MMPI-2 relevant for contemporary populations, a large, nationally representative sample of subjects was randomly solicited from several regions of the United States to serve as the normative population. New T-score transformations were developed based on the MMPI-2 normative sample, which contained 2,600 subjects (1,138 males and 1,462 females). The normative sample closely approximates the 1980 U.S. Census in terms of age, gender, minority status, social class, and education. The new MMPI-2 norms are comparable to the original MMPI norms, based on linear T-scores (see Butcher et al., 1989), although a given raw score for a scale will result in a slightly lower T-score (an average of about 5 points) according to contemporary norms. Most MMPI code types (about 80 percent) remain the same, regardless of which normative population is used for comparison. The high degree of similarity between the MMPI validity and clinical scores in the original MMPI and the new MMPI-2 allows for the use of previous empirical research in interpreting scores based on the new norms. The MMPI-2 normative approach also equates T-score ranges so that a given T-score has the same meaning across the clinical scales. In the past, conservative clinical interpretation with the original MMPI usually employed cutoff scores above a T-score of 70, although some interpretations were possible at lower elevation ranges (Graham & McCord, 1985). Clinical research with the MMPI-2 shows that interpretations of the clinical scales are significant at elevations of T > 65.

Revision of the MMPI Booklet

After the new normative data had been collected, Form AX was further revised to reduce the item pool by eliminating many objectionable, obsolete, and nonworking items. New norms were then developed for the final version of the revised MMPI (MMPI-2), which contains 567 items, including most of the original items in the standard validity and clinical scales. These scales were kept relatively intact to preserve the substantial research that has accumulated on the instrument. To broaden and strengthen the instrument, 108 new items were added to the booklet.

A number of new scales have been developed for the MMPI-2 to increase its research potential and clinical utility. These scales are described in more detail in Chapters 4 and 5. The remainder of this chapter provides a brief introduction to MMPI-2 interpretation.

MMPI-2 Validity Data: Couple's Behavior Ratings

In the MMPI restandardization study, a number of people solicited for the MMPI-2 normative study were asked to invite their spouses to participate in the study. A total of 822 heterosexual couples were administered the MMPI-2. Each participant also completed a marital adjustment questionnaire (Spanier's Dyadic Adjustment Scale) and was asked to complete a behavior rating questionnaire on his or her spouse. The 110-item Couple's Rating Form contained a wide range of behaviors, attitudes, and impressions that people would be expected to know about their spouses. These ratings provided an important source of validity data on the MMPI-2 scales. Validity information based on the couple's ratings is included in this chapter to show that the MMPI-2 clinical scales are applicable with a "normal" range of individuals as well as within patient groups. The data presented here include the items that have the highest correlations with the clinical scales. Also included are correlations with a set of factor scales developed to summarize the Couple's Rating Form data (Butcher et al., 1989).

PART ONE: THE VALIDITY SCALES

The validity scales of the MMPI-2 (the Cannot Say score, the Lie or L scale, the Infrequency or F scale, and the Defensiveness or K scale) shown on the left-hand side of the profile sheet were originally included in the inventory to provide the clinician with information about the client's approach to the test. The validity scales indicate the presence of invalidating attitudes and provide the interpreter with clues to the validity of the test. Moreover, the validity scales, regardless of the range of scores, can provide the clinician with information that reflects the accessibility and openness of the examinee. Research with the original MMPI has shown that the validity indicators also provide information about the personality of the client. There are well-established empirical correlates for each of the validity scales. For a more detailed discussion of the construction and operation of the MMPI-2 clinical and validity scales, consult John Graham's text (1990).

The MMPI revision committee added three new validity scales to the MMPI-2 to aid in the evaluation of invalidating attitudes. These scales— the Back Side F and two response inconsistency scales, True Response Inconsistency (TRIN) and Variable Response Inconsistency (VRIN)— are detailed in the following discussion.

The Cannot Say Score (?)

The Cannot Say score is not a scale in the strict sense of the word, but is simply the total number of unanswered or doubly answered items on the record. It is not widely used today, because most subjects are encouraged to answer *all* the items. In earlier work with the MMPI, when subjects were given the option of omitting items, the Cannot Say score needed to be evaluated carefully.

How many items can be omitted without invalidating the record? Clinical practice has suggested that records with 20 or more omitted items within the first 370 should be interpreted with caution; records with 30 or more unanswered items within the first 370 attenuate and invalidate the test. The client needs to answer all items if the supplementary and content scales are to be scored. Consequently, it is good practice always to evaluate the Cannot Say score before proceeding to the interpretation. In the event that a large number of items have been left unanswered, it makes sense to return the booklet and answer sheet to the client, if possible, and have the record completed.

Reasons for Cannot Say score elevations include reading difficulties, guardedness on the part of the patient, confusion and distractibility resulting from the patient's clinical state (e.g., an organic disease, intoxication, etc.), severe psychomotor retardation accompanying depression, rebellion or antagonistic behavior (often found among uncooperative subjects such as prisoners or adolescents), obsessional or overly intellectualizing subjects who ruminate a great deal about the content, and people taking the MMPI-2 in personnel selection settings.

The Lie Scale (L)

The Lie scale was included in the validity scale grouping as a means of assessing general frankness in responding to the test items. The scale consists of 15 items that were selected on the basis of "face validity." The item content is obvious—for example, "I do not always tell the truth." When a number of these items (usually about 8 or 9) are answered falsely, the individual appears to be claiming a greater amount of virtue and presenting himself or herself more favorably than most others do. Profiles with elevations on this scale should be interpreted with caution because the individual's generalized response to claim excessive virtue, or deny socially undesirable faults, has likely distorted the profile. High scorers on L generally distort responses to items on the clinical scales as well, producing profiles that underestimate the number and extent of problems a client may have.

Several possible reasons can be found for high scores on the L scale. A person who is trying to present a favorable impression (i.e., someone taking the test in a personnel selection situation or a domestic court custody case) may claim a great deal of virtue to impress the evaluator. People with limited intelligence or who lack psychological sophistication may also produce high L scores in their attempt to look good to the evaluator. And some subcultural groups (such as ministers who represent church bodies) as well as some ethnic minority groups may present a favorable image on psychological tests. Some clients with neurotic disorders, such as somatization disorders, try to present a favorable (defensive) self-image to others.

Several personality characteristics are associated with elevations on the L scale. Individuals who score high on L appear to be naive and low in psychological mindedness; they tend to be defensive and are characterized by denial and "hysteroid" thinking. They are often rigid in their thinking and adjustment and have a strong need to "put up a good front."

The Infrequency Scale (F)

The F scale was devised as a measure of the tendency to admit to a wide range of psychological problems or to "fake bad." An individual who scores high on the F scale is admitting to a wide range of complaints that are infrequently endorsed by the general population and reflect a tendency to exaggerate problems.

The F scale consists of 60 items that range in content and are related to physical problems, bizarre ideas, antisocial behavior, and deviant personal attitudes. The following examples illustrate the range of item content on the F scale (typical exaggerated responses are given parenthetically):

"I believe in law enforcement."   (F)

"Evil spirits possess me at times."   (T)

"I loved my mother."   (F)

"Someone has been trying to rob me."   (T)

The construction of the F scale was simple and empirical. The scale consists of those items that were infrequently endorsed by the normative population (usually less than 10 percent). Although this is one of the longest MMPI-2 scales, normal subjects usually endorse only about four items. Thus a high score on the F scale reflects a tendency to exaggerate problems. Excessive endorsement of the items on this scale suggests that a person is attempting to present the most unfavorable picture of himself or herself.

Many reasons can be found for high scores on the F scale, usually reflecting confusion, disorganization, or exaggeration. Some of the more frequent situations producing elevated F scores are these:

1. Random response to the items. Since there are 60 items on the F scale, haphazard or random responding would result in about half of the items (or 30) being endorsed.
2. Deviant response set due to taking or falsely claiming mental illness. People who attempt to feign mental illness typically do not know which items to endorse and tend to *overrespond* by endorsing too many items. Actual patients are more selective in their response pattern.
3. Poor reading level and the person's inability to understand the items may result in an elevated F score.
4. Adolescent subjects typically have higher F scores than adults. This results, in part, from adolescent identity problems and possibly from some exaggerated responding as well.
5. Acutely psychotic or organically impaired people who are confused or disorganized may produce elevated F scores. The F scale is often associated with severity and chronicity of problems.
6. Persons in stressful situations may produce elevated scores on F.

7. Individuals who produce high F scores may be attempting to get the attention of the clinician. Thus, high F scores may represent a "plea for help."

What Range of F Score Invalidates an MMPI-2 Profile? Although a T-score of 70 is typically taken as the critical elevation suggesting invalidity of the performance, this is not the case for the F scale. Clinicians do not typically begin to concern themselves with profile invalidity until the F score gets to about the 90 T-score level, depending on the setting. In some settings, particularly at admission into an inpatient psychiatry unit or at incarceration in a correctional institution, it is appropriate to interpret (with caution, of course) profiles with an F score at about 90–109 T-score points.

The Back Side F Scale [F(B)]

An additional validity measure, the F(B) scale or Back Side F scale, was developed for the MMPI-2 to detect deviant responding to items located toward the end of the item pool. Some subjects may modify their approach to the items part way through the item pool and answer in a random or otherwise invalid manner. The items on the F scale are presented in the first part of the inventory, before item number 370; therefore, the F scale or the F-K index may not detect dissimulation later in the booklet. The 40-item F(B) scale was developed in much the same way as the original F scale—by including items that had low endorsement percentages among the normal population. There are several ways the F(B) scale can be usefully interpreted.

If the F scale exceeds the previously mentioned criteria for validity, then no additional interpretation of F(B) is needed, because the MMPI-2 would be considered invalid by F scale criteria. If the T-score of the F scale is considered valid and the F(B) is below T = 89, then a valid response approach is indicated, and the clinical profile can be interpreted. However, if the T-score of the F scale is considered valid and the F(B) is above T = 90, then an interpretation of F(B) is needed. In this case, cautious interpretation of the clinical and validity scales is possible; however, interpretation of scales such as the MMPI-2 Content Scales, which require valid response to the later-appearing items, needs to be deferred.

The Subtle Defensiveness Scale (K)

Meehl and Hathaway (1946) wanted to develop a measure that would detect more subtle kinds of defensive responding than were detected by the obvious content of the L scale. They wanted to identify the "false positive" test misses by taking into account different degrees of defensiveness. About 22 of the K items were obtained by comparing the responses of normal subjects with those of 50 psychiatric patients with elevated L scores whose clinical scales were in the normal range (i.e., patients who were excessively defensive). Eight other items were included to counteract the tendency of certain types of patients to score excessively low on the scale without psychological justification. Twenty-four of the 30 K items are highly correlated with the Edward's Social Desirability Scale, a measure of social favorability.

In interpreting the MMPI-2, the K scale serves both as an indicator of invalidity and as a means of correcting for test defensiveness. Elevations on the K scale (particularly above a T-score of 70) reflect test defensiveness. For example, individuals who seek to present a highly favorable view of themselves, such as those attempting to indicate that they are not in need of psychological treatment or a parent seeking custody of children in court, try to make good impressions on the MMPI-2 by denying problems. The result is an elevated K score. The K scale is correlated with other psychological variables, such as social class and education level. It is important to take the subject's social class and education into account when interpreting the K scale. Individuals from higher social classes typically produce higher K scores (between 55 and 65). Consequently, the interpretation of test defensiveness in higher social status groups should not be applied until the T-scores reach 70.

It has also been noted that other personality factors, such as self-acceptance, independence, self-esteem, and nonauthoritarian values, have been associated with moderate elevations on the K scale.

Defensive profiles (K over T = 70) in situations that call for frankness and openness, such as in a clinical context, reflect the following characteristics: aloofness, rigidity, unwillingness to cooperate with the evaluation, denial of problems, and the presence of an unrealistic self-image.

Extremely low scores on K in cases where a moderate score is expected (e.g., in keeping with an individual's high social status) may be indicative of dissatisfaction, cynicism, "masochistic confessing," and poor response to treatment.

Response Inconsistency Scales

Two additional validity scales have been included in the MMPI-2. Both of these scales, True Response Inconsistency (TRIN) and Variable Response Inconsistency (VRIN), were developed to assess the possibility that a person is responding to the items in a psychologically inconsistent manner.

True Response Inconsistency Scale. The TRIN scale is comprised of 20 pairs of items for which a combination of two true or two false responses is semantically inconsistent. For example, responding to the items "Most of the time I feel blue" and "I am happy most of the time" as both true, or both false, is inconsistent. Eleven of the 20 item pairs are scored as inconsistent only if the client responds true to both items. Six of the item pairs are scored inconsistent only if the client responds false to both items. Three additional pairs are scored inconsistent if the client responds either both true or both false. The TRIN scale is scored by subtracting the number of inconsistent false pairs from the number of inconsistent true pairs, and then subtracting that number from 9 (the total number of possible inconsistent false pairs). This procedure yields an index ranging from 0 to 20. Extreme scores on either end of this range reflect a tendency to either indiscriminately answer false, that is "nay-saying," at the low end of the range, or indiscriminately answer true, that is "yea-saying," at the upper end of the distribution.

Variable Response Inconsistency Scale. The VRIN scale is made up of 49 pairs of items for which one or two of four possible configurations (true–false, false–true, true–true, false–false) represent semantically inconsistent responses. For example, answering true to "I do not tire quickly" and false to "I feel tired a good deal of the time," or vice versa, represent semantically inconsistent responses. The scale is scored by summing the number of inconsistent responses. Scores may range from 0 to 49. The VRIN scale may be used to help interpret a high F score. For example, a high F score, together with a low-to-moderate VRIN score rules out the possibility that the F score reflects random responding or confusion. The VRIN scale can also be used in place of the Test–Retest (TR) scale, which consisted of responses to the 16 repeat items that appeared on the original MMPI.

Patterns of Test Invalidity

The MMPI-2 validity scales, and their various combinations, can be used effectively to detect unusual response patterns and to determine if the profile can be safely interpreted. Two distinctly different patterns of invalidity follow:

1. *Illustration 1: Profile revealing a defensive response pattern.* The validity configuration shown in Figure 2-1, marked by high elevations on the L and K scales with relatively little problem checking as reflected in the low F scale score, is a relatively common pattern when an individual is attempting to present an overly favorable impression to gain a positive review or to be seen as "without psychological problems." Persons with this validity configuration are reporting no psychological problems, in fact, denying the presence of any unusual mentation or negative thoughts. The pattern is an exaggerated assertion of "excellent" mental

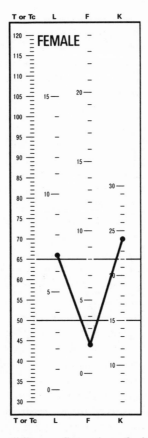

Figure 2–1. MMPI-2 validity configuration of a highly defensive person.

health and positive virtue that is atypical in clinical populations. For example, a parent who is being evaluated by forensic psychologists to determine suitability to have custody of children or individuals entering
treatment against their will commonly produce this pattern. People with
this validity pattern are presenting themselves as inaccessible and unwilling to disclose personal information.

   2. *Illustration 2: Profile claiming psychological problems.* The second illustration comes from a profile of a malingerer who sought to demonstrate
psychological problems to gain benefits in a court suit claiming "psychological injury." In this profile (see Figure 2-2), the individual is indicating
an extreme number of psychological and physical problems to substan-
tiate extensive injury. This exaggerated "plus-getting" is reflected in the
high elevation on the F scale. In addition, note that the L and K scores
are quite low, indicating a lack of defensiveness in the profile.

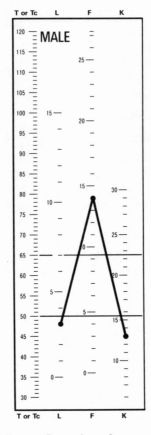

Figure 2–2. MMPI-2 validity configuration of an exaggerated response pattern.

PART TWO: CORRELATES OF THE CLINICAL SCALES

Scale 1: Hypochondriasis (Hs)

Scale 1 was designed to measure hypochondriasis—a pattern of "neurotic" concern over physical health. This was one of the first scales developed for the MMPI in 1940. In the construction of the Hs scale, items were selected that differentiated 50 cases of "relatively pure, uncomplicated hypochondriacal patients" from members of the Minnesota normative sample. Great care was taken by Hathaway and McKinley to exclude psychotics from the clinical criterion group. After initial empirical item selection, the scale was revised in an attempt to correct for the excessive number of psychiatric cases who obtained high scores on the scale without having clear hypochondriacal features in their clinical picture. The Hs scale contains 32 items whose content ranges over a variety of bodily complaints (e.g., "I have a great deal of stomach trouble"; "I feel weak all over much of the time"; and "I am troubled by attacks of nausea and vomiting"). Persons endorsing a large number of these items are presenting an abnormal number of physical complaints or are showing concerns that cannot be attributed to a specific physical disorder. The complaining picture is vague and nonspecific, and is usually suggestive of psychological factors in the clinical profile. Some elevation on scale 1 can accompany actual physical disorders, but a score of 65 or higher is believed to reflect a psychological or "character" problem.

The Hs scale is usually interpreted in conjunction with other clinical scales, particularly the scales in the "neurotic triad"—scales 2 and 3 (Depression and Hysteria). Correlates for the Hs scale include excessive bodily concern, fatigue, experience of pain, a pessimistic outlook on life, complaining behavior, and reduced efficacy in life.

The interpretation of elevations on the Hs scale as indicating somatic concern among physically healthy subjects was borne out in the couple's rating study for the MMPI Restandardization Project (Butcher, et al., 1989). The correlates for Hs in the normative sample of males and females centered on worries over health (i.e., reporting headaches, stomach trouble, and other ailments, and appearing generally worn out to their spouses).

Scale 2: Depression (D)

The Depression scale was developed as a measure of symptomatic depression as reflected in a general frame of mind characterized by poor morale, lack of hope in the future, dissatisfaction with one's status in life, and presence of psychic and somatic symptoms of depression. The D scale contains 57 items that were selected in two ways: Most of the items were obtained through their power to differentiate the criterion group of depressed patients (50 manic-depressive patients in the depressive phase) from a group of normal subjects. A number of items were included to minimize the D scale elevations of psychiatric patients whose diagnoses were not depression. The item content of scale 2 reflects much of the behavior that is suggestive of clinical depression (e.g., "My sleep is fitful and disturbed"; "I have a good appetite" [F]; "I brood a great deal"; "I cry easily"). The items deal with a lack of interest in things, denial of happiness, a low degree of esteem or personal worth, and an inability to function.

It should be noted that scale 2 is the most frequent peak score found in psychiatric profiles. It was designed as a symptom measure that is sensitive to "current" mood. Among its other uses, the D scale is valuable as an indicator of change in the clinical picture. Clinicians using the MMPI have long been aware of the need to understand the D scale in terms of the configural relationships with other scales. The same level of elevation on this scale can have a different clinical meaning depending

upon other scale elevations. Correlates for the D scale include such behaviors as feeling depressed, feeling pessimistic, having low self-esteem,
feeling dysphoric, having a negative attitude toward the future, being
guilt prone, and being indecisive.

Interpretation of elevated Depression scores for normal subjects received substantial empirical support from the couple's rating study in the
MMPI Restandardization Project (Butcher et al., 1989). High D males
and females were viewed by their spouses as generally maladjusted, lacking energy, lacking in self-confidence, and as persons who get sad or blue
easily, give up easily, are concerned that something bad is going to hap-
pen, lack interest in things, and act bored and restless.

Scale 3: Hysteria (Hy)

Scale 3 was developed as an aid in the diagnosis of conversion disorder
and as a possible measure of the predisposition to develop this disorder.
Conversion disorder or somatization disorder (i.e., development of physical symptoms such as loss of voice or psychogenic seizures) typically occurs only under stressful conditions. The criterion group used in the
development of this scale comprised 50 patients who had been diagnosed with psychoneurosis or hysteria, or who had been observed to
have hysterical features in their clinical pattern. This was a rather difficult criterion group to obtain in the early period of MMPI scale development. The final Hy scale consists of 60 items whose content falls
broadly into two general areas—*physical problems* and *social facility* items
(e.g., "My sleep is fitful and disturbed" [T]; "I feel weak all over much
of the time" [T]; "It is safer to trust nobody" [F]; "At times I feel like
swearing" [F]). The empirical correlates for elevations on this scale include such behaviors as being prone to develop physical symptoms under stress, presenting vague physical complaints, being repressed and
lacking in anxiety, and being socially outgoing and coquettish in relation
to others.

Scale 4: Psychopathic Deviate (Pd)

The Pd scale was designed to measure personality characteristics suggestive of antisocial or psychopathic personality disorders. The characteristics to be measured in this scale included general social maladjustment,
disregard for rules or mores, difficulties with the law or authority, absence of strongly pleasant experience, superficiality in interpersonal relations, inability to learn from punishing experiences, and the presence
of an impulsive and uncontrolled behavioral history. The clinical criterion group used in the development of scale 4 comprised patients who
were being seen in a psychiatric setting and who had been diagnosed as
having a psychopathic personality of the asocial or amoral type, analo-

gous to antisocial personality disorder in the *Diagnostic and Statistical Manual* (DSM III-R). Patients with psychotic or neurotic features were not included in the clinical group. Most of the patients were between the ages of 17 and 22 years, and the majority were female. Each patient had manifested a long history of offenses, including stealing, lying, truancy, sexual promiscuity, forgery, and alcohol problems.

In contrasting this criterion group with the Minnesota normative sample, which was made up of older and more rural adults, some biases were obvious. A group of college subjects was also used in further refinement of the scale, because they more closely approximated the criterion group in terms of age and marital status. Use was made of two other groups: additional psychiatric patients who fit the criterion and 100 male inmates at a federal prison.

The Pd scale consists of 50 items that sample a wide range of content dealing with alienation from the family, school difficulties, and broader authority problems; poor morale; sexual problems as well as other personal shortcomings; assertion of social confidence and poise; and denial of social shyness or anxiety. The last two types of items, as in the Hy scale, appear somewhat incongruous and contradictory to the first four and appear to reflect social extraversion. The empirical correlates for the Pd scale include antisocial behavior, impulsivity, poor judgment, a tendency to externalize blame, socially outgoing behavior, a manipulative personality in relationships, and an aggressive stance in interpersonal situations.

The person with a high Pd score is usually considered unable to profit from experience, lacks definite goals, is likely to have a personality disorder diagnosis (antisocial or passive-aggressive), is dissatisfied, shows absence of deep emotional response, feels bored and empty, has a poor prognosis for change in therapy, blames others for problems, intellectualizes, and may agree to treatment to avoid jail or some other unpleasant experience, but is likely to terminate therapy before change is effected.

Interpretation of elevated Pd scale scores for normal subjects received substantial empirical support from the couple's rating study in the MMPI Restandardization Project (Butcher et al., 1989). Normal-range subjects from the MMPI-2 normative sample who score high on Pd are viewed by their spouses as antisocial, impulsive, moody, and resentful. They were reported to take drugs other than those prescribed by a doctor, have sexual conflicts, and swear and curse a lot.

Scale 5: Masculinity–Femininity (Mf)

The Mf scale was added to the MMPI item pool a few years after the clinical scales were developed. It was added for the purpose of identifying the personality features of sex role identification problems. This scale is *not* a pure measure of masculinity–femininity and is factorially complex because it contains two item groups—one measuring masculine interests and the other measuring feminine interests (Johnson et al., 1984). This scale is the *least* well defined and understood of the MMPI clinical scales. Problems with the Mf scale result from several factors. Empirical item selection was not strictly followed (see Terman and Miles, 1936), and the criterion group of male inverts consisted of only 13 cases (although the group was very homogeneous and included neither neurotics nor psychotics) (Hathaway, 1980). Scale derivation consisted of borrowing items from the Terman and Miles Inventory that showed promise of differentiating sexual inverts. Since the Minnesota normative population had not responded to these items, another normative population was used (54 soldiers and 67 female airline employees).

Items were further screened to determine how well they differentiated males from females. This was followed by a third set of comparisons to differentiate feminine men from "normal" men. A further attempt to develop a corresponding scale for female inverts by contrasting normal females with female patients was not successful.

The most serious problem with the Mf scale, however, is the nature of the construct(s) being measured by the scale. A great deal of controversy has surrounded the use of personality scales to measure "masculinity" or "femininity." The MMPI Mf suffers from some of the same problems as other gender identification scales.

The original Mf scale consisted of 60 items that deal with interests, vocational choices, aesthetic preferences, and activity–passivity. The same scale is used for both sexes, but is scored in the opposite direction for females. In the MMPI-2 four controversial and objectionable items were deleted, leaving the present Mf scale with 56 items.

The Mf scale is highly correlated with education, intelligence, and social class; consequently, any interpretations based on Mf scale elevations must take these factors into account. Correlates for high Mf scores in males include sensitivity in an interpersonal situation, insecurity in male roles, having broad cultural interests, and passivity in interpersonal relationships. Low Mf males, on the other hand, are viewed as presenting an overly masculine image, somewhat narrow in interests, insensitive in interpersonal relationships, and more interested in action than reflection.

Fewer data exist on Mf scores for females; however, recent data reported by Graham (1990) show that education level should also be kept in mind when interpreting Mf scores for females. Correlates of high Mf scores for females suggest rejection of traditional female roles, preference for male-oriented activities, and interpersonal insensitivity. Low Mf women tend to be viewed as more traditional in interests and somewhat passive and dependent in relationships.

Scale 6: Paranoia (Pa)

The Pa scale was originally designed to assess the presence of attitudes and beliefs that would reflect paranoid thinking and behavior or would measure suspicious, mistrusting tendencies that often accompany other personality disorders, affective disorder, and schizophrenia. The criterion group of patients for developing the Pa scale were persons who had developed fairly well-defined delusional systems (although the diagnostic label *paranoia* was rarely applied to them). More often they were diagnosed as paranoid state, paranoid condition, or paranoid schizophrenia. In most cases, the symptoms manifested by the criterion group patients involved the presence of ideas of reference, delusions of grandiosity, feelings of persecution or suspiciousness, rigidity, and excessive interpersonal sensitivity.

Although the Pa scale provides useful information when evaluated in configuration with other clinical scales, it does not fulfill its original purpose of differentially diagnosing paranoid disorders. The Pa scale does not always detect the presence of paranoid or delusional thinking. Although persons who score high on scale 6 usually show paranoid ideation and delusions, persons who score low on this scale are often seen as behaviorally paranoid. Persons who score low on scale 6 may be viewed as being *too* cautious in their interpretations and do not endorse the more blatant items on the scale.

The Pa scale consists of 40 items with both blatantly psychotic items such as "Evil spirits possess me at times" or "I believe I am being plotted against" and very subtle items such as "I am more sensitive than most people" and "Once in a while I think of things too bad to talk about." This scale measures psychological processes such as interpersonal sensitivity, proclamation of high moral virtue, having feelings that are easily hurt, denial of suspiciousness, complaints about the shortcomings of others (cynicism), and excessive rationality.

The Meaning of Elevations of the Pa Scale. It should be kept in mind that elevated Pa scores in the normal population are quite different from elevated scores obtained by psychiatric patients. The correlates of scale 6 change markedly in character as the elevation goes from moderate (T = 60–65) to high (T = 66 and above). In clinic populations, moderate elevations on scale 6 suggest an individual who expresses hostility through "righteous indignation." Clinic patients with elevated Pa scores tend to be rigid, argumentative, suspicious, and brooding. Correlates for individuals scoring high on Pa include externalization of blame, use of projection as a defense, mistrust, suspicion of others, unusual thinking, hypersensitivity, and guarded relationships.

Scale 7: Psychasthenia (Pt)

The Pt scale was devised as an aid in diagnosing the neurotic syndrome *psychasthenia,* or the obsessive–compulsive syndrome. The syndrome psychasthenia is not presently a part of psychiatric nomenclature, but the personality features measured by this scale—obsessions, compulsions, anxiety or worrying, unreasonable fears, guilt feelings, etc.—appear in many other psychiatric disorders (e.g., depression, neurotic reactions, and psychoses). There is a great deal of evidence to indicate that the Pt scale is a good indicator of general maladjustment, tension, anxiety, and ruminative self-doubt.

The construction of this scale involved two steps. First, items were selected through empirical separation of a criterion group of 20 patients from the normative group. Next, this preliminary scale was refined through a statistical analysis of its internal consistency in which items were accepted that correlated highly with the total score on the empirically derived item set.

The scale consists of 48 items that deal with symptoms relating to anxiety, irrational fears, indecisiveness, low self-esteem, and self-devaluation. The utility of this scale in profile interpretation comes primarily from its configural relationship with other scales and as a measure of "acuteness" of disturbance. For example, the higher the Pt scale elevation in relation to the Schizophrenia (Sc) scale, the more likely it is that the individual's problems are acute rather than chronic.

A peak score on scale 7 is not particularly frequent, even among psychiatric groups. When it occurs as the highest point, it tends to measure neurotic anxiety. Correlates for the Pt scale include anxiety, tension, feelings of inadequacy, difficulties in concentration, indecision, and rumination.

Interpretation of elevated Pt scores for normal subjects received substantial empirical support from the couple's rating study in the MMPI Restandardization Project (Butcher et al., 1989). Normal range men and women with high Pt scores were viewed by their spouses as having many fears, being nervous and jittery, being indecisive, lacking in self-confidence, and as having sleeping problems.

Scale 8: Schizophrenia (Sc)

Scale 8 was constructed to assess the disorders categorized under the broad grouping of schizophrenia. Several subtypes present a wide range of behavioral manifestations. This was one of the most difficult MMPI scales for Hathaway and McKinley to construct, in part because of the behavioral heterogeneity in the *schizophrenia syndromes,* but mainly because of the inclusion of such behavioral features as depression and hypochondriasis on earlier groups of items that separated the criterion group. The criterion patients for scale 8 were 50 persons who had been diagnosed schizophrenic with various subclassifications. The Sc scale (which consists of 78 items) is composed of a number of preliminary subscales derived from the four subclassifications of schizophrenia: catatonic, paranoid, simple, and hebephrenic.

The item content on the Sc scale deals with social alienation, isolation, complaints of family alienation, bizarre feelings and sensations, thoughts of external influence, peculiar bodily dysfunctioning, general inadequacy, and dissatisfaction.

The Sc scale has been found to be extremely valuable in diagnosing schizophrenia in adult psychiatric populations. There are some problems, however, in interpreting Sc scale elevations in adolescent populations, because the mean elevation for adolescents is high—probably due to the typical stress and identity crises experienced by even normal adolescents.

One should be cautioned against a narrow interpretation of scale 8 in any group and avoid calling all high 8s schizophrenic. Depending on configural relationships with other scales, elevations on scale 8 provide a great deal of information if one gets away from a narrow "diagnostic" or labeling frame of reference.

People in a normal population who score high on scale 8 reveal characteristics that can be informative. While a high score (T > 65) is somewhat rare in the normal population, it reflects unconventionality and alienation. High scorers feel a great deal of social distance and tend to doubt their own worth and identity. Persons who have T-scores that exceed 70 usually have schizoid mentation—although they are not necessarily psychiatrically disturbed. Correlates for the Sc scale include confusion, disorganization, unusual thinking, alienation, preoccupation, isolation, and withdrawal. Individuals with high ranging scores are often reported to be psychotic.

Scale 9: Mania (Ma)

The Ma scale was developed as an aid in the assessment of the personality pattern of hypomania. This condition refers to a milder degree of manic excitement than that which typically occurs in the bipolar manic-depressive or manic disorders. The features that characterize this syndrome are overactivity and expansiveness, emotional excitement, flight of ideas, elation and euphoria, overoptimism, and overextension of activities.

Patients characterized by this pattern often manifest behavior that can be seen as psychopathic, and both psychopathic behavior and manic features are frequently common. Elevated 9 profiles are frequently obtained along with elevations on scale 4. Hypomanic behavior as reflected by elevations on scale 9 resembles the symptoms found in manic conditions, but it is usually less blatant and less extreme. In the development of this scale, the criterion group comprised patients who were less acutely disturbed than those with major affective disorders. Patients with the delirium and confusion of a manic state would not have been able to complete the test. The criterion group consisted of 24 patients who were not psychotic or manifesting agitated depressions, but who were classified as hypomanic. The 46 items on the Ma scale deal with expansiveness, egotism, irritability, lack of inhibition and control, amorality, and excitement.

People in the normal range who score high on scale 9 (T = 60–65) tend to be warm, enthusiastic, expansive, outgoing, and uninhibited; they are active and possess an unusually high drive level. Individuals who obtain low scores on the Ma scale often show low energy—listlessness, apathy, and low self-confidence. It should be noted that scale 9 is one of the most frequent peak scores in a normal population. Approximately 10 to 15 percent of subjects in normal-range groups obtain scores above T = 65.

In psychiatric populations, scale 9 is frequently found to be the lowest score, reflecting low morale and lack of energy. The behavioral correlates associated with elevations on the Ma scale include overactivity, expansiveness, energetic behavior, unrealistic views about personal abilities, disorganization, excessive speech, failure to complete projects, and a tendency to act out in impulsive ways.

Interpretation of elevated Ma scale scores for normal-range individuals received substantial empirical support from the couple's rating study in the MMPI Restandardization Project (Butcher et al., 1989). High Ma wives were rated by their husbands as follows: wears strange or unusual clothes, talks too much, makes big plans, gets very excited or happy for little reason, stirs up excitement, takes many risks, and tells people off about their faults. High Ma males, as viewed by their wives: acts bossy, talks back to others without thinking, talks too much, whines and demands attention, and takes drugs other than those prescribed by a doctor.

Scale 0: Social Introversion (Si)

The concept of social introversion–extroversion (I–E) has had a long history—dating back to Jung (1923)—and a number of inventories have been devised to measure this personality dimension. The Si scale was not one of the original MMPI scales, but it is now included on the profile as a measure of introversion–extroversion. This scale was originally developed by Drake (1946) and published as the Social I–E scale. The items were selected by contrasting college students' scores on the subscale for social introversion–extroversion in the Minnesota T–S–E Inventory (which measures social extroversion). The preliminary items were those that differentiated 50 high- from 50 low-scoring females, and the scale was cross-validated on males. The development of this scale differed from that of other MMPI scales in that the criterion groups were *not* from a psychiatric population.

The Si scale included in the MMPI contains 69 items and is designed to measure uneasiness in social situations, social insecurity and self-depreciation, denial of impulses and temptations, and withdrawal from interpersonal contacts.

Hostetler, Ben-Porath, Butcher, and Graham (1989) developed three homogeneous content subscales for the Si scale through an item factor analysis approach. The subscales for Si—Si1 (Shyness), Si2 (Social Avoidance), and Si3 (Self–Other Alienation—are discussed in detail in Chapter 5.

This scale is a very useful measure of an individual's ease or comfort in social situations. In addition, it serves as an effective measure of the inhibition or expression of aggressive impulses. The scale operates as a suppressor scale in studies of delinquency; that is, elevations on Si are associated with low rates of delinquency. The configural relationships involving the Si scales are very important. Elevations on Si enable the interpreter to evaluate the meaning of various other scales on the profile.

The Si scale is also one of the most stable scales on the MMPI-2 with a long-term reliability of .736 over a 30-year time span (Leon et al., 1979). Correlates for high scores include the following: socially withdrawn, shy, reserved in social situations, unassertive, overcontrolled, and submissive in relationships. Individuals with low scores on the Si scale tend to be extroverted, outgoing, manipulative in social relationships, gregarious, and talkative.

Interpretation of elevated Si scale scores for normal subjects received substantial empirical support from the couple's rating study in the MMPI Restandardization Project (Butcher et al., 1989). High scoring subjects were viewed by their spouses as follows: acts very shy, lacks self-confidence, avoids contact with people, is unwilling to try new things, and often puts himself or herself down.

CAUTIONS TO KEEP IN MIND WHEN INTERPRETING MMPI-2 PROFILES

Several general considerations should be followed when interpreting MMPI-2 profiles.

1. *Be aware of the population base rate.* The population from which the profile was obtained should be taken into consideration when interpreting the profile. Specific populations tend to draw similar profile groups. Consequently, the interpreter should be aware of the types of profiles

typically obtained in a given setting. For example, in alcohol treatment programs, profiles with significant elevations on scales 2 and 4 are common, while profiles with high ranging 4, 9, and 8 are frequently obtained in correctional settings. Knowing the types of cases that typically occur in a given setting enables the clinician to moderate and focus interpretations appropriately.

2. *Refer to scale "numbers" (e.g., scale 4) when discussing an MMPI-2 scale rather than referring to the original scale names (e.g., Psychopathic Deviate scale).* The use of the original scale names is confusing to many people since some scale names have become archaic (e.g., the Psychasthenic scale). The actual scale has taken on considerably more detail and more explicit meaning as empirical research has accumulated. It is therefore more exact to discuss the scales in terms of their number.

3. *Interpret the pattern or "configuration" of scales rather than a scale-by-scale analysis of individual MMPI-2 scores.* It was originally thought that the MMPI scores would reflect the specific pathology measured by each scale and that an elevated score could be "read" as reflecting a particular scale's problem—for example, a scale elevation on Depression would reflect problems of depression. Early MMPI researchers soon realized, however, that *more than one* scale was frequently elevated with some clinical problems. The pattern of scores or the profile configuration then came to be the important focus in MMPI-2 interpretation. An experienced MMPI-2 interpreter usually takes into account the shape of the profile as much as the elevation of the scores in interpreting the profile.

4. *Clinical scales in the MMPI-2 should be considered as having interpretive significance above a T-score level of $T = 65$ and having some suggestive correlates between a T-score of 60 and 64.*

SUMMARY

This chapter provides an overview of the MMPI-2, beginning with a discussion of the early work on the original MMPI and a brief introduction to the MMPI Restandardization Project and the MMPI-2. The chapter also includes a summary of the MMPI-2 validity and clinical scales for individuals who need to review the development and correlates of the basic MMPI-2 scales. Chapter 3 directly addresses the use of these scales in treatment planning.

3

Hypotheses about Treatment from MMPI-2 Scales and Indexes

The focus of this chapter is on the correlates pertaining to psychological treatment that can be culled from the MMPI-2 validity scales, clinical scales, and selected MMPI-2 code types. The general descriptions were drawn from both the empirical and the clinical literature on the MMPI-2 and from the author's clinical experience with the MMPI-2 in treatment planning. The major goal is to present the MMPI-2 scale and profile classification system as a lens through which the clinician can view clients' problems. In the first part of this chapter the client's response attitudes and orientation toward therapy through the validity scales and patterns are discussed; the second section surveys the treatment implications for the MMPI-2 clinical scales; and the final part summarizes information related to a number of selected MMPI-2 profile code types.

HYPOTHESES ABOUT PATIENT CHARACTERISTICS FROM THE MMPI-2 VALIDITY SCALES

The MMPI-2 validity scales provide some of the most useful interpretive hypotheses about patients being evaluated in treatment. In using the MMPI-2 as a pretreatment measure, the clinician makes several assumptions about the patient, about people in the patient's support network, and about the treatment program itself. The manner in which a person being tested approaches the MMPI-2 items can provide valuable clues about that person's test-taking attitudes in comparison with those of other people seeking psychological treatment. Two basic questions need to be asked by the clinician about each candidate for testing: (1) *Is this person cooperating with the treatment program by responding to the MMPI-2 items in a frank and self-disclosing manner?* (2) *Does this person need to be in therapy?* The first question can be directly assessed from the range and pattern of scores on the MMPI-2 validity indicators. The second question is more clearly addressed by clinical scale score and profile information.

In the summary of treatment information obtainable from the MMPI-2, some of the hypotheses may appear to be negative, uncomplimentary, and pessimistic. These examples are not, however, meant to suggest bases for a decision either to refuse to initiate therapy or to terminate it. My purpose in presenting some of the extremes is to encourage therapists to be aware of possible problems and pitfalls. Certain behaviors represent challenges, and the MMPI-2 can assist the clinician in recognizing them.

Interpreting Patient Attitudes Toward Treatment

The MMPI-2 validity scales—namely, the ?, L, F, and K scales—serve as indicators of how patients view their own clinical situation, how well they have cooperated with the assessment, and how accessible they are to the therapist. Specific indications of treatment readiness can be obtained directly from elevations on the MMPI-2 response attitude scales and from the *configurations* or relative elevations on the validity scales. First, we will examine possible treatment hypotheses indicated by the four individual validity indicators. Afterward, we will discuss the context of the validity scales by looking at the entire configuration of a profile.

Cannot Say Score (?). The Cannot Say scale is useful in treatment planning because it reflects the patient's level of cooperation. The clinician assumes that the person is interested in being understood and is being cooperative in taking the test. People taking the test are asked to answer all questions; most can comply even though some items are less than relevant to their particular case. Those who omit more than 8 to 10 items within the first 370 (the MMPI-2 validity and clinical scales are scorable from the first 370 items) are being more cautious and evasive than is expected under the conditions of pretreatment evaluation. If the number of omissions is between 11 and 19, then it is likely that the person would have considerable difficulty participating in a discussion of personal problems. Records with 20 or more omitted items among the first 370 suggest that a treatment-ready attitude is very unlikely. In such cases the therapist is probably going to need to deal with the client's reticence very early. Treatment termination before benefits can accrue is likely.

L Scale. People with a T-score of 55–64 on the L scale are engaging in overly virtuous self-descriptions that could be counterproductive in therapy. A self-perception that is highly principled, virtuous, and above fault should be a signal to the therapist that frank, direct, and open communication is going to be difficult. This difficulty in frank expression may derive from a number of factors, including membership in special population subgroups such as ministers or airline pilots, who have a strong need to project responsibility and uprightness; individuals who are somewhat indignant about being assessed; or "neurotic" individuals who have unrealistic views of their motives and values.

If the L scale is elevated at a T-score of 65 or more in a treatment evaluation context, then therapy is unlikely to proceed well, progress will be slight, and premature termination is likely. People with unrealistically high claims to virtue are much too rigid and "perfect" to change their self-perceptions much. They typically see little need to discuss their problems or to change their behavior.

F Scale. In addition to its role as a validity indicator, the F scale operates as a barometer of psychological distress. The lower the scale elevation (e.g., $T < 50$), the less likely it is that the individual is experiencing, or at least reporting, problems. Without recognized symptoms, there is little intrinsic motivation for seeking help, so it is unlikely that a person with an F score in this range would seek counseling.

If the F scale is between 51 and 59 T-score points, then the individual may be reporting symptoms of distress that could require psychological treatment. The level of distress, however, is considerably below that of most people who seek help. As we shall see in a later section, the configuration of validity scale scores is often more important in evaluating treatment readiness than the elevation of the validity scale scores. Consequently, for our present discussion a slight elevation on the F scale can be viewed as a problem-oriented self-review only if the F scale is higher than both the L and K scales.

When the F scale range is between 60 and 79 the individual is engaging in appropriate symptom expression, particularly if F is greater than L and K.

When the F scale range is between 80 and 90 the person is expressing a high degree of distress, confusion, and a broad range of psychological symptoms. Prompt attention to such a complaint pattern is suggested. This range also indicates that the patient is reporting a multiproblem situation and a lack of resources with which to deal with the problems. Such patients may be under a great deal of stress and may have lost perspective on their problems. This is the fairly common "plea for help pattern" seen in emergency settings or crisis contacts.

MMPI-2 records with an F score above $T = 91$ are technically invalid. A person with such a score has grossly exaggerated the symptom picture to the point that little differential information is available. Several hypotheses are available for protocols with such extensive distress or symptom presentations.

1. High F scale records are frequently obtained in inpatient settings (psychiatric), particularly at admission, when a person is confused, disoriented, or frankly psychotic. In such cases the clinical scale profile may still yield interpretable and useful information.

2. The high F scale pattern is found when a person is seeking to be viewed as "disturbed" so that his or her needs will be given attention. This type of record is seen, for example, with incarcerated felons, who may seek to be viewed as having symptoms but who do not know how to present an internally consistent pattern suggestive of psychological problems.

The Back Side F or F(B) Scale. As noted in Chapter 2, the F(B) scale is important in the interpretation of the MMPI-2 scales with items toward the end of the test booklet. Because clinical and validity scales can be scored from the first 370 items, the F(B) scale has little relevance for their interpretation. For the scales described in Chapters 4 and 5, however, the F(B) scale has a great deal of importance.

K Scale. The K scale, if interpreted properly, can be a useful indicator of treatment readiness or, in some cases, hesitance to become involved in treatment. In general, in its lower ranges—usually below T = 40–45—the K scale reflects an openness to emotional expression; in its upper ranges—usually above T = 70—it suggests an aloofness toward problem expression and discussion of emotions. The K scale is somewhat more complicated than this, however, and must usually be interpreted in conjunction with information about social class and educational level. Several interpretive hypotheses for level of K score are given in Table 3-1.

Patterns of Response Attitudes: Treatment Implications

The MMPI-2 validity scales provide much information concerning attitudes toward treatment if their relative elevations are considered. In the paragraphs that follow several validity configurations are presented and illustrated with their treatment implications.

1. *The highly virtuous, "proper," and unwilling participant.* This validity configuration includes relatively high elevations on both L and K. Both scales are elevated above scale F, but the elevation is less important than the shape of the configuration. For this pattern of "naive" defensiveness, the L and K will be higher than T = 60, with F lower than T = 60. In this pattern L is greater than K (see Figure 3-1).

This configuration reveals attitudes that are contrary to easy engagement in therapy. Overly virtuous self-appraisal and test defensiveness suggest that the client rigidly maintains attitudes of perfectionistic thinking and a reluctance or refusal to engage in self-criticism. Such respondents view their psychological adjustment as "good" and feel little need for discussing problems. In fact, they feel a need to keep up a good front and to preserve their social image. Rigid beliefs, perfectionistic mental

Table 3–1. Interpretations of K as a Function of Social Class in
Treatment Planning

T-Score Range of K	Interpretations	
	Low Social Class	Middle to High Social Class
30–44	Some problem admission and symptom expression Problem-oriented responding	Overly complaining Symptom exaggeration Lack of defenses Attempting to gain attention through symptom expression
45–55	Expected level of K for this SES	Some admission of symptoms Apparent willingness to discuss problems
56–63	Somewhat reluctant to express problems Somewhat defensive	Expected range of scores for ths level of SES with *no* problems
64–69	Pretest defensiveness Unwillingness to discuss feelings Uses denial as a defense	Somewhat reluctant to discuss personal problems
70 +	Highly defensive Outright distortion of self-presentation Attempting to manipulate others through symptoms characterized by extreme symptom denial	Defensive Evasive Unwilling to express feelings Disinclined to express symptoms Some denial of symptoms

sets, and moralistic attitudes may be prominent in treatment interactions. In early treatment sessions such patients tend to stand off or remain aloof. They thus appear to be distant, unrealistic, and uninvolved in their own problem.

A similar test configuration results when respondents attempt to use the test to manipulate other people's view of them. For example, a parent seeking custody of a child will often present such a favorable self-image. Individuals in pain treatment programs for psychogenic pain may take a similar self-protective stance. Thus, this validity profile is accompanied by an unrealistic self-appraisal and produces an inflexible mind-set, a combination that suggests considerable difficulty in treatment engagement. It may be difficult for a therapist to pass beyond the "smiling barrier."

2. *The reluctant, defended, and unwilling participant.* Unlike the pattern of resistance just described, prospective patients with this pattern are less moralistic and defiantly virtuous in their self-presentation; they are nonetheless reluctant to disclose their problem in therapy. The pattern

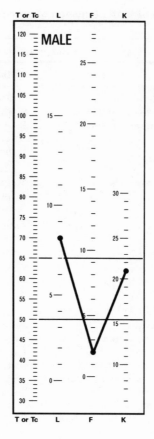

Figure 3–1. Validity pattern of a person presenting an overly virtuous self-picture.

of behavior marked by the K-dominated validity configuration is one of denial, assertion of a positive social image, and presentation of positive mental health. This configuration is illustrated in Figure 3-2.

The behavior reflected in this profile suggests a subtle defensive attitude that denies any psychological need. Individuals with this pattern view (or at least describe) themselves quite positively. They are reluctant to disclose personal weakness and appear resistant in therapy. Two types of patients are commonly found with this validity pattern:

a. Patients who are in the later stages of successful therapy. The K score usually increases in elevation once a person has regained— or gained—effectiveness in functioning.
b. Patients who are reluctantly entering treatment at the insistence of another individual such as a spouse or a court official.

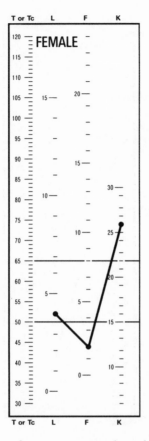

Figure 3–2. Validity pattern of a person presenting a highly defensive response pattern.

3. *Exaggerated symptom expression—the need for attention to problems.* This exaggerated response pattern is frequently found among individuals seeking psychological help. They appear to be presenting a great number of problems and drawing attention to their need for help. In such cases there is an urgency in the complaint pattern and an indication that the patients feel vulnerable to the demands of their environment and that they do not have strength to cope with their problems. This validity configuration has been referred to as a "plea for help" pattern, and is depicted in Figure 3-3.

One feature of this clinical picture that has implications for treatment is its amorphous quality. The problems being presented are nonspecific and the difficulties involve several life areas. As a consequence, the patient may be unable to focus on specific issues in the treatment sessions. People with this MMPI-2 validity pattern appear prone to develop "crises" that seem, at times, to consume all of their energies and adaptive resources.

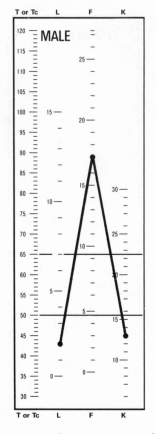

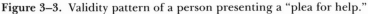

Figure 3–3. Validity pattern of a person presenting a "plea for help."

4. *Open, frank problem expression.* Moderate elevation on the F scale in the context of lower L and K scores reflects a problem-oriented approach to self-appraisal and a relatively easier engagement in psychological treatment than the first two configurations discussed. In addition, such patients can focus on symptoms more effectively than the previously described high F scorers, and they are relatively more inclined to discuss their problems. This pattern clearly describes the willing, appropriate pretreatment MMPI-2 validity configuration presented in Figure 3-4.

THE NEED FOR TREATMENT AS REFLECTED BY THE MMPI-2 CLINICAL SCALES

Scale 1: Hypochondriasis

People whose highest clinical scale elevation is on the Hypochondriasis (Hs) scale are reporting a great deal of somatic distress and are attempt-

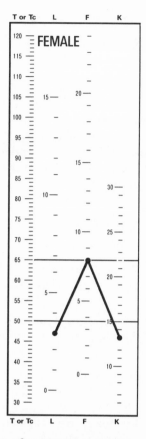

Figure 3–4. Validity pattern of a person presenting a clear problem-oriented response pattern.

ing to get the therapist to pay attention to their perceived physical ailments. They typically do not consider themselves to have psychological adjustment problems.

Their poor response to verbal psychotherapy may be due to several factors, such as a desire to seek physical (medical) solutions, low motivation for behavioral change, or a cynical attitude toward life. They are usually found to be willing to tolerate psychological strain before change is considered. These people often are expert "doctor shoppers" who have great experience with many therapies and are quite critical of treatment staff. They may show hostility toward a therapist whom they perceive as not giving enough support.

Such patients may respond to behavioral treatment for chronic pain, but noncompliance and early termination of treatment are frequent problems. The therapist should be aware that medication use or abuse is common and that there may be a strong element of secondary gain from the symptom pattern. Thus, a reduction in symptoms may actually be deflating to the patient.

Scale 2: Depression

High elevations on the Depression (D) scale reflect considerable expression of poor morale, low mood, and lack of energy to approach daily activities. People with this peak score have taken the test with a clear problem-oriented approach and are open—indeed receptive—to discussing their problems with a therapist. The MMPI-2 profile here reflects the following possible hypotheses:

> The patient is expressing a need for help.
>
> Distress and the motivation for relief are high.
>
> He or she needs to resolve immediate, situational stress.
>
> A supportive treatment setting is an important part in the early stages of therapy.
>
> An activity-oriented approach to treatment may be effective at improving mood and rekindling the patient's interest in life.

Good response to verbal psychotherapy has been well documented in research studies involving the D scale. People whose D score is their highest scale tend to become engaged in therapy, remain in treatment, and show improvement at follow-up. Consequently, good treatment prognosis in people with suitable verbal skills is expected for high scorers on the D scale.

Antidepressant medication may aid symptom relief among high D patients. Behavioral or cognitive–behavioral therapy may help alter life attitudes and unrealistic evaluations of life. Patients with high-ranging, persistent depression scores may respond to electroconvulsive shock therapy if less drastic approaches prove ineffective.

Scale 3: Hysteria

People with the Hysteria (Hy) scale as the peak score present themselves as socially facile, moral, inhibited, and defensive. Most important, they appear to be subject to developing physical health problems under stress. High Hy individuals do not usually seek psychological treatment for their problems. Instead, they view themselves as physically ill or vaguely prone to illness and will frequently go to physicians for reassurance or "treatment," even though the actual organic findings are minimal. This MMPI-2 pattern suggests the following treatment hypotheses:

Defensive attitudes held by high Hy patients may thwart psychological treatment.

Patients tend to resist psychological interpretation and seek medical or physical solutions to their problems.

They may be naive and have low psychological mindedness.

They tend to gloss over personal weaknesses.

Since they are well defended, they do not appear to "feel" much stress; thus, they may be unmotivated for change.

They seemingly enjoy receiving attention for their symptoms; thus, the role of secondary gain factors in their symptom picture should be evaluated.

They seek reassurance.

People with this clinical pattern may gain some symptom relief with mild, directive suggestion; these patients often respond well to placebo.

Individuals with this profile code may be interested in medical solutions, at times drastic ones such as elective surgery, and may actually become disabled through extensive, repeated surgery (e.g., for back pain).

Significant change may come only through long-term treatment; however, these people tend to drop out of therapy prematurely.

Scale 4: Psychopathic Deviate

People with prominent elevations on the Pd scale are typically uninterested in seeking treatment or changing their behavior. They seldom choose treatment for themselves and seek therapy in response to the demands of others—for example, a spouse, family, or the court. They generally see no need for changes in their behavior and are inclined to see others as having the problems. They tend to feel little anxiety about their current situation.

They typically have many problems and pressures resulting from previous impulsive behavior. They may also have legal difficulties, interpersonal relationship problems, and other problems resulting from poor judgment.

Substance abuse is likely to be a factor, and treatment may need to include alcohol or drug abuse assessment and referral. Addiction problems may continue during treatment and be kept from the therapist.

In therapy, as in other relationships, patients with high Pd scores tend to be manipulative, aggressive, deceptive, exhibitionistic, and self-oriented. They are inclined to act out conflicts and may engage in therapeutically destructive behavior. They often leave therapy prematurely and without significant improvement.

Scale 5: Masculinity–Femininity

The Mf scale, though not originally developed as a clinical scale, provides useful information for treatment planning. The scale assesses a person's level of cultural awareness and openness to new ideas. The Mf scale has different interpretive significance depending upon the level of elevation and the gender of the client. The following hypotheses should be considered.

In males.

1. *The man with a score below T = 45* may be viewed as a poor candidate for individual, insight-oriented psychotherapy. Individuals with this pattern tend to show low verbal skills, interpersonal insensitivity, or a lack of interest in discussing their problems with others. They are more "action oriented" than reflective in their general approach to life. They show low psychological mindedness, have a narrow range of interests, and are noninsightful, and so are usually not interested in psychological matters or therapy.

2. *The man with a score of T = 65–70* demonstrates sensitivity, introspection, and insightfulness, characteristics that suggest openness to experience and amenability to individual psychotherapy. He may show some passivity and dependency and wish to be taken care of. He may also show some dependency in long-term therapy.

3. *The man with a score above T = 75* has a strong possibility of passivity and heterosexual adjustment problems that may severely affect his interrelationships. The person might show a severe narcissism that could interfere with some types of therapy (e.g., directive, short-term treatment).

There is some suggestion that he has problems dealing with anger, which could prove difficult in therapy. Passivity and an impractical approach to life may prevent him from trying new roles and alternative behaviors that might emerge out of therapy.

In females

1. *The woman with a score below T = 40* has an ultrapassive life-style suggestive of low treatment potential. There may be a need to remain "weak, dependent, and passive" in relationships. She may show masochistic and self-deprecating, self-defeating behavior in relationships that could be difficult to alter.

Patients with high 4–6 profiles with low Mf are thought to be passive–aggressive in interaction style and may strive to control others through procrastination and nagging. Seemingly overcompliant and partially compliant behavior may interfere with implementing treatment plans.

Dependency and lack of assertiveness may be a central problem for low Mf women. They might respond to assertiveness training if appropriate.

2. *The woman with a score above T = 70* is overly aggressive and

maladaptively dominant, behaviors that may contraindicate verbal psychotherapy. This woman tends not to be very introspective or to value self-insights. She generally has difficulty expressing emotions and articulating problems. She may be rebellious, brusk, and cynical in dealing with others.

Scale 6: Paranoia

The Pa scale is a very important scale for use in treatment planning because it assesses the client's trust in interpersonal relationships, flexibility toward personal change, and attitudes toward authority figures. High Pa clients are generally not viewed as good candidates for psychotherapy because they tend to see others as responsible for their problems. They are often argumentative, resentful, and cynical. They may enjoy interpersonal encounters and verbal combat, and may even challenge the therapist. They tend to be aloof, defensive, and do not confide in the therapist, which could prevent the therapeutic relationship from proceeding to one of mutual respect, warmth, and empathic feeling. The patient may have inaccurate beliefs that are rigidly maintained even against contrary evidence.

High Pa patients tend to terminate therapy early; many do not return after the first visit because they believe that the therapist does not understand them.

Scale 7: Psychasthenia

The Pt scale assesses a person's level of felt discomfort, tension, and cognitive efficiency. People with peak scores on this scale generally express a great need for help for their nervousness and tension. They may seek medical solutions for their physical problems, which are probably associated with intense anxiety. They appear to be quite motivated for symptom relief. Their anxiety may be debilitating, causing them to be grossly inefficient and indecisive. They may need antianxiety medication to enable them to function and fall asleep at night.

Psychotherapy and a supportive, structured environment may be effective in allaying the anxiety and intense guilt of such patients. Cognitive restructuring therapy may facilitate dramatic behavior changes if the sources of anxiety or panic states are known. Directive, action-oriented treatment may assist them in redirecting their maladaptive cognitive behavior. Systematic desensitization therapy may serve to reduce tension. In some cases, patients (especially if Si is $T > 60$) may benefit from assertiveness training. These patients have a strong tendency to intellectualize and ruminate. Insight-oriented treatment may be unproductive if it only serves to encourage discussion about their problems without implementation of newly learned adaptive behavior.

Patients with extremely high elevations on this scale ($T > 90$) may show considerable interpersonal rigidity and unproductive rumination. Consequently, the therapist may experience some frustration over their seeming unwillingness or inability to implement "well worked through insights" into actual behavioral change. The high Pt individual is often so self-critical that he or she engages in a degree of self-critical, perfectionistic behavior that impedes progress in treatment.

Scale 8: Schizophrenia

Peak scale elevations on Sc generally suggest a problem-oriented focus in initial treatment sessions. The level of elevation, however, needs to be considered in terms of other scales. Increasing elevation of this scale suggests relative differences in the amount of unusual thinking, unconventional behavior, and problem severity and chronicity. It is useful for the therapist to evaluate the severity of potentially relevant information in this scale as shown in the following.

1. *A score of T = 70–79* indicates a chaotic life-style. Disorganized life circumstances may produce a multiproblem situation that is difficult to pinpoint in therapy. The patient may be experiencing extensive anxiety and emotional disarray while seeking relief for symptoms.

Interpersonal difficulties may interfere with establishing rapport in treatment. Preoccupation with the occult or superstitious beliefs may undermine psychological treatment, and the patient may show immature, self-destructive behavior and act out conflict rather than deal with it in therapy sessions. Such patients may avoid emotional commitments and not respond well to therapy. They may feel that no one understands them. Their problems tend to be chronic and long-term; thus, lengthy treatment is anticipated.

2. *Scores of T = 80 and above* suggest severe confusion and disorganization in high Sc patients, who may require antipsychotic medication. Hospitalization is sometimes required if the patient is unable to handle his or her affairs. Withdrawal and bizarre thought processes may deter psychotherapy. As outpatients, such patients may benefit from structured treatment programs such as halfway house contacts, outpatient follow-up, or day-treatment programs to provide some structure to their lives.

Scale 9: Mania

It is useful to consider the relative elevation on the Ma scale to appraise an individual's motivation for and accessibility to treatment. The range of scores is explored in the paragraphs that follow.

1. *Scores below T = 45* indicate difficulty in psychological treatment because the patients feel unmotivated, inadequate, depressed, hopeless, and pessimistic about the future. They may be experiencing multiproblem situations and have difficulty getting mobilized to work on these various problems. An activity-oriented therapy program may provide the appropriate structure for treatment if it is not overly demanding.

2. *Scores of T = 46–69* reflect self-assurance. If the Ma score is the highest peak in the profile, then the respondent is presenting a statement of self-assurance, self-confidence, and denial of problems. People with this pattern typically do not seek treatment. For all practical purposes, this should be considered a normal range profile. Treatment recommendations are usually not made.

3. *Scores above T = 70* indicate distractibility and overactivity, which may make individuals with this profile difficult, uncooperative patients. They may not be able to focus on problems and tend to overuse denial to avoid self-examination. They are inclined to be narcissistic and they make unrealistic grandiose plans. They frequently make shallow promises and set goals in treatment that are never met. They are manipulative and disregard scheduled therapy times with ease—they are frequently "too busy" to make the session. They avoid self-examination by generating projects and ideas to occupy their time.

Their low frustration tolerance may produce stormy therapy sessions punctuated by irritable and angry outbursts. Their problems with self-control lead them to act out their impulses. They may have problems with alcohol abuse that require evaluation and treatment.

Si Scale: Social Introversion–Extroversion

The Si scale is one of the most useful scales in pretreatment planning because it addresses several aspects of interpersonal adjustment. The Si scale reflects problems of social anxiety and maladjustment, inhibition and overcontrol, and comfort in relationships. The level of elevation in the Si scale provides valuable clues to an individual's capacity to form social relationships as well as readiness to become engaged in a process of self-disclosure.

1. *Low Si (scores below T = 45)* identify patients who may not see the need for treatment. They tend to feel little or no anxiety and do not feel uncomfortable enough to change. They usually are rather superficial in their social relations and may be too glib to form deep emotional relationships. They are exhibitionistic and dominant and not reflective or interested in inward scrutiny. They may act out and experience problems of poor control.

2. *Moderate Si (scores of T = 60–69)* reflect difficulty in forming per-

sonal relationships. Treatment sessions are often slow in tempo. Patients are shy and inhibited and may have great difficulty expressing themselves. They are quite insecure and conforming; thus, they may expect the therapist to be directive and dominate the sessions. Group treatment methods or social skills training may be useful in teaching them to relate more effectively with others.

3. *High Si (scores of T = 70 or greater)* suggest probable difficulty in developing an effective therapeutic relationship. These clients are quite inhibited and may be unable to articulate their feelings; they are very slow to trust the therapist. Treatment sessions are typically slow-paced, with long silences. Patients may appear unmotivated and passive, yet quite tense and high-strung. Such people are overcontrolled and can have great difficulty making changes in their social behavior or in putting into practice new modes of responding outside the treatment setting.

MMPI-2 CODE TYPES

The literature on MMPI-2 code types provides additional hypotheses for treatment planning. The following brief summaries of descriptive hypotheses associated with MMPI-2 code types may be useful for understanding patient behaviors in the early stages of treatment. The code type information provided here is for those types in which all relevant scales are greater than T = 65.

12/21

Individuals with the 12/21 profile type are not good candidates for traditional insight-oriented therapy. They tend to somatize problems; they tolerate high levels of stress without motivation to change; they resist psychological interpretation of their problems; and they seek medical solutions to problems.

1234

Alcohol or drug abuse problems are characteristic of people with the 1234 profile. Chemical dependency treatment may be required, and medical attention for ulcers or related gastrointestinal problems may also be necessary. Sometimes tranquilizers are prescribed for such patients because they show tension in addition to other evident psychological problems. Use of tranquilizers should be minimized or discouraged, however, because such patients have addictive tendencies. Psychotherapy, when attempted, is often a long and difficult process since these clients tend to resist psychological interpretations, blame others for their problems, and see no need for personal change. Acting out problems commonly occur. The long-range prognosis is usually considered poor.

13/31

Individuals with the 13/31 profile are resistant to psychological treatment. They seek medical explanations for their difficulties, deny the validity of psychological explanations, are defensive, avoid introspection, show lack of concern for their physical symptoms, and show little motivation to alter their behavior. They may respond to mild direct suggestion and placebo in a medical setting. Brief stress-inoculation training may be successful if resistance is overcome. Long-term commitment to therapy is usually required for treatment of personality problems. Treatment resistance and lack of motivation for change may result in early termination of therapy.

14/41

Individuals with the 14/41 profile code tend to have long-standing personality problems and are inclined to have relationship problems, excessive somatic complaints, and patterns of aggressive behavior. Their symptomatic behavior can often be viewed as manipulative and controlling. They are likely to be resistant to psychological treatment and may fail to comply with treatment plans.

Insight-oriented treatment is likely to be somewhat stormy. Treatment sessions become tense because of the patients' high level of hostility and aggressiveness, which may at times be directed toward the therapist.

23/32

The 23/32 pattern reveals considerable tension and stress, but affected patients may have difficulty articulating the sources of their problems. They tend to excessively employ ego-defensive mechanisms, such as repression, to maintain their social "image," and they may have some problems in early stages of insight-oriented treatment. They often describe vague somatic problems such as weakness or dizziness. They generally view these complaints as their main problem and have difficulty going beyond the felt symptom itself. They tend to seek medical treatment such as pain medications or tranquilizers as the solution to problems caused by conflictive relationships. They may "energize" themselves through self-medication.

The degree of depression in people with this profile is usually high, and some symptomatic relief is considered necessary. Sometimes antidepressant medication is required to reduce tension and distress. Supportive psychological treatment might be successfully applied.

24/42

The treatment setting and referral problems are extremely important factors in interpreting the 24/42 MMPI-2 profile code. Since this is the mean and most frequent code type appearing in alcohol and drug treatment programs, an assessment for substance abuse is important. An acceptance and admission by the individual of such a problem is crucial in making positive life changes. People with this profile are often viewed as having long-standing personality problems that make them resistant to treatment. Therapy on an outpatient basis often ends in termination before behavior changes result. Some outpatients with this profile type fail to recognize or acknowledge their alcohol or drug abuse problems. Consequently, the therapist should be aware of possible substance abuse.

Some people with this pattern may respond to treatment in a controlled context that reduces acting out. Group treatment may be more successful than individual therapy.

27/72

People with either a 27 or a 72 code type are usually in such psychological distress that they seek help and are amenable to psychotherapy. Initial therapy sessions may be oriented toward problem expression and help-seeking behaviors. Reassurance and advice may be sought directly by such clients because they often feel that they do not have the personal resources to deal with their life circumstances.

Low self-esteem and self-defeating behavior may prevent such patients from taking action to remedy their problem circumstances. They usually seek considerable support, are introspective, and can be ruminative and overly self-critical in sessions. They generally establish interpersonal relationships easily, although this is apparently easier for 27s than for 72s, who are more anxious. People with the 72 code are quite prone to guilt and are overly perfectionistic. Their obsessive ruminations can be very unproductive in verbal psychotherapy. They tend to be obsessive about the need for change but have considerable difficulty actually trying out new behaviors.

Both 27s and 72s tend to experience acute disabling symptoms. Psychotropic medication might be required to reduce the acute symptoms: antianxiety medication for 72s (where anxiety is problematic) and antidepressants for 27s (where depression is primary). Of course, both anxiety and depression could be present in a 27 or a 72.

274/427/724

The 274 MMPI-2 code is rather different from the 27/72 code, largely due to the presence of personality problems reflected in the Pd (scale 4) configuration. Acute distress, possibly of a transitory and situational nature, is usually present. The presence of Pd indicates an antisocial life-style, which might have produced the depression by an injudicious pattern of self-indulgence. This profile code is commonly found among people who have alcohol or drug abuse problems. This possibility should be verified in early therapy sessions because a long-standing problem could suggest a poor prognosis.

Persons with this profile code are generally not very responsive to individual insight-oriented treatment. In outpatient settings they tend to leave treatment prematurely, cannot tolerate anxiety in treatment, and act out (for example, by engaging in drinking bouts between sessions). They often show a "honeymoon effect"; that is, they have gains early in treatment but slip as their frustration mounts. They may respond best to environmentally focused changes and directive goal-oriented treatment. Group treatment methods in a controlled setting (e.g., alcohol treatment programs) may produce therapeutic gains.

28/82

Individuals with the complex MMPI-2 profile code 28/82 require careful consideration in terms of treatment planning since several major diagnostic problems are possible, as discussed in the paragraphs that follow.

1. *Psychotic behavior.* Problems reflected in this group are bizarre ideation, delusional thinking, social withdrawal, extreme emotional lability, and anger. Social relationship problems are usually evident.

2. *Affective disorder.* Mood disorder and social withdrawal are characteristic problems of this disorder.

3. *Personality disorder.* Emotional instability reflected in acting-out behavior, social relationship problems, and lability are present. Borderline personality is a likely diagnostic summary for patients with these problems.

Regardless of clinical diagnosis and treatment setting, several factors are important for the potential therapist to consider.

Relationship problems. People with this profile tend to have difficulty dealing with interpersonal relationships. This is likely to be manifest in stormy therapeutic relationships as well.

Anger expression problems. The 82/28 profile type tends to experience marked emotional control problems, including loss of control and expression of anger. Unmodulated anger toward the therapist is common during periods of emotional intensity.

Social withdrawal. Persons with the 28/82 profile may experience considerable ambivalence toward relationships. It is often difficult for them to enact new relationship "tactics" learned in therapy.

Individuals with this profile code tend to have several problems in their life. It is often difficult for them to focus on a problem area for any time before other aspects of their lives begin to fall apart. A therapist can provide a point of stability for such patients, who often require long-term treatment to work through their extensive problems. Many people with this profile require psychotropic medications (i.e., antidepressant and antipsychotic compounds) to control their emotions and thoughts, particularly in periods of intense crisis.

34/43

Patients with the 34/43 code typically enter therapy with problems in which their own lack of emotional control, particularly anger, is the salient feature. Their impulsive life-style and stormy interpersonal style are as likely to characterize therapy sessions as the other aspects of their lives. Self-control issues and acceptance of responsibility for their problems are likely to be central issues in treatment.

Clients with this pattern are often found to be resistant to psychological treatment because they project blame. Their conflict-producing interpersonal dynamics result in a rather rocky therapeutic course. Early termination in anger and acting out in frustration are common for such patients.

People with this profile may not seek treatment on their own but enter therapy at the insistence of a spouse or the court. Outpatient psychotherapy may often be problematic because of emotional immaturity and a tendency to blame others for their own shortcomings. A motivation to change is sometimes lacking.

Some people with this pattern get into legal problems and require treatment in a more controlled setting. Group treatment has been shown to be effective for some patients with this extensive behavioral problem.

46/64

People with the 46/64 MMPI-2 profile code are generally antagonistic toward psychological treatment. They tend not to seek help on their own but are usually evaluated in mental health settings at the request or insistence of someone else. As a consequence, they are often hostile, uncooperative, suspicious, and mistrustful of the motives of others. Treatment relationships are usually rocky and initially very difficult to form. These people usually view their problems as being caused by someone else, and they project the blame for their circumstances on others.

Patients with this pattern are usually hostile and aggressive, and they commonly have a number of environmental difficulties as well. Treatment plans should be realistic. Because they are typically argumentative and they tend to defend and justify their actions to a considerable degree, therapy sessions with such patients are often marked by extreme resistance and lack of cooperation. Treatment often ends abruptly when the client becomes angry and frustrated. The therapist should be aware of the possibility of angry acting out by clients with the 46/64 profile code.

47/74

The 47/74 MMPI-2 profile code suggests some characteristic behaviors that are very pertinent for treatment planning, particularly the individual's tendency toward cyclic acting out followed by superficial remorse. Individuals with this pattern are generally found to show long-standing personality problems that center on an impulsive–compulsive pattern of self-gratification and consequent guilt. In the early stages of treatment, such strong behavioral trends may find the patient seemingly cooperative, remorseful, and goal-directed. Over time, however, the guilt appears to diminish and the desire for pleasure again appears to dominate. Thus, the "early gains" and sincere attitude toward change melt away, leaving the unswerving acting-out component in the character pattern to disrupt treatment.

Many 47/74 persons are found in alcohol and drug treatment programs or in other treatment settings (e.g., programs for those with eating disorders such as bulimia) where the impulsive–compulsive life-style appears with some frequency. Therapists should be cautious about the early and "easy" gains and be aware of personality factors that may lie in wait for their turn at ascendancy.

48/84

Long-standing problems of unconventional, unusual, or antisocial behavior are likely to characterize early treatment sessions with the 48/84 profile type. Patients usually have substantial environmental and relationship problems, as well as intrapsychic difficulties. Individual psychological treatment planning with the 48/84 may be confounded by other problems—for example, drug or alcohol abuse—which need to be addressed if treatment is to proceed effectively.

If the treatment approach is verbal psychotherapy, the early treatment sessions are likely to be chaotic, with numerous complicated involvements and little productive focusing. The treatment relationship, like other interpersonal involvements the person has, is likely to be stormy and difficult. Verbal psychotherapy, because of the 48/84's aloofness, unconventionality, and relationship-formation deficits, is likely to be unproductive at worst and difficult at best. Acting-out behavior is likely to complicate treatment planning as well as other aspects of life. The client's lack of trust may lead to early termination of therapy.

482

Patients with the 482 profile typically lack insight into their behavior and tend to have a low capacity for insight-oriented treatment. If depression is a strong component in the symptomatic picture, as is likely to be the case, they may respond to antidepressant medication. Underlying character disorder and addiction potential should be evaluated before medication is prescribed. Antipsychotic medications may be required to control possible thought disorder in 482s. Commitment to an inpatient facility may be necessary to protect such patients from injuring themselves or others.

Long-term change in the basic personality structure is unlikely to result from treatment. Symptomatic relief and emotional support may enable the individual to return to previous marginal adjustment.

49/94

Patients with the 49/94 code are usually less interested in treatment and the complex task of self-analysis and behavior change than they are in self-gratification and hedonistic pursuits. Persons with this profile code usually find their way into psychological treatment at the behest of another person, such as a spouse, employer, or the court. They are generally not motivated to discuss personal problems even though they are usually articulate and expressive. Their lack of anxiety usually proves to be a deficit that deters genuine change.

Individuals with this code are frequently found to be controlling and turn their "charm" and manipulative skill to the therapist in order to gain favor or attention.

At times, the most effective treatment approach for 49/94s is difficult to determine, since manipulating and "conning" other people is an important adaptive strategy for 49s. It behooves the therapist to be forewarned of such tactics, whatever the proposed treatment approach. It is effective to confront this behavioral style when it becomes manifest. Individuals with this profile code usually do not respond well to punishment.

Outpatient treatment for the 49/94 often ends in premature termination when he or she becomes bored with the sessions. Since acting-out behavior is common among 49/94s, therapy can be disrupted by poor judgment and indiscreet behavior on the client's part.

Individual insight-oriented treatment may be "enjoyed" briefly by 49s, but treatment may be terminated early, often abruptly. Group treatment methods (in controlled environments) have reportedly been effective; behavior modification procedures may be useful as well in helping the patient learn more adaptable behaviors.

68/86

Severe psychopathology characterizes the 68/86 profile type with both cognitive and emotional disturbances. Consequently, the therapist may have several important decisions to ponder in treatment planning.

Should the patient be treated on an inpatient or outpatient basis? Many people with this profile code require careful monitoring and external direction. The question of whether hospitalization is needed should be answered with the potential for dangerousness to self or others given consideration. Outpatient treatment can be complicated by regressed or disorganized behavior. Day treatment is often effective at helping these patients manage their daily activities.

Paralleling the question of an appropriate setting for treatment is the question of the need for psychotropic medication. The individual should be evaluated for medication needs if this has not been done. Major tranquilizers to control psychotic thinking are often helpful. Long-term, marginal adjustment is a problem; thus, frequent brief contacts for "management" therapy can be helpful. Insight-oriented therapy on an outpatient basis should proceed with caution since self-scrutiny may exacerbate problems and result in regression.

Regardless of the treatment setting and therapeutic approach, several factors influence treatment planning for the 68/86:

1. *Problems of relationship formation.* Individuals with this profile code are unskilled socially and may never have had a satisfactory interpersonal experience.
2. *Problems of mistrust* (projection). Suspicion and mistrust are characteristic of the way such people interact with others. They manage conflict and anxiety by projecting blame onto others.
3. *Cognitive distortion.* People with this profile show cognitive defects and may operate with a different form of logic than does the therapist. This poses a particular problem for cognitively based therapy. Delusions and hallucinations may be present.
4. *Impulsivity—poor judgment.* Patients may act impulsively and their behavior will at times be bizarre.
5. *Preoccupation with nonnatural causation.* Many people with this pattern give as much credence to the occult (astrology, numerology, etc.) as they do to natural causes. Treatment suggestions or plans might be subverted as a result of an unusual belief system.
6. *Pan-anxiety.* Patients are usually extremely anxious, although their affect might be flat or blunted.
7. *Regression.* The individual's behavior might be extremely regressed and requires careful management.

78/87

Since patients with the 78/87 profile code are usually experiencing intense anxiety and psychological deterioration, the therapist may need to begin therapy by providing a supportive atmosphere of reassurance to lower the client's level of distress. People with this profile are generally "crisis prone" and appear to have little resiliency and few resources with which to manage their daily affairs. Structure and a directive crisis management approach might be effective in helping the 78/87 manage intense stress. Many people who experience this level of tension and disorganization require psychotropic medication for relief of anxiety; referral for an evaluation of medication is indicated.

Insight-oriented psychological treatment may aggravate psychological problems and produce further deterioration in functioning. There is a tendency for this type of patient to over-intellectualize. A problem-focused treatment approach may be more effective in helping such patients deal with their problems. Social skills or assertiveness training may be appropriate if the patient is not psychotic. This approach may be productive since the 78/87 client is frequently lacking in social skills.

83/38

Patients with the 83/38 profile often report obscure, intractable somatic complaints. Relationship problems and lack of insight into psychological problems may contraindicate individual insight-oriented therapy. These patients may be responsive to pharmacological treatment and supportive/directive therapy.

96/69

Antipsychotic medication is likely to produce the most dramatic change in patients with the 96/69 profile codes. Traditional insight-oriented treatment is difficult because 69s show extensive relationship problems and lack of trust. Problem-focused treatment is most successful if the patient comes to trust the therapist.

89/98

Major tranquilizers are likely to be the most effective treatment for the 89/98 profile patient if the diagnosis is major affective disorder. Lithium may be useful in controlling affective disorder. Prolonged hospitalization may be necessary for patients who lack behavior control. Traditional psychotherapy is usually ineffective since these clients cannot focus on problems. Some 89s suffer from severe personality disorders that are entrenched and unresponsive to insight-oriented psychotherapy.

4

MMPI-2 Supplementary Scales in Treatment Evaluation

A number of supplementary or special purpose scales have been developed for the MMPI. Several of these scales, which have special relevance for treatment evaluation, are discussed in this chapter. Individuals interested in a more detailed discussion of these scales should consult Graham's (1990) MMPI text.

THE EGO STRENGTH SCALE (Es)

Rather early in MMPI history, clinical researchers saw promise in using the MMPI for predicting a client's response to psychological treatment and for determining which personality characteristics lead to treatment success or end in treatment failure. One interesting attempt to develop a specific scale to measure personality characteristics associated with successful outcome in therapy resulted in development of the Ego Strength Scale (Es). The Es scale was developed by Barron (1953) as a scale to use in predicting whether an individual is likely to respond well to therapy.

The Es scale was developed by empirical scale construction procedures. Barron divided a sample of 33 patients into 17 patients who had been judged by their therapists to have clearly improved and 16 who were judged to be unimproved. The test responses of the patients were obtained before the therapy had begun. The scale was proposed as a pretreatment measure of prognosis for therapy. As the Es scale began to be used, and content analysis and intercorrelational studies followed, the meaning of the scale came to be viewed as a measure of adaptability and personal resourcefulness or the ability to manage stressful situations rather than as a predictor of treatment response.

In the revision of the MMPI, the MMPI Restandardization Committee deleted a number of items that were outmoded or objectionable. Sixteen items from the Es scale were among those deleted in the revision; consequently, the MMPI-2 version of Es contains 52 items.

An examination of the content of the Es scale suggests that no single unitary personality dimension is represented by the scale, but it is the sum of a number of complex adjustment factors. The Es scale contains items that can be grouped into the following categories by content: physical functioning and physiological stability; psychasthenia and seclusiveness; moral posture; sense of reality; personal adequacy and ability to cope; phobias; and miscellaneous other content.

In some respects, the Es scale is a measure of problem denial or whether a person is able to manage current stressors. Early correlational research related high scores on the Es scale to such factors as resourcefulness, vitality, self-direction, psychological stability, permissive morality, outgoingness, and spontaneity. High scorers on the Es scale typically show more positive changes in treatment than do low scorers according to Graham (1987). Graham has summarized the correlates for the Es scale as follows:

A number of personality characteristics have been associated with high and low scores on the Es scale. People with high Es are thought *not* to be experiencing chronic psychopathology and are viewed as more stable, reliable, and responsible than others. They are considered to be tolerant in their views of others and to lack prejudice. They show a high degree of self-confidence and may be outspoken and sociable. Individuals with high scores on Es are thought to be resourceful, independent, and grounded in reality. Socially, they are thought to be effective in dealing with others and easily gain social acceptance. Individuals with high Es scores often seek help because of situational problems. They can usually manage verbal interchange and confrontation in psychotherapy without deteriorating psychologically.

Individuals who score low on the Es scale are considered to have low self-esteem and a poor self-concept. They feel worthless and helpless and have difficulty managing daily affairs. In an interview they may appear confused and disorganized and are likely to have a wide range of psychological symptoms, such as chronic physical complaints, chronic fatigue, fears, or phobias. They are likely to appear withdrawn, seclusive, overly inhibited, rigid, and moralistic. They are often seen by the therapist as maladaptive, unoriginal, and stereotyped in behavior. They are likely to demonstrate exaggerated problems or a "cry for help," have work problems, and show more susceptibility to experiencing day-to-day crises. Their problems are more likely to be viewed as characterological rather than situational in nature. They are likely to express a desire for psychotherapy and feel the need to resolve their many problems; however, it may be difficult for them to focus on problems. Readers interested in a more extensive discussion of the Es scale should see Graham (1990).

► Case: The Value of Using the Es Scale in Treatment Planning

Sybil, the patient whose MMPI profile is shown in Figure 4-1, is a 37-year-old single woman who lives with her parents. Her father is a semi-invalid but financially well-off retired businessman. Her mother, a successful attorney and partner in a large law firm, travels a great deal on business. Sybil was a rather reclusive woman with a substantial history of mental illness. She has been hospitalized on three occasions for depression and in each instance improved to the point that she could resume her limited activities. She did not finish college because of an early and seemingly poorly planned marriage. Her husband left town after 6 months without telling anyone where he was going. After several years, with her parents' prompting, she obtained an annulment of her marriage. She has not dated anyone since her husband left. Her MMPI profile (an extremely elevated 28) shows severe psychopathology. She appears to be quite depressed at the present testing and has problems with her thinking and emotions. She is confused, disorganized, and has been experiencing auditory hallucinations. She is also experiencing intense moods that are characterized by anger and despair. She shows some suicidal preoccupation. In the past, she has attempted to kill herself on two occasions.

Her poor prognosis for outpatient, insight-oriented psychological treatment is shown by her extremely low score on the Es scale (T = 35). Her Es score suggests that she has a very poor self-concept, low morale, is confused and fearful, and has chronic problems.

Problems in Interpreting the Es Scale in Treatment Planning

Although the Es scale provides the clinician with a measure of the patient's adjustment level and ability to cope with life stressors, it does not fulfill the original hope of being a predictor of treatment amenability that one could use in pretreatment evaluation to appraise potential treatment success. As an index of adjustment, it appears to be a redundant measure of general maladjustment measures, of which there are several in the MMPI, such as the Pt scale.

One difficulty in using the Es scale in clinical interpretation is that the scale contains a generally heterogeneous group of items, making substantive interpretation difficult. There are several items on the Es scale that have little content relevance to treatment prediction. These items were probably included on the scale as a result of chance, since the original scale construction used small sample sizes. For example, in the original MMPI the item "I like Lincoln better than Washington" has neither appropriate content nor empirical validity for the construct being assessed. The most useful interpretations for the Es scale in treatment prediction were noted by Graham (1987):

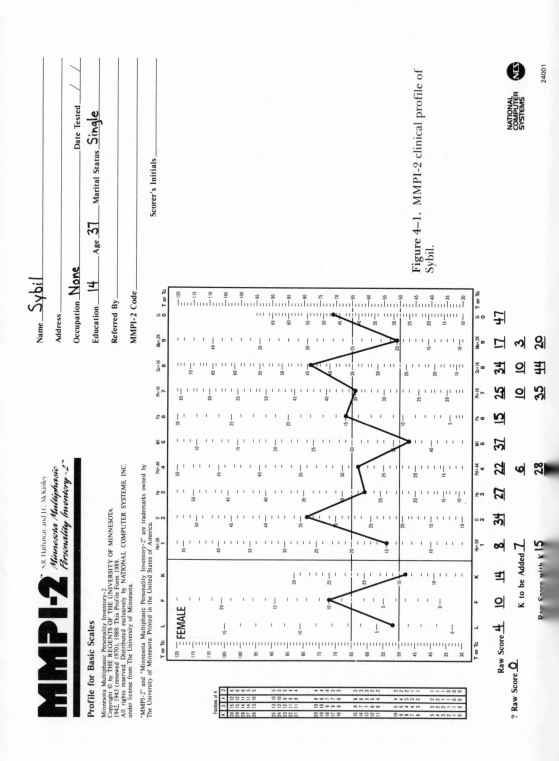

Figure 4–1. MMPI-2 clinical profile of Sybil.

In summary, people with low Es scores do not seem to be very well put together. Such individuals are likely to be seriously maladjusted psychologically. Problems are likely to be long-standing in nature; personal resources for coping with problems are extremely limited; and the progress for positive change in psychotherapy is poor. (pp. 170–171)

MACANDREW ALCOHOLISM SCALE (MAC-R)

Alcohol and other addictive substances are prominent in contemporary society, and abuse of them is commonplace. Many individuals with psychological symptoms find temporary relief from the pressures of living through the use and abuse of these substances. Consequently, clinicians find that an assessment of the way in which their patients learn or fail to learn to deal with alcohol and other drugs is an important assessment question in a pretreatment diagnostic study. Many people who eventually develop alcohol or drug abuse disorders begin their abuse in an effort to deal with their psychological distress. The substance abuse pattern they develop comes to be viewed as an effort to manage their psychological distress. It becomes an important aspect in any pretreatment psychological assessment, then, to determine if alcohol or drug use is a pertinent or potentially confounding problem.

MacAndrew (1965) was interested in developing a psychological assessment measure that would differentiate between alcohol abusing and non–alcohol abusing people who also had some psychological problems. He contrasted a group of 200 male alcoholics with a group of 200 male psychiatric patients from the same facility who did not have an alcohol abuse problem. The scale he developed, the MAC scale, contained 51 items. MacAndrew cross-validated the scale on a different sample and found comparable classification rates (82 percent). Since MacAndrew's original work, numerous other researchers (for example, Apfeldorf & Huntley, 1975; Rhodes, 1969; Rich & Davis, 1969; and Schwartz & Graham, 1979) have found high classification rates for the MAC scale, but these were not as high as MacAndrew's cross-validation.

Although MacAndrew initially found 51 items to discriminate significantly between alcoholics and nonalcoholics, he recommended the use of only 49 items, dropping two obvious alcohol items since he thought that alcoholics would deny these items. Most of the research on the MAC scale has employed the 49-item scale, and the norms now used are based on that set. Initially, MacAndrew recommended a cutoff score of 24 as indicative of alcohol abuse problems. This cutoff is probably too low because it is less than one standard deviation above the mean of the original Minnesota normals. A more conservative cutoff score is therefore recommended. A general rule of thumb for interpreting the MAC scale is provided as follows:

1. For males, a raw score of 26 to 28 suggests that alcohol or drug abuse problems are possible; a raw score of 29 to 31 suggests that alcohol or drug abuse problems are likely; a raw score of 32 or more suggests that alcohol or drug abuse problems are highly probable.
2. For females, a raw score of 23 to 25 suggests that alcohol or drug abuse problems are possible; a raw score of 26 to 29 suggests that alcohol or drug abuse problems are likely; a raw score of 30 or more suggests that alcohol or drug abuse problems are highly probable.

In the MMPI restandardization the MAC scale was modified slightly because it contained four items that were eliminated as objectionable. To keep the same number of items on the scale, 49 items, four new items were substituted for the objectionable items (see Butcher et al., 1989). These items were selected through procedures similar to those Mac-Andrew originally used in developing the scale—empirical discrimination between a group of alcoholics and a group of psychiatric patients.

The content of the MAC scale suggests that high-scoring individuals may have the following characteristics: they are socially extroverted, present themselves as self-confident, are assertive and exhibitionistic, enjoy taking risks, show concentration problems, and have a history of acting-out behavior such as school problems. An example of the utility of the MAC score can be seen in the following case (see Figure 4-2).

▶ Case: A Study of the MAC Scale

John W., a 48-year-old postal employee, was referred for a psychological evaluation by his physician, who suspected that he might be experiencing some psychological problems. He has been reportedly missing a great deal of work over the past year and has attempted to obtain medical permission for his numerous absences. He has been to see the physician on several occasions, in recent months for "medical problems," but a physical basis for his problems has been ruled out. Mr. W. was somewhat reluctant to make an appointment with the psychological staff since he viewed his problems as physical, not psychological. He was defensive on the MMPI, although he presented a general picture of somatic concern and physical weakness. His MAC raw score of 29 suggested the possibility that his problems could result, in part, from an underlying drug or alcohol abuse problem. In interview, when this possible problem was raised with him, he denied that he drank alcohol to excess and acknowledged only moderate use. Further discussion about his modes of "tension relief," however, did reveal that he had been taking Doriden (a highly addictive central nervous system depressant) for several years in order to sleep. His daily use of this medication suggested the likelihood of an addictive disorder; yet a referral to psychological treatment was refused.

MMPI-2™

Minnesota Multiphasic Personality Inventory -2™

S.R. Hathaway and J.C. McKinley

Profile for Basic Scales

Name John W.

Address

Occupation Post Office   Date Tested   /   /

Education 13   Age 48   Marital Status M

Referred By

MMPI-2 Code

Scorer's Initials

MALE

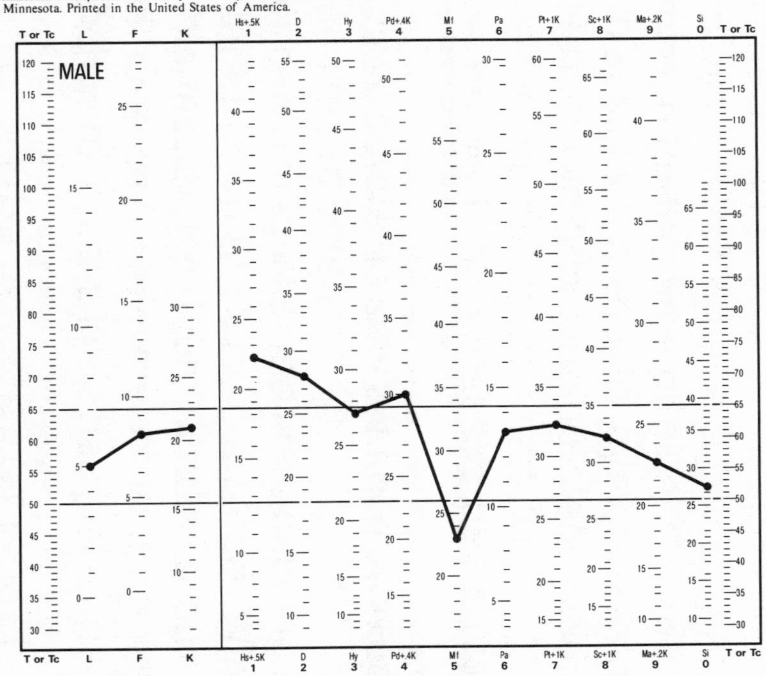

	L	F	K	Hs+.5K 1	D 2	Hy 3	Pd+.4K 4	Mf 5	Pa 6	Pt+1K 7	Sc+1K 8	Ma+.2K 9	Si 0
Raw Score	5	8	21	11	28	27	22	23	13	11	11	19	28
K to be Added				11			8			21	21	4	
Raw Score with K			22	22			30			32	32	23	

? Raw Score

Figure 4–2. MMPI-2 clinical profile of John.

75

Predictive Limitations of the MAC Scale

Research has shown that black Americans typically score in the alcoholic range on the MAC scale and that classification rates are not as good as with white populations (Walters et al., 1983; Walters et al., 1984). In clinical practice, the ranges listed earlier should be set 2 points higher for minority Americans.

Studies on the use of the MAC scale to predict adolescent alcohol and drug problems have reported inconsistent findings. Most reports have found the scale to be useful with adolescent groups (Wisniewski et al., 1985). Wolfson and Erbaugh (1984) found that the MAC scale was useful in differentiating alcohol and drug abusing adolescents, with and without a significant substance abuse history, using a cutoff score of 24 for females and 26 for males. This produced an overall hit rate of 74 percent for females and 68 percent for males; however, Klinge, Lachar, Grissell, and Berman (1978) found that the MAC scale was limited in usefulness with adolescents.

The assessment of substance abuse problems is clearly central to treatment planning. In cases where a new patient has a high MAC-R score, the therapist should be aware of the potential complications that could occur in the course of therapy when the individual becomes frustrated and acts out with excessive substance abuse.

Another valuable use of the MAC-R score in treatment planning involves application of the finding that a number of patients in treatment for substance abuse (about 15 percent) have low scores—less than a raw score of 24 for males and 21 for females—when it would be expected that their MAC-R scores would be high. The low MAC-R score typically indicates that a person is experiencing alcohol or drug abuse problems as secondary to other psychological problems. Treatment of the other problems may be necessary to clear up the substance abuse problems.

THE O-H SCALE (MEGARGEE)

An important psychological characteristic that has been of interest to both practicing clinicians and researchers alike is whether people are able to control their emotions and impulses without aggressively expressing them. In particular, psychologists have been interested in those who seem to be able to assert self-control up to a point but may, at times, especially under high stress, explode or otherwise lose control and suddenly act out their aggressions in a violent, uncontrollable manner. If one were able, on the basis of a psychological test, to predict if an individual were so emotionally overcontrolled that he or she might fail to modulate his or her emotions under some conditions, such predictions could be of value in treatment assessment.

The Overcontrolled-Hostility (O-H) scale was developed by Megargee, Cook, and Mendelsohn (1967) as a predictor of assaultiveness among prisoners. The authors were interested in identifying people who were chronically overcontrolled in their expression of aggression but who may act out in an extremely aggressive manner at times. Megargee et al. developed the 31-item O-H scale by obtaining MMPI items that significantly discriminated extremely assaultive prisoners, assaultive prisoners, prisoners convicted of nonviolent crimes, and men who had not been convicted of crimes. A high score on the O-H scale suggests a more overcontrolled, assaultive person.

Megargee et al. (1967) reported that prisoners who had high scores on O-H were chronically angry but maintained rigid control over their emotions. Several practical correlates for the O-H scale have been reported in the research literature: lack of overt anxiety (Lane & Kling, 1979); absence of depression (Walters et al. 1982); denial or repression of interpersonal conflict (Lane & Kling, 1979); and rigid control of emotional expression (Deiker, 1974).

The factor structure of the O-H scale has been studied by Walters and Greene (1983), providing some additional clues to the possible meanings of scale elevations on O-H. They found that five major factors accounted for most of the variance on the O-H scale: anxiety or depression; defensiveness and denial; chronic hostility and anger; persistent dreaming and reporting of dreams; and compliance and nonassertiveness.

Meaning of O-H Scale Elevations

Since the O-H scale was developed with convicted felons in correctional settings, the extension of the scale's use outside of prison populations should be cautious and tentative at best. Moreover, the scale may be less valuable in predicting aggressive behavior than in helping to explain the behavior of individuals with a known history of extremely aggressive behavior. The O-H scale cannot be used as a simple predictor of "overcontrol" of emotions or nonaggressiveness in general settings. For example, a high score on the scale does not necessarily mean that a person will not act out in an aggressive manner, only that he or she typically *denies* aggressive actions.

In using the O-H scale in nonprison settings, the interpreter should be wary of making predictions about whether the individual is or is not "hostile." Most applicants for jobs produce high O-H scores, which does not mean that they are hostile; rather, they are denying hostile intent or actions. The O-H scale does not allow the practitioner to determine whether the subject will or will not act out (acting out behavior can occur with either low or high O-H scale elevations). It suggests to the clinician that, in cases where acting-out behavior has occurred, it is likely that the behavior occurred in the overcontrolled hostility personality pattern.

Graham (1987) summarized the O-H scale correlates as indicating that the individual typically does not respond to provocation by showing nonpunitiveness, reporting fewer angry feelings, expressing less verbal hostility in reaction to frustration, appearing socialized and responsible, having strong needs to excel, being dependent on others, being trustful, and describing a nurturant and supportive family background.

High O-H scores for a person seeking treatment suggest that the individual is "oversocialized," reports few angry feelings, and tends to react to frustrating events in overcontrolled ways. This degree of constriction and inhibition is likely to make therapy, at least initially, somewhat superficial and devoid of affect until the individual begins to openly share feelings. The therapist should also be alert to the possibility that the high O-H scoring patient may be unable to control or modulate intense emotions, particularly anger, that might emerge in sessions or outside of therapy during the course of treatment.

RESPONSIBILITY SCALE (Re)

In many pretreatment evaluations it is desirable to assess whether the person entering therapy assumes responsibility for himself or herself and whether he or she approaches social relationships in a responsible manner. People tend to respond to treatment and are more willing to alter their negative behaviors if they care about themselves and others. One possible measure that reflects whether a person possesses social responsibility is the Re scale developed by Gough, McClosky, and Meehl (1952). They developed the Re scale empirically by employing groups of subjects who had been rated (by peers or by teachers) as "most" or "least" responsible in their group. Responsible individuals were viewed as those who were willing to accept the consequences of their own behavior, were viewed as dependable and trustworthy, were thought to have high integrity, and were believed to possess a sense of obligation to others. Four groups of subjects were employed in the study (50 college men and 50 college women, 123 social science students from a high school, and 221 ninth graders). The MMPI items that became the Re scale were those that empirically discriminated the most responsible from the least responsible subjects. The item content centered on espousing conventional behavior versus rebelliousness, social consciousness, emphasis upon duty and self-discipline, concern over moral issues, possession of personal security and poise, and disapproval of favoritism and privilege. The MMPI Restandardization Committee, in the final item selection for MMPI-2, eliminated 2 items from the Re scale as objectionable, bringing the total number of items on Re in the MMPI-2 to 32. The reduction in items did not result in a reduction in scale reliability. The test–retest correlations for Re reported for the MMPI-2 (Butcher, 1989) was .85 for males and

.74 for females. This is consistent with the test–retest reliabilities (.85 for males and .76 for females) reported by Moreland (1985) for the original MMPI.

Individuals who score high on Re, a T-score above 65, are viewed as having a great deal of self-confidence and a generally optimistic, positive view toward the world. They are considered by others as conventional and conforming. They are seen as having a strong sense of justice and a deep concern over ethical and moral problems. They are thought to have a strong sense of fairness and justice, tend to set high standards for themselves, and pride themselves on managing their responsibilities well.

On the other hand, low scorers (below a T-score of 40) are viewed as *not* accepting responsibilities well. They are considered undependable, untrustworthy, and lacking in integrity. The low Re person is usually viewed as not having leadership potential because he or she lacks social concern and interest in others.

High scores on the Re scale in one's therapy patient can provide some reassurance that the client is likely to more seriously approach his or her relationships and daily activities with more self-confidence and social concern than people who make up the lower end of the distribution of Re scores. Low scorers, on the other hand, are likely to be more unconventional in their approach to others and too caught up in their own turmoil to concern themselves with "doing what is the right thing" with regard to others. Low Re clients are often those who are likely to behave in selfish, nonsocially oriented ways. They may require more assistance from the therapist in defining the boundaries of reality and in seeing the social consequences of their behavior.

THE COLLEGE MALADJUSTMENT (Mt) SCALE (KLEINMUNTZ)

Therapists or counselors working in a college counseling setting are often at a loss to evaluate the nature and extent of problems being experienced by college students seeking help. Not only are the prospective student-clients manifesting symptoms of psychological disorder or personality problems but they may also be experiencing a great deal of situational turmoil that is sometimes difficult to separate from more long-standing pathology. For example, many college students experience transitional problems related to working through autonomy and independence issues with their parents or simply encounter some of the trials of becoming involved in peer relationships which can cause them great, though perhaps temporary, discomfort. As a result of turbulent situational problems, it may be difficult for the clinician to gain an accurate assessment of the individual.

The use of a college-specific assessment measure within the MMPI-2 might aid the clinician in obtaining an appropriate appraisal of students' problems. One measure developed to assess college maladjustment, the Mt scale developed by Kleinmuntz, might be a valuable addition to the college counselor's initial assessment strategy because it provides a specific appraisal of college students.

Kleinmuntz (1961) developed the Mt scale as an aid in discriminating emotionally adjusted college students from those who are maladjusted. The items for the scale were derived by contrasting maladjusted male and female students (obtained from a student counseling clinic) who were seen in therapy for at least three sessions from 40 male and female well-adjusted students (students being evaluated in the context of a teacher certification program). In the original scale development 43 items were identified that separated the groups. Items were keyed so that endorsement of an item increased the probability that the individual was in the maladjustment group. The MMPI revision process (see Butcher et al., 1989) eliminated 2 items on the Mt scale; consequently, the revised version of the scale on MMPI-2 contains 41 items.

The Mt scale has been shown to have high test–retest reliability: Kleinmuntz (1961) reported a test–retest reliability of .88; Moreland (1985) reported 6-week test–retest correlations ranging from .86 for females to .89 for males; and Butcher et al. (1989) reported 1-week test–retest correlations for males to be .91 and for females to be .90.

The Mt scale is thought to measure severe psychopathology in college students (Wilderman, 1984), and research has addressed the question of how effectively the scale predicts future emotional problems. Kleinmuntz (1961) concluded that the scale is more appropriate for detecting existing psychopathology than for predicting future emotional problems.

Students who score high on the Mt scale are viewed as being generally maladjusted, anxious, worried, ineffective in dealing with current situations, having tendencies to procrastinate rather than to complete tasks, and tending to have a pessimistic, negative outlook on life.

The college counselor whose counselee has high Mt scores needs to be aware that the student is reporting substantial psychological problems and probably requires a treatment program that addresses the significant personal problems and goes beyond simple academic counseling.

SUMMARY

This chapter has presented information about several MMPI-2 supplementary scales that have relevance and possible utility in treatment-oriented assessment. The Es scale, developed for the purpose of providing a measure of treatment potential, actually provides more information about a person's present ability to tolerate stress. Low scores on Es appear to reflect an inability to deal effectively with current problems. The MAC-R scale measures addiction potential—an important assessment concern in most pretherapy evaluations. The O-H scale, developed as an indicator of emotional—particularly aggressive—control can provide the clinician with an assessment of the possibility that the client typically deals ineffectively with emotions and tends to overcontrol emotions to the point of being unable to modulate their appropriate expression. The Re scale can provide the clinician with information about how a client assumes responsibility and conforms to the values of society. Finally, for clinicians working in college counseling settings, the Mt scale might provide a perspective on the level of maladjustment experienced by college students who seek counseling.

5

MMPI-2 Content Indicators in Evaluating Therapy Patients

The traditional interpretive approach for MMPI scales and profile codes involves the application of empirical correlates to scale scores and patterns. These empirically derived behaviors provide a solid basis for clinical description and prediction of behavior from the individual's self-report. The major strengths of this approach lie in the extensive external validation of the MMPI scales and profile codes; they provide valid and reliable test correlates that can confidently be applied to a broad range of treatment cases. One disadvantage to the MMPI empirical scale approach is that the heterogeneous item content of the scales make face valid or intuitive interpretative statements difficult at times. In other words, items that empirically separate groups or prove themselves to be valid predictors may not "hang together" or be intuitively related to what the patient tells the therapist. The empirical correlates of the clinical scales, with rather heterogeneous content, may not be as intuitively understandable as are interpretations that are based on content-homogeneous scales.

There are a number of valuable content indicators for the MMPI-2 that can add immeasurably to the therapist's information about a client. By viewing the patient's responses to item content, the therapist can obtain valuable clues to the person's specific feelings, attitudes, problems, and resources.

Content interpretation is based on different assumptions from that of MMPI empirical scale elevations or code type analyses. One major assumption underlying content interpretation is that the subject *wishes* to reveal his or her ideas, attitudes, beliefs, and problems, and *cooperates* with the testing. People taking the MMPI under clinical conditions usually provide accurate personality information. Subjects taking the MMPI under pressure, court order, or in employment-selection situations, however, may distort their responses to create a particular impression. In these cases the content themes may not accurately portray the individual's problems.

This chapter addresses several approaches to summarizing important content themes in the patient's MMPI-2 and provides the therapist with clues to how this substantive information can be employed to shed light on the patient's view of his or her problems. Three important ways of evaluating content themes in the MMPI-2 will be described and illustrated in this chapter: "critical" items, rationally derived content subscales, and the MMPI-2 content scales.

THE CRITICAL ITEM APPROACH

The most direct approach to assessing content themes in the MMPI is to examine the patient's actual responses to individual items. The *critical item approach*, as this strategy has been called, involves using individual MMPI items as a means of detecting specific content themes or special problems the patient is reportedly experiencing. The critical item approach assumes that the patient responds to items as symptoms or problems, and reports his or her feelings accurately. The critical item or pathognomic indicator is one of the earliest approaches to personality test interpretation. In fact, Woodworth (1920), in his pioneering work on the *Personal Data Sheet,* included what he called "starred items," or pathognomic contents, that were believed to have particular significance if answered in a pathological direction.

Of course, evaluation of specific items by reading through the record is a cumbersome and confusing way of attempting to understand the content, since there are too many bits of information to readily organize and integrate. Consequently, the clinician needs some ways of organizing or hierarchically arranging the items in order of importance before examining specific items. Early critical item approaches, such as the Grayson Critical Items or the Caldwell Critical Items, were largely developed by their authors by simply reading through the items and selecting those believed to reflect particular problems. Neither of these early sets of critical items were ever validated to determine if the specific items used were tapping uniquely important problems. The items were simply adapted for clinical or computerized psychological test use on the basis of the clinician's hunch that the item measured highly significant or "critical" problem areas.

There are two sets of MMPI-2 critical items that were empirically derived to aid the clinician in assessing specific problems of concern: the Koss–Butcher Critical Item list and the Lachar–Wrobel Critical Item List.

The Koss–Butcher Critical Items

Koss and Butcher (1973) were concerned that the existing sets of critical items were being used as indicators of specific pathology without an empirical data base for such predictions. That is, the Grayson and Caldwell item groupings were initially developed by a rational examination of the item pool and were not actually empirically related to clinical problems in a valid way. Koss and Butcher (1973), Koss, Butcher, and Hoffman (1976), and Koss (1979) conducted empirical investigations of item responses and their relationships to psychiatric status for patients at admission to a psychiatric facility. They evaluated the effectiveness of the Grayson and Caldwell critical item lists for detecting crisis states and developed a new set of empirically based critical items that discriminated among presenting problems experienced by psychiatric patients at admission.

Koss and Butcher (1973) first defined several "crisis situations" that were frequently found among individuals seeking admission to a psychiatric facility. They interviewed several clinicians as to what were important crises that would require evaluation in clinical settings. Six crisis situations were thought to be particularly important because of their frequency or their significance. They were:

1. Suicidal depression
2. Anxiety state
3. Threatened assault
4. Alcoholic crisis
5. Paranoia
6. Psychotic distortion

Koss and Butcher then reviewed presenting problems for more than 1,200 cases admitted to the Minneapolis Veteran's Administration Hospital and grouped together individuals with similar problems. Then they performed an item analysis to detect MMPI items that discriminated the various crisis groups from each other and from a control group of general psychiatric patients. The resulting Koss–Butcher Critical Item list contains items that validly discriminated the crisis conditions.

The Koss–Butcher Critical Item list was expanded in the MMPI revision to incorporate new item contents of importance in the assessment of two major problem areas: substance abuse and suicidal threats. A number of new items have been added to the MMPI-2 for assessment of special problem areas, including four new items that empirically separate alcohol and drug abusing patients from other groups, which have been added to the Alcohol Crisis Item group, and four new items dealing with depression and suicide, which have been added to the Depressed-Suicidal Crisis group.

The Lachar–Wrobel Critical Items

In a subsequent study, Lachar and Wrobel (1979) replicated about two-thirds of the Koss–Butcher list and developed an expanded critical item list to include several other crisis categories (see Lachar & Wrobel, 1979).

Use of Critical Items

The most appropriate use of critical items is for detecting specific problems or attitudes the patient is reporting that might not be reflected in the clinical profile elevations. In this way significant themes are highlighted and can be used to illustrate inferences from the clinical scales or code type information. A case illustration highlights the effectiveness with which groups of similar items can reflect particularly pertinent problem areas.

▶ **Case: Use of Critical Items in Evaluating Specific Problems**

Charles D., a 48-year-old divorced post office employee, was referred for psychological evaluation by his physician, who had some concerns that he was clinically depressed. He was an introverted, shy man who had very little personal contact with other people. He had been working ineffectively for several months and had been absent from work a great deal. He had no close friends. When he was seen by the physician he reported extreme fatigue, lethargy, lack of energy, and a loss of interest in life.

After his referral to a psychotherapist, he was administered the MMPI-2 (see profile in Figure 5-1). In spite of the fact that his clinical profile elevation was not marked, he nevertheless reported a number of significant problems, as noted in his endorsement of Koss–Butcher Critical Items (see Table 5-1). He endorsed most of the items on the Depressed-Suicidal cluster, reflecting a considerably depressed mood and little interest in life. Given his highly dysphoric mood, suicidal ideation, and lack of a support network, outpatient treatment was not thought to be feasible. Instead, it was recommended that he be hospitalized in an inpatient program for treatment of his major affective disorder.

Limitations of the Critical Item Approach to Content Interpretation

The clinician needs to understand that, although the critical item approach can provide important clues to specific problems the patient is experiencing, there are some clear limitations to this approach to MMPI interpretation.

1. *Limited range of problems.* The types of problems shown by the critical items are, of course, limited by the range of problems reflected in the

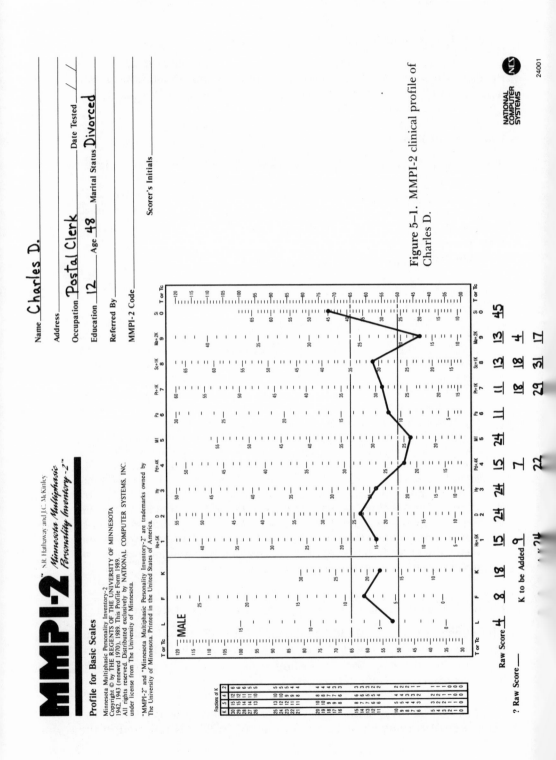

Name _Charles D._

Address _____

Occupation _Postal Clerk_ Date Tested _/_/_

Education _12_ Age _48_ Marital Status _Divorced_

Referred By _____

MMPI-2 Code _____

Scorer's Initials _____

Figure 5–1. MMPI-2 clinical profile of Charles D.

86

Table 5-1. Critical Item Content on the Depressed Suicidal Group Endorsed by Charles D.

---

38. I have had periods of days, weeks, or months when I couldn't take care of things because I couldn't "get going." (T)
65. Most of the time I feel blue. (T)
71. These days I find it hard not to give up hope of amounting to something. (T)
95. I am happy most of the time. (F)
130. I certainly feel useless at times. (T)
146. I cry easily. (T)
215. I brood a great deal. (T)
306. No one cares much what happens to you. (T)
233. I have difficulty starting to do things. (T)
273. Life is a strain for me much of the time. (T)
303. Most of the time I wish I were dead. (T)
388. I very seldom have spells of the blues. (F)
411. At times I feel I am no good at all. (T)
454. The future seems hopeless to me. (T)
485. I often feel that I'm not as good as other people. (T)
506. I have recently considered killing myself. (T)
520. Lately I have thought a lot about killing myself. (T)
524. No one knows it but I have tried to kill myself. (T)

---

categories employed. The critical item lists employed here address relatively few problem areas. Patients may be experiencing severe and debilitating problems that are not represented in published critical item lists.

2. *Unreliability of brief measures.* Responses to items can be very unreliable and should not be given the weight in interpretation that clinical scales and code types are given. Patients sometimes mismark or answer items incorrectly. The response to a particular item could be a mistake.

Critical item responses should be seen as possible hypotheses about specific problems that the patient might be experiencing. Clinicians should attempt to obtain more reliable information—for example, by the patient's response to scales—about suggested interpretations obtained from critical item responses.

MMPI-2 CONTENT SUBSCALES

The discussion in this section focuses on two sets of MMPI-2 content subscales or item groups containing similar content within an MMPI scale. The first group of subscales described are the Harris-Lingoes MMPI-2 subscales for D, Hy, Pd, Pa, Sc, and Ma. The second group of subscales are the MMPI-2 Si subscales developed by Hostetler, Ben-Porath, Butcher, and Graham (1989).

Rationally Derived Content Subgroups: The Harris-Lingoes Subscales

The Harris-Lingoes subscales are item subsets that were developed for six of the MMPI empirical scales by rational analysis. Harris and Lingoes (1955) constructed their item subgroups by reading through the items on the D, Hy, Pd, Pa, Sc, and Ma scales, and rationally grouping the items according to content themes. The authors did not provide subscales for scales 1 (Hs) and 7 (Pt), because these scales were believed to be "naturally" homogeneous in content and not subject to further reduction into subthemes. The Hs scale contains strictly somatic problems, and the Pt scale is comprised of anxiety indicators. A listing of the Harris-Lingoes subscales is given in Table 5-2.

The Harris-Lingoes content subscales are used to provide the interpreter with clues to the specific problem dimensions that contribute to the high elevations on the scale. For example, if the patient has a high score on scale 8, say a T-score of 80, an inspection of the Harris-Lingoes subscales might show that the individual's score on Subjective Depression is contributing substantially to the overall score. The relative prominence of Subjective Depression in the individual's clinical picture suggests that themes related to low mood should be given priority in the test interpretation.

The Harris-Lingoes subscales are interpreted according to the content of the specific scale on which they are contained. Interpretation proceeds by examining the relative contribution of the subscales to the overall elevation found on the significantly elevated clinical scale. For example, if the D scale is elevated above a T-score of 65, then the most prominent subscale elevations (those also above T = 65) would be considered salient for interpretation.

The value of clarifying the meanings of MMPI-2 scale elevations by evaluating subscale content can be seen in the case illustration that follows. The MMPI-2 Pd scale elevations are usually thought to be stable and unchanging over time. The case illustrated in Figure 5-2 provides some useful, additional interpretive information about scale 4.

▶ **Case: Understanding Clinical Scale Elevation Through Homogeneous Content Groups**

Susan F., a 35-year-old office worker, was referred for marital therapy by her physician. After the first two sessions it became clear that her husband, an aggressive and self-centered man, was unwilling to come to therapy. Su-

Table 5–2. Description of the Harris-Lingoes Subscales for the MMPI-2

Scale 1   Hypochondriasis: NONE

Scale 2   Depression

D1—Subjective Depression   32 items
High scores suggest: feeling depressed, unhappy, nervous; lacks energy and interest; not coping well; problems in concentration and attention; feels inferior; lacks self-confidence; shy and uneasy in social situations

D2—Psychomotor Retardation   14 items
High scores suggest: immobilized, withdrawn; lacks energy; avoids people; denies hostility

D3—Physical Malfunctioning   11 items
High scores suggest: preoccupied with physical functioning; denies good health; wide variety of somatic complaints

D4—Mental Dullness   15 items
High scores suggest: lacks energy; feels tense; has problems in concentration and attention; lacks self-confidence; feels life is not worthwhile

D5—Brooding   10 items
High scores suggest: broods, ruminates; lacks energy; feels inferior; feels life is not worth living; easily hurt by criticism; feels like losing control of thought processes

Scale 3   Hysteria

Hy1—Denial of Social Anxiety   6 items
High scores suggest: socially extroverted and comfortable; not easily influenced by social standards and customs

Hy2—Need for Affection   12 items
High scores suggest: strong needs for attention and affection; sensitive, optimistic, trusting; avoids confrontations; denies negative feelings toward others

Hy3—Lassitude–Malaise   15 items
High scores suggest: uncomfortable and not in good health; tired, weak, fatigue; problems in concentration; poor appetite; sleep disturbance; unhappy

Hy4—Somatic Complaints   17 items
High scores suggest: multiple somatic complaints; utilizes repression and conversion of affect; little or no hostility expressed

Hy5—Inhibition of Aggression   7 items
High scores suggest: denies hostile and aggressive impulses; sensitive about response of others

Scale 4   Psychopathic Deviate

Pd1—Familial Discord   9 items
High scores suggest: views home situation as unpleasant and lacking in love, support, understanding; family critical and controlling

Pd2—Authority Problems   8 items
High scores suggest: resents authority; trouble in school and with law; definite opinions about right and wrong; stands up for beliefs

Table 5–2. Continued

Pd3—Social Imperturbability   6 items
High scores suggest: comfortable and confident in social situations; exhibitionistic; defends opinions

Pd4—Social Alienation   13 items
High scores suggest: feels misunderstood, alienated, isolated, estranged; lonely, unhappy, uninvolved; blames others; self-centered, insensitive, inconsiderate; verbalizes regret and remorse

Pd5—Self-Alienation   12 items
High scores suggest: uncomfortable, unhappy; problems in concentration; life not interesting or rewarding; hard to settle down; excessive use of alcohol

Scale 6   Paranoia

Pa1—Persecutory Ideas   17 items
High scores suggest: views world as threatening; feels misunderstood, unfairly blamed or punished; suspicious, untrusting; blames others; sometimes delusions of persecution

Pa2—Poignancy   9 items
High scores suggest: sees self as high-strung, sensitive, feeling more intensely than others; feels lonely, misunderstood; looks for risk and excitement

Pa3—Naiveté   9 items
High scores suggest: extremely naive and optimistic attitudes toward others; trusting; high moral standards; denies hostility

Scale 7   Psychasthenia: NONE

Scale 8   Schizophrenia

Sc1—Social Alienation   21 items
High scores suggest: feels misunderstood, mistreated, family situation lacking in love and support; lonely, empty; hostility, hatred toward family; never experienced love relationship

Sc2—Emotional Alienation   11 items
High scores suggest: depression, despair; wishes he or she were dead; frightened, apathetic

Sc3—Lack of Ego Mastery, Cognitive   10 items
High scores suggest: fears losing mind; strange thought processes; feelings of unreality; problems with concentration, attention

Sc4—Lack of Ego Mastery, Conative   14 items
High scores suggest: feels life is a strain; depression, despair; worries; problems coping with everyday problems; life not interesting, rewarding; given up hope; may wish he or she were dead

Sc5—Lack of Ego Mastery, Defective Inhibition   11 items
High scores suggest: feels out of control of emotions, impulses; restless, hyperactive, irritable; laughing or crying episodes; may not remember previously performed activities

Sc6—Bizarre Sensory Experiences   20 items
High scores suggest: feels body changing in unusual ways; hallucinations, unusual thoughts, external reference; skin sensitivity, weakness, ringing in ears, etc.

Table 5–2. Continued

Scale 9 Hypomania

Ma1—Amorality 6 items
High scores suggest: sees others as selfish; dishonest and feels justified in being this way; derives vicarious satisfaction from manipulative exploits of others

Ma2—Psychomotor Acceleration 11 items
High scores suggest: accelerated speech, thought processes, motor activity; tense, restless; feels excited, elated without cause; easily bored; seeks out excitement; impulse to do harmful or shocking things

Ma3—Imperturbability 8 items
High scores suggest: denies social anxiety; not especially sensitive about what others think; impatient, irritable toward others

Ma4—Ego Inflation 9 items
High scores suggest: unrealistic self-appraisal; resentful of demands made by others

san decided to continue therapy herself and remained in treatment (cognitive–behavioral therapy) for about 6 months, making substantial improvement in her mood and changes in her life. After divorcing her husband, she became romantically involved with another man who was apparently more mature, better adjusted, and supportive than her ex-husband. Toward the end of treatment she was readministered the MMPI-2 prior to treatment termination. Her second MMPI-2 (Figure 5-3) showed a marked change in two scales, Pd and D. Even the Pd scale, with its reputation for persistence over time, had diminished considerably at retest. The reasons for this reduction are evident when one views the Harris-Lingoes subscales for scale 4 (see Table 5-3). The high elevations on the Pd and D scales at the initial testing were largely reflecting problems she was experiencing in her marital relationship; the problems were expressed through the content of the Family Problems and Subjective Depression subscales. When her relationships improved, her response to the second MMPI-2 showed diminished problems.

Clinicians using the MMPI-2 in evaluating clients in marital therapy might find that their clients' Pd scale elevations (a frequent finding among marital therapy clients) can result from situationally based marital or family problems.

Limitations of Subscale Interpretation

There are some limitations to using the Harris-Lingoes content subgroups in MMPI-2 interpretation, particularly if the application involves comparing the T-scores of subjects' subscales. Many of the Harris-Lingoes subfactors contain relatively few items, so the scale is likely to be relatively unreliable as a result of its brevity. Thus, the Harris-Lingoes

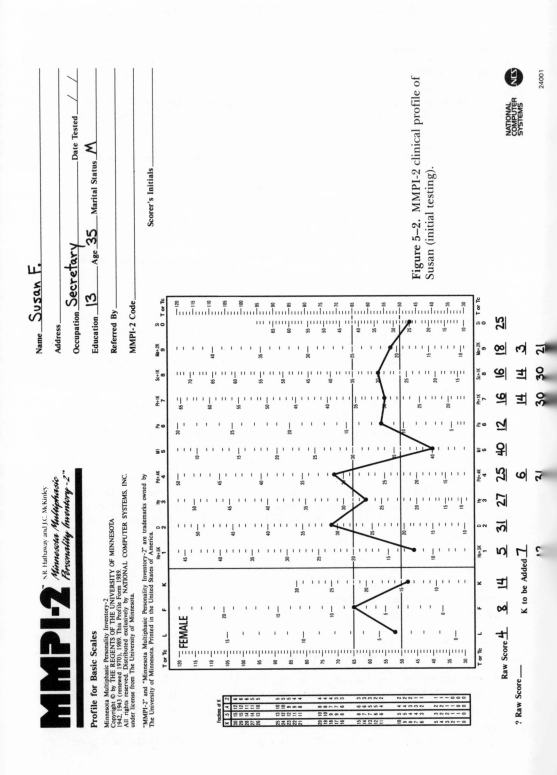

Figure 5–2. MMPI-2 clinical profile of Susan (initial testing).

Table 5–3. Harris-Lingoes *Pd* Subscale Scores for Susan's Test and Retest on the MMPI-2

	T-Scores First Testing	T-Scores Second Testing
Pd1	80	57
Pd2	54	54
Pd3	58	. 54
Pd4	67	59
Pd5	55	67

scales are not as psychometrically reliable as longer scales and should only be used clinically as a guide to content interpretation and not as a psychometric predictor. For the most part, the Harris-Lingoes subscales are used to highlight or help the clinician focus on specific problems that are producing elevations on the clinical scales. The most prominent Harris-Lingoes elevation for a particular clinical scale can be used by the clinician to determine which of the empirical correlates for that clinical scale elevation should be given the most prominence in the clinical report. The clinician should not interpret *all* subscale scores that appear to be elevated. Unless the clinical scale is elevated (greater than a T-score of 65) and holds a prominent place in the profile code, the Harris-Lingoes subscales should not be interpreted. This strategy reduces the number of inconsistent or potentially contradictory statements in the diagnostic report.

The Si Subscales

Originally, the Mf and Si scales were not included in the Harris-Lingoes subclassification approach to the item content because these scales were not considered to be "clinical" scales and were less frequently included in clinical interpretation approaches. Recognizing the need for item subgroups on these scales, Serkownek (1975) developed a set of subscales for the original MMPI; however, these item groups were not considered sufficiently homogeneous by the MMPI Restandardization Committee (Butcher et al., 1989) to enable effective content interpretation and were not included in the MMPI-2 manual.

Hostetler, Ben-Porath, Butcher, and Graham (1989) developed a set of homogeneous subscales for the Si scale following a multistage approach involving both rational and empirical procedures. They initially conducted a series of factor analyses to identify homogeneous factors in the items comprising the scale. The scales were refined by using item–scale correlations and rational analyses. The final set of three subscales (see Table 5-4) were highly homogeneous (internal consistencies ranged

MMPI-2™
S.R. Hathaway and J.C. McKinley

Minnesota Multiphasic Personality Inventory-2™

Profile for Basic Scales

Minnesota Multiphasic Personality Inventory-2
Copyright © by THE REGENTS OF THE UNIVERSITY OF MINNESOTA
1942, 1943 (renewed 1970), 1989. This Profile Form 1989.
All rights reserved. Distributed exclusively by NATIONAL COMPUTER SYSTEMS, INC.
under license from The University of Minnesota.

"MMPI-2™" and "Minnesota Multiphasic Personality Inventory-2" are trademarks owned by
The University of Minnesota. Printed in the United States of America.

Name Susan F. [Re-test]

Address

Occupation Secretary   Date Tested

Education 13   Age 36   Marital Status Divorced

Referred By

MMPI-2 Code

Scorer's Initials

FEMALE

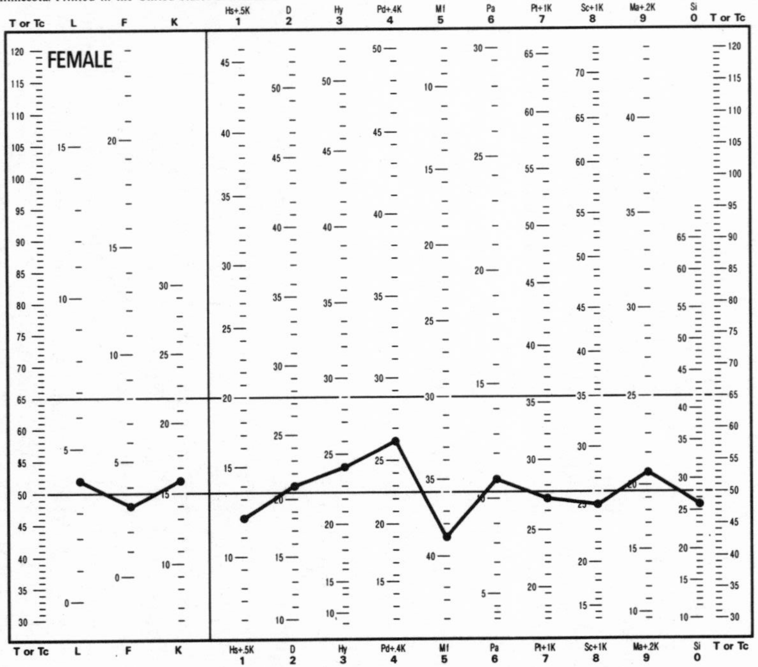

	L	F	K	Hs+.5K 1	D 2	Hy 3	Pd+.4K 4	Mf 5	Pa 6	Pt+1K 7	Sc+1K 8	Ma+.2K 9	Si 0
Raw Score	4	3	16	4	21	24	20	39	11	11	11	18	26
K to be Added				8			6			16	16	3	
Raw Score with K				12			26			27	25	21	

? Raw Score ___

Figure 5–3. MMPI-2 clinical profile of
Susan (retest).

94

Table 5–4. Composition of the Si Subscales

Shyness/Self-Consciousness (Si1):	
True:	158, 161, 167, 185, 243, 265, 275, 289
False:	49, 262, 280, 321, 342, 360
Social Avoidance (Si2):	
True:	337, 367
False:	86, 340, 353, 359, 363, 370
Alienation (Self and Others) (Si3):	
True:	31, 56, 104, 110, 135, 284, 302, 308, 326, 328, 338, 347, 348, 358, 364, 368, 369

Note: Numbers are MMPI-2 booklet items numbers.
Source: Ben-Porath et al. (1989).

from .75 to .82) and reliable (test–retest reliabilities ranged from .77 to .91).

Ben-Porath, Hostetler, Butcher, and Graham (1989) report external correlates for the Si subscales. The correlates given in Table 5-5 were obtained from the MMPI-2 normative study (Butcher et al., 1989). The 822 normal marital couples from the MMPI-2 normative study rated each other on a number of personality variables. The most significant correlates for the Si subscales are informative. High scores on the Shyness subscale (Si1) are associated with such behaviors as acts very shy, avoids contact with people for no reason, does not enjoy parties, is not talkative, and does not laugh and joke with other people. High scores on Social Avoidance (Si2) are viewed by spouses as follows: avoids contact with people, does not enjoy parties, and acts to keep people at a distance. High scorers on Self and Social Alienation (Si3) are viewed as having considerable psychological problems. They are seen as lacking in self-confidence, lacking an interest in things, being nervous and jittery, showing poor judgment, acting bored and restless, thinking others are talking about them, being suspicious of others, putting themselves down, lacking creativity in solving problems, giving up too easily, blaming themselves for things that go wrong, and being unrealistic about their own abilities.

Interpretation of the Si subscales follows the same general strategies as that for the Harris-Lingoes subscales. Given significant elevations on the Si scale, an examination of the subscales could provide clues to the types of important content themes that contributed to the scale elevation. The relative prominence of these content themes gives the clinician interpretive descriptions to highlight in the diagnostic study.

The Si subscales (Hostetler et al., 1989; Ben-Porath et al., 1989) suggest the following personality characteristics to keep in mind for treatment planning.

Table 5–5. Correlation of Si Subscales with Spouses Ratings

Item	Si1	Si2	Si3
Men (*n* = 822)			
Acts very shy.	.38	.15	.03
Avoids contact with people for no reason.	.23	.20	.08
Is friendly.	−.22	−.15	−.10
Talks too much.	−.19	−.13	.05
Laughs and jokes with people.	−.19	−.17	−.01
Acts to keep people at a distance.	.18	.17	.11
Enjoys parties, entertainments, or having friends over.	−.18	−.31	−.04
Is self-confident.	−.18	−.03	−.15
Lacks an interest in things.	.18	.08	.21
Gives up too easily.	.11	.01	.19
Is creative in solving problems and meeting challenges.	−.12	.03	−.19
Is unrealistic about own abilities.	.08	.01	.19
Is pleasant and relaxed.	−.10	.01	−.18
Women (*n* = 822)			
Acts very shy.	.33	.18	.13
Avoids contact with people for no reason.	.28	.20	.18
Enjoys parties, entertainments, or having friends over.	−.25	−.32	−.14
Acts to keep people at a distance.	.21	.24	.13
Is self-confident.	−.25	−.11	−.29
Gets nervous and jittery.	.13	.03	.25
Gives up too easily.	.14	.06	.24
Lacks an interest in things.	.15	.07	.24
Has many fears.	.11	.05	.23
Is creative in solving problems and meeting challenges.	−.18	.01	−.23
Shows sound judgment.	−.07	.03	−.22
Puts own self down.	.18	.11	.22
Acts bored and restless.	.08	.03	.22
Is unrealistic about own abilities.	.13	.08	.20
Worries and frets over little things.	.12	.06	.20
Has a very hard time making any decisions.	.12	.01	.20
Gets very sad or blue and is slow to come out of it.	.13	.07	.20
Thinks others are talking about her.	.13	.02	.20
Is suspicious of others.	.05	.02	.19
Blames self for things that go wrong.	.11	.11	.18
Lacks control over emotions.	.05	.05	.18
Is very concerned about death.	.10	.08	.18

Shyness (Si1). High scorers feel shy around others, feel easily embarrassed, feel ill-at-ease in social situations, and feel uncomfortable as they enter new situations. Therapy is probably viewed by them as no different from other social contexts. High scorers on Si1 are likely to have initial problems feeling comfortable and relating to the therapist.

Social Avoidance (Si2). High scores on this subscale reflect a great dislike of group activities, concerns about group participation, active efforts to avoid being in a crowd, dislike of parties and social events, and a strong aversion to interpersonal contacts. Individuals with high Si2 subscale scores are likely to report considerable difficulty with other people and with entering social or group situations. Some forms of behavior therapy in which the individual is encouraged to participate in social activities may be difficult to initiate since the individual has a prominent, pathologic aversion to group settings. Various cognitive–behavioral approaches may be considered for these people.

Self–Other Alienation (Si3). High scores on this subscale reflect characterological personality traits that make the individual vulnerable to failure in social interactions. High scores reflect low self-esteem, low self-confidence, self-critical tendencies, self-doubt about personal judgment, and a feeling of being ineffective at determining one's own fate. High scores also reflect nervousness, fearfulness, and indecisiveness. In addition, high scores indicate that the person is suspicious of others, considers others to be malevolent, and thinks others are talking about him or her. High scores on Si3 show great self-doubt and concern about others. Such intense feelings of alienation are likely to be deterrents to treatment motivation and, if present, need to be preempted from producing a negative treatment outcome.

An attempt to develop similar subscales for the Mf scale was unsuccessful because of the lack of enough homogeneous subsets of Mf items to produce psychometrically sound scales.

RATIONAL–STATISTICAL CONTENT SCALES: THE MMPI-2 CONTENT SCALES

Wiggins (1966) developed a set of MMPI content scales that were representative of the major content dimensions in the MMPI item pool and that were psychometrically sound enough to operate as scales. Wiggins started with the 26 content categories defined by Hathaway and McKinley (1940) and later reduced the number of content groupings to 13 clusters of items. He applied internal consistency procedures to this revised set of items, producing 13 scales with a homogeneous item content and with a large enough number of items to provide high scale reliability.

The Wiggins content scales, which have been widely used and researched over the past 20 years, have provided valuable information for the MMPI interpreter. The scales are not available in the MMPI-2, however, since many of the items comprising the scales were deleted from the inventory as outmoded or objectionable.

The MMPI-2 Content Scales

A new set of MMPI content scales was developed for the revised version of the MMPI by Butcher, Graham, Williams, and Ben-Porath (1989). These investigators developed 15 new content scales using the original items contained in the MMPI clinical and validity scales, some special scales, and many of the new items that were included in the revised version of the MMPI.

The MMPI-2 content scales were developed in stages. First, three raters independently sorted the 704 items in the experimental booklet of the revised MMPI (Form AX) and grouped similar items into related item groups. Next, provisional content scales were developed by including only items that all three raters agreed belonged in each of the content groupings. Next, using one of the normal samples collected for the MMPI restandardization study, the authors computed item–scale correlations for all of the 704 MMPI items with the total score for each of the provisional content scales. This procedure was implemented to eliminate items that had low item–scale correlations and to detect other possible items that were highly correlated with the provisional scale.

In the next step the homogeneity and internal consistency of the items on the working version of the content scales were computed. Items were kept on a scale if they correlated at a .50 level with the total score. One final step was undertaken to assure discriminant validity among the content scales: Items on a particular scale would be dropped if they correlated more highly with the total score of another scale.

The MMPI-2 normative sample of 1,138 males and 1,462 females was used in the development of the norms for the MMPI-2 content scales. An important feature of these new norms is that they were adjusted to fit the same uniform distributions as the clinical scales, making T-scores on the two sets of scales highly comparable. This was not the case with the Wiggins scales. The final MMPI-2 content scales are described in Table 5-6.

Unlike the Harris-Lingoes subscales, the MMPI-2 content scales can safely be used psychometrically since they contain a sufficient number of items and substantial scale reliabilities. Interpretation of content scale scores typically proceeds by profiling the scores (see Figure 5-5) and inspecting the scale elevations for deviations. Content scale scores in the 65 T-score range and above are considered clinically interpretable. Inter-

Table 5–6. Description of the MMPI-2 Content Scales

1. *Anxiety* (ANX, 23 items)   High scorers on ANX report general symptoms of anxiety, including tension, somatic problems (i.e., heart pounding and shortness of breath), sleep difficulties, worries, and poor concentration. They fear losing their minds, find life a strain, and have difficulties making decisions. They appear to be readily aware of these symptoms and problems, and are willing to admit to them.

2. *Fears* (FRS, 23 items)   A high score on FRS indicates an individual with many specific fears. These specific fears can include blood; high places; money; animals such as snakes, mice, or spiders; leaving home; fire; storms and natural disasters; water; the dark; being indoors; and dirt.

3. *Obsessiveness* (OBS, 16 items)   High scorers on OBS have tremendous difficulties making decisions and are likely to ruminate excessively about issues and problems, causing others to become impatient. Having to make changes distresses them, and they may report some compulsive behaviors like counting or saving unimportant things. They are excessive worriers who frequently become overwhelmed by their own thoughts.

4. *Depression* (DEP, 33 items)   High scores on this scale characterize individuals with significant depressive thoughts. They report feeling blue, uncertain about their future, and uninterested in their lives. They are likely to brood, be unhappy, cry easily, and feel hopeless and empty. They may report thoughts of suicide or wishes that they were dead. They may believe that they are condemned or have committed unpardonable sins. Other people may not be viewed as a source of support.

5. *Health Concerns* (HEA, 36 items)   Individuals with high scores on HEA report many physical symptoms across several body systems. Included are gastrointestinal symptoms (e.g., constipation, nausea and vomiting, stomach trouble), neurological problems (e.g., convulsions, dizziness and fainting spells, paralysis), sensory problems (e.g., poor hearing or eyesight), cardiovascular symptoms (e.g., heart or chest pains), skin problems, pain (e.g., headaches, neck pains), respiratory troubles (e.g., coughs, hay fever, or asthma). These individuals worry about their health and feel sicker than the average person.

6. *Bizarre Mentation* (BIZ, 24 items)   Psychotic thought processes characterize individuals high on the BIZ scale. They may report auditory, visual, or olfactory hallucinations and may recognize that their thoughts are strange or peculiar. Paranoid ideation (e.g., the belief that they are being plotted against or that someone is trying to poison them) may be reported as well. These individuals may feel that they have a special mission or special powers.

7. *Anger* (ANG, 16 items)   High scores on the ANG scale suggest anger control problems. These individuals report being irritable, grouchy, impatient, hotheaded, annoyed, and stubborn. They sometimes feel like swearing or smashing things. They may lose self-control and report having been physically abusive toward people and objects.

8. *Cynicism* (CYN, 23 items)   Misanthropic beliefs characterize high scorers on CYN. They expect hidden, negative motives behind the acts of others; for example, believing that most people are honest simply for fear of being caught. Other people are to be distrusted, for people use each other and are only friendly for selfish reasons. They likely hold negative attitudes about those close to them, including fellow workers, family, and friends.

Table 5–6. Continued

9. *Antisocial Practices* (ASP, 22 items)   In addition to holding similar misanthropic attitudes to high scorers on the CYN scale, high scorers on the ASP scale report problem behaviors during their school years and other antisocial practices like being in trouble with the law, stealing, or shoplifting. They report that they sometimes enjoy the antics of criminals and believe that it is all right to get around the law, as long as it is not broken.

10. *Type A* (TPA, 19 items)   High scorers on TPA are hard-driving, fast-moving, and work-oriented individuals, who frequently become impatient, irritable, and annoyed. They do not like to wait or be interrupted. There is never enough time in a day for them to complete their tasks. They are direct and may be overbearing in their relationships with others.

11. *Low Self-Esteem* (LSE, 24 items)   High scores on LSE characterize individuals with low opinions of themselves. They do not believe that they are liked by others or that they are important. They hold many negative attitudes about themselves including beliefs that they are unattractive, awkward and clumsy, useless, and a burden to others. They certainly lack self-confidence, and find it hard to accept compliments from others. They may be overwhelmed by all the faults they see in themselves.

12. *Social Discomfort* (SOD, 24 items)   SOD high scorers are very uneasy around others, preferring to be by themselves. When in social situations, they are likely to sit alone, rather than joining in the group. They see themselves as shy and dislike parties and other group events.

13. *Family Problems* (FAM, 25 items)   Considerable family discord is reported by high scorers on FAM. Their families are described as lacking in love, quarrelsome, and unpleasant. They even may report hating members of their families. Their childhood may be portrayed as abusive, and marriages seen as unhappy and lacking in affection.

14. *Negative Work Attitudes* (WRK, 33 items)   A high score on WRK is indicative of behaviors or attitudes likely to contribute to poor work performance. Some of the problems relate to low self-confidence, concentration difficulties, obsessiveness, tension and pressure, and decision-making problems. Others suggest lack of family support for the career choice, personal questioning of career choice, and negative attitudes toward co-workers.

15. *Negative Treatment Indicators* (TRT, 26 items)   High scores on TRT indicate individuals with negative attitudes toward doctors and mental health treatment. High scorers do not believe that anyone can understand or help them. They have issues or problems that they are not comfortable discussing with anyone. They may not want to change anything in their lives, nor do they feel that change is possible. They prefer giving up rather than facing a crisis or difficulty.

Source: Adapted from J. N. Butcher, J. R. Graham, C. L. Williams, and Y. Ben-Porath (1990). *Development and use of the MMPI-2 content scales.* Minneapolis, Minn.: University of Minnesota Press.

pretation of the content scales typically involves applying content descriptions for high or low scores in the profile.

One caution regarding interpretation of content scale scores is in order. Some confusion could result from scale scores, such as Depression (DEP), being confused with the clinical scale with a similar name, the Depression (D) scale. It is possible to obtain an elevated score on D and a moderate or even low score on DEP. This could result in an internal inconsistency in interpretation unless the clinician is aware that the two scales actually measure different clinical attributes in spite of their common name. The reason for this potential inconsistency is that, although the names are similar, the constructs and correlates of the scales are actually somewhat different.

An illustration of the use of content scales and the MMPI-2 clinical scales is provided in the following discussion. (See the MMPI-2 clinical profile shown in Figure 5-4 and the content scale profile shown in Figure 5-5.)

The content scale profile shown in Figure 5-5 was produced by a 43-year-old man who was reporting some acute family problems. He sought help from a psychologist when his wife threatened to report his past incestuous relations with his oldest daughter if he did not give up his current relationship with his 19-year-old secretary. His most highly elevated score was on the Family Problems scale, suggesting that he viewed his problems as largely resulting from his family situation. The high score on Antisocial Practices (ASP) suggests that he cpossesses attitudes that are antisocial in character; he tends to violate rules and to disregard societal norms. Finally, he obtained a high score on the Negative Treatment Indicators scale, suggesting that he possesses attitudes that are contrary to cooperating with a treatment effort. He shows a high resistance to change.

Two new content scales—the Negative Treatment Indicators scale (TRT) and Negative Work Attitudes scale (WRK)—may have particular significance for treatment evaluation and the individual's potential for rehabilitation. A more detailed discussion of these scales follows.

Treatment Planning with the MMPI-2 Content Scales

The MMPI-2 content scales provide a direct assessment of many of the individual's problems and personal attitudes that require attention in treatment sessions. Elevated scores on these scales provide important clues concerning the focus of therapy since they summarize problems the individual considers important in his or her case.

Negative Treatment Indicators scale (TRT). The TRT scale was developed as a means of assessing the individual's potential to cooperate with treatment and to detect the presence of personality factors or attitudes in the

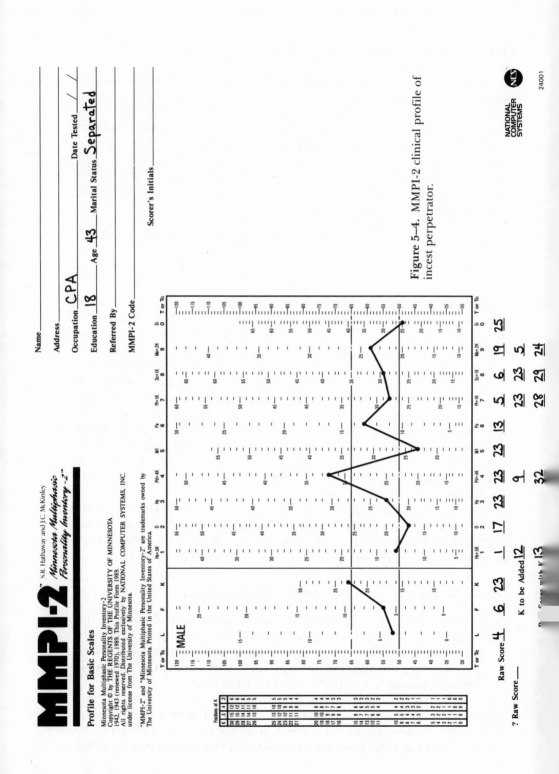

Figure 5–4. MMPI-2 clinical profile of incest perpetrator.

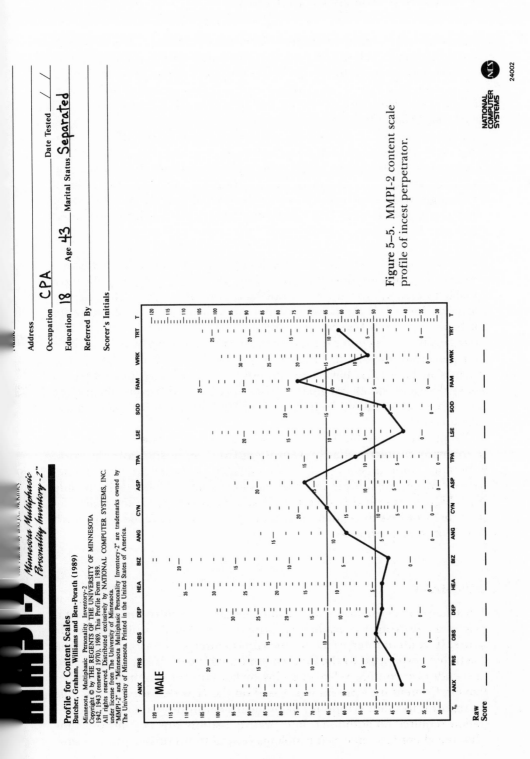

Figure 5-5. MMPI-2 content scale profile of incest perpetrator.

client that reflect an unwillingness or inability to change. The item content on the scale includes attitudes or beliefs that reflect a rigid and noncompliant orientation toward personal change, such as a lack of insight into one's own motives, an unwillingness to discuss problems with others, a dislike of health providers, an inability to work out problems, and alienation from others.

High scorers on this scale are presenting the view that they are unwilling or unable to change their life situation at this time and that they are pessimistic about the future. A therapist armed with this information in the early stages of treatment might attempt to deal with the individual's negative treatment views before they result in early termination of therapy. Note the high TRT score obtained by the individual reported in Figure 5-5.

Negative Work Attitudes scale (WRK). Many individuals experiencing psychological problems find that their work deteriorates or that they are unable to maintain productive attitudes toward life. The WRK scale was developed to assess the possibility that the individual possesses attitudes or habits that would be counterproductive to rehabilitation efforts. The items on the scale center on the person's attitude toward work or his or her perceived inability to function in productive activities. The content themes include such beliefs or attitudes as inability to function or to make decisions, quick resignation when faced with difficulty, feelings of low success expectation, feeling weak and helpless, and possessing a dislike for work.

People who score high on this scale are presenting the view that they have many problems that prevent them from being successful at work. Therapists should be aware that work-related problems are or could become central problems in any person's life situation. Therefore, people with high scores on this scale may have a poor prognosis for achieving treatment success since their environmental pressures are likely to absorb much of their energies.

SUMMARY

This chapter focused on content interpretation—a different interpretative strategy from the traditional approach to MMPI scales and code types. In content interpretation, the clinical interpreter assumes that the client has responded to the item content in an open, frank manner and has endorsed content relevant to his or her current symptoms and behavior. Content interpretation is based on the view that the client is able to report important symptoms or problems truthfully. Content interpretation requires no additional interpretive assumptions beyond the view that the client has endorsed problems central to his or her present situation. The content scales or indexes are interpreted on face value; that is, the content measure is viewed as a "summary statement" concerning the client's present symptoms, mood, personality characteristics, and current behavior.

Three major approaches to MMPI-2 content interpretation were summarized and illustrated. The use of MMPI-2 Critical Items was presented, along with a discussion of the limitations of this approach. It is important to remember that Critical Items are best viewed as hypotheses for further evaluation, and not as psychometrically sound measures of personality and behavior.

The use of MMPI-2 subscales (Harris-Lingoes) for six of the clinical scales (D, Hy, Pd, Pa, Sc, and Ma) was described and illustrated along with three new subscales for Si. These subscales contain content homogeneous item groups that can aid the clinician in understanding the scale elevation on the parent scale by determining the relative contribution of each content theme to the overall scale score. Care should be taken in the psychometric use of the content subscales because they are relatively short.

Finally, the interpretation of the MMPI-2 content scales was described and illustrated. These scales have the advantage over other content approaches in that they contain strong psychometric properties and can therefore be interpreted psychometrically. They also address important, clinically useful content dimensions for understanding patient symptoms and behavior. These dimensions were not previously tapped by the MMPI because they rely on new items written specifically for assessing previously neglected content areas. Most relevant to the topic of this book is the new Negative Treatment Indicators (TRT) scale.

6

Use of Computer-Generated MMPI-2 Reports in Treatment Planning

Many clinicians find that computer-based psychological test interpretations are valuable aids in pretreatment planning for several reasons. First, psychological test results can be processed rapidly and the information from the MMPI-2 can be immediately available to be incorporated in therapy planning early in the intervention, even in the initial session. Second, a computer-based MMPI-2 interpretation can provide extensive personality information in a readily usable form without the need for the therapist to search through the empirical research for each patient's profile. The automated MMPI-2 report summarizes the most valid test correlates in a readable format. Finally, the automated MMPI-2 report is an informative, interesting format for use in providing test feedback to clients, a process that is discussed in more detail in Chapter 7.

The theoretical basis for computer-generated MMPI predictions was provided by Meehl (1954), who showed the power of actuarial prediction and personality description over intuitive test analysis procedures. Meehl's view of actuarial prediction was that test interpreters, basing their decisions on empirical experience, would outperform clinicians making decisions following intuitively based decision procedures. One of Meehl's students, Halbower (1955), demonstrated convincingly that empirically established test correlates could be accurately applied to new cases meeting the test criteria. Meehl's compelling argument on the strength of the actuarial procedure over clinically based decisions influenced a number of investigators to develop "actuarial tables" for personality descriptions using MMPI scales and combinations of scales (Altman, Gynther, Warbin, & Sletten, 1973; Arnold, 1970; Boerger, Graham, & Lilly, 1974; Fowler & Athey, 1971; Gilberstadt & Duker, 1965; Graham, 1973; Gynther, 1972; Gynther, Altman, & Sletten, 1972; Gynther, Altman, & Warbin, 1973; Gynther, Altman, & Warbin, 1973a, 1973b, 1973c; Gynther, Altman, Warbin, & Sletten, 1972; Gynther, Altman, Sletten, & Warbin, 1973; Halbower, 1955; Kelly & King, 1978; Lewandowski & Graham, 1972; Marks & Seeman, 1963; Marks, Seeman, &

Haller, 1974; Meikle & Gerritse, 1970; Persons & Marks, 1971; Sines, 1966; Warbin, Altman, Gynther, & Sletten, 1972). Research on MMPI profile patterns has established a validated and extensive interpretive base for the instrument for a number of patient types. Correlates for the MMPI scales are robust and can be automatically applied, even by mechanical procedures such as a computer, to cases that meet test score criteria.

HISTORY OF COMPUTER-BASED MMPI INTERPRETATIONS

Computer-based MMPI interpretation has a long history. The first computer-based interpretation of the MMPI following the actuarial approach was initiated at the Mayo Clinic (Pearson & Swenson, 1967) in the early 1960s. In this system, more than 100 statements of preestablished test correlates were programmed to print out descriptions of the patient who produced specified profile types. The computer output included an MMPI profile, along with a listing of up to six of the relevant descriptors. This computer interpretation system, though limited in scope, was readily accepted by the psychology and medical staffs at the Mayo Clinic. In the 1970s several other more comprehensive and sophisticated MMPI interpretation programs were developed. Later computer-based MMPI programs typically provided information in a narrative report format, rather than a listing of correlates as the Mayo System provided, and incorporated more extensive information.

Today, computer-based interpretation of psychological tests has become a widely accepted clinical tool. The computer-based MMPI report has become a central part of many clinician's diagnostic appraisal of their clients' problems. Using the computer-based report as an "outside opinion" of the client's problems can be very valuable to the process of providing feedback to clients. We will now turn to a discussion of procedures and practices of computer-based MMPI-2 interpretation.

AVAILABILITY OF VARIOUS ADMINISTRATIVE FORMATS FOR COMPUTER-BASED MMPI-2 REPORTS

There are a number of options available for administering and processing MMPI-2 protocols to obtain a computer-based MMPI-2 report.

Mail-In Service

For clinicians with a low volume of patients and ample time to process their MMPI-2 test results (e.g., if the therapist sees the patient on a weekly basis), mailing in the MMPI-2 to National Computer Systems for processing is probably the easiest test-processing option. The test is administered to the client in a paper–pencil form, and the answer sheet is mailed to National Computer Systems, where it is processed within 24 hours of receipt. The report is then sent back to the clinician by return mail. Express mail delivery or FAX machine reporting of results is possible if needed.

Test Processing by Data Phone

Clinicians with a microcomputer and a modem (for telephone communication purposes) can obtain rapid turnaround of their MMPI-2 reports. The client is administered the MMPI-2 in booklet form and responds to the questions on an answer sheet. The answer sheet is processed at the site by having a clerical person type the answers, in a proscribed format, into the computer. The answers are then sent by telephone to the National Computer Systems. The processed report is sent back to the clinician immediately by telephone and is printed out in the practitioner's office.

In-Office Processing by Microcomputer

Clinics or practitioners with access to a microcomputer can obtain immediate processing of the MMPI-2 answer sheet in their own office without sending the MMPI-2 answer sheet by mail or the individual's answers by telephone. Patients respond to the inventory by marking their answers on an answer sheet. A clerical person enters the individual's responses into the computer following a simple procedure using software provided by the test scoring service. The test answers are then processed by microcomputer and a report is printed out immediately. A "scorebox" or mechanism to allow for the software to be correctly read is required for this application.

Optical Scanning of MMPI-2 Answer Sheets

Clinics or practitioners with a relatively high volume of assessments (e.g., 10 to 15 cases a week) would find the use of an optical scanner for scoring MMPI-2s a valuable addition to their assessment program. The optical scanner reads the answer sheet and communicates the scores directly to the microcomputer. The scores are processed and a report is immediately produced.

The costs incurred in purchasing a table-top optical scanner, about $3,500, can be quickly compensated for in the savings of clerical time in processing. The scanner is relatively bug-free and operates with very low maintenance cost.

Computer Administration and Processing of Patient Responses

Another possible MMPI-2 administration format is the computer-administered test. The MMPI-2 items are presented on the video screen, and the subject is instructed to respond to them on the computer keyboard. Once the individual has completed the inventory, the microcomputer scores the test and generates a report, which is printed on an attached printer. This administration format is usually interesting to the client and easy to take. However, this is a somewhat inefficient use of the computer in that it usually requires the individual about an hour and a half to two hours to take the test in this manner. This ties up the computer for that period and only one person at a time can take the test.

Adaptive Computer Administration of the MMPI. Although not available at this time, computer-adaptive test administration is likely to be available for the MMPI-2 in the future. This test-administration format employs the flexibility of the computer in deciding which items on the inventory to administer. The full MMPI-2 would not be administered; only items that add to the information about the client are given. Each client would be administered a different form depending on their answers to previous items.

This concept is analogous to the way a clinical interview is conducted. An interviewer does not usually ask the same questions of all clients. Instead, the questions are contingent on answers the subject has previously given. For example, if the interviewee has responded "no" to the question "Are you married?" the interviewer would not ask any further questions about the client's being married. If the subject responded "yes" to the question, then he or she would "branch" into questions concerning the nature and quality of the marriage.

Researchers in the area of personality questionnaires are only beginning to determine the ways and means of branching personality inventory items so that only pertinent items are administered to each client. Several studies have demonstrated that appropriate "branching" or adaptive strategies could be developed for MMPI-type items (Clavelle & Butcher, 1977; Butcher, Keller, & Bacon, 1985; Ben-Porath, Slutske, & Butcher, 1989; Ben-Porath, Waller, Slutske, & Butcher, 1988). Several successful MMPI-2 adaptive strategies have been developed, and work is under way to develop practical, effective procedures for implementing them.

HOW COMPUTER-BASED INTERPRETATION PROGRAMS FOR THE MMPI-2 WORK

Computerized psychological test reporting programs are expert systems or forms of "artificial intelligence" in which computer programs simulate the cognitive processes of clinicians interpreting the MMPI-2. The general procedure or model on which MMPI-2 interpretation systems operate is quite simple. The data base for MMPI-2 interpretations comes from several sources, such as the established empirical literature for MMPI scales and indexes, correlates for specially constructed "supplementary" scales such as the Mf, MAC, Si, Es, and predictive decisions or personality descriptions based on scale relationships or *indexes* (e.g., the Megargee Rules for correctional settings or the Goldberg Index). More comprehensive interpretation systems also attempt to integrate information from the content themes presented by the subject as reflected through the MMPI-2 content scales, the Harris-Lingoes content subscales, or the critical items. And the clinical experience of the system developer also becomes a part of the program interpretation.

The MMPI-2 computer programs usually allow for the following operations.

1. *Scoring and processing answer sheets.* Scoring of relevant scales[1] and compilation of MMPI-2 indexes from raw scores are addressed first, and then profiles are drawn. The appropriate test variables, such as code types, are obtained to serve as the indexing variables for the report. Finally, special aspects such as relevant critical item content are listed on the printout.
2. *Organizing relevant variables.* The index variables are used to search stored data bases (reference files, look-up tables, and classification or decision rules) to locate the relevant personality and symptom information for the client being assessed.
   a. The initial step involves determination of profile validity and elimination of invalid records.
   b. Searching stored data files for prototypal information on the case.
   c. Integrating test information into a unified report.
3. *Communicating the results in a readable format.* Printing out a narrative report that addresses the believability of the report and provides a summary of the individual's symptomatic status, personality characteristics, and significant problems.
4. *Highlighting special problems or issues.* The computer system might also provide additional information about the client based on responses to particular item or scale relationships that address specific problems.
5. *Indicating appropriate cautions.* The American Psychological Associ-

---

1. Only systems that have been licensed by the copyright holder—The University of Minnesota Press—can score the MMPI-2 by computer. Unlicensed interpretation systems can produce MMPI interpretations, but the raw scores need to be obtained by hand scoring of the answer sheet.

ation has recommended guidelines for computerized psychological assessment. Appropriate qualifying statements concerning computer-based psychological reports need to be included in the report to prevent its misuse.

As you will see in a later section, MMPI computer interpretations vary in terms of their comprehensiveness and accuracy in describing and predicting individual behavior. Users need to be careful in deciding which available scoring and interpretation program to use.

RELATIVE ACCURACY OF COMPUTER INTERPRETATION SYSTEMS FOR THE MMPI

Research studies comparing the relative accuracy of computer-based reports with reports written by a trained clinician are not available. It is not known whether computer-based MMPI reports are more or less accurate than reports developed by a clinician. Most of the early computer-report evaluation research employed rather vague "satisfaction" ratings to determine whether a report was valid (Moreland, 1985). There have been several recent empirical validation studies involving the validity of the Minnesota Report. Moreland and Onstad (1985) found that reports produced on actual patients were judged significantly more accurate than randomly generated reports.

The most comprehensive empirical validation studies of computer-based MMPI reports were conducted by Eyde, Fishburne, and Kowal (1987) and Fishburne, Eyde, and Kowal (1988). These investigators compared the relative accuracy of seven MMPI computerized reports: Applied Innovations, Behaviordyne, Caldwell Report, Psych Systems, Minnesota Report (NCS), Western Psychological Services, and Tomlinson Reports. The investigators submitted protocols on several patients to each computer-assessment firm. They disassembled the computer-generated statements, disguised their origin, and gave these statements to raters (familiar with the actual cases) to rate for accuracy. Once the accuracy ratings were complete, the investigators reassembled the reports and computed accuracy ratings. The results of their study are summarized in Figure 6-1. The shaded box in the lower right-hand corner of the figure contains the most accurate reports emerging from the ratings. The Minnesota Reports were among those judged to be accurate enough for clinical use. The high degree of variability in accuracy level shown by this study provides a note of caution for clinicians selecting a computer-based assessment program.

We will now turn to a discussion of one MMPI system—The Minnesota Report distributed by National Computer Systems.

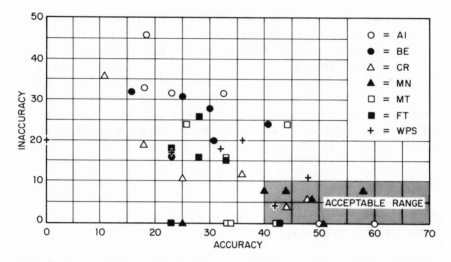

Figure 6–1. Scatter diagram of median percentages for hit rate of CBTI systems for three MMPI profile types for matched black/white cases. Note: 7/2, subclinical normal and unique cases (1, 2/1, 1/3, 8/1, 2, 2/8, 3, 4/2, 6, 8/6, 9/6, & 8/9) rated by 12 raters.

ILLUSTRATION OF COMPUTER-BASED ASSESSMENT: THE MINNESOTA CLINICAL REPORT

The Minnesota Report, a computerized interpretation for the MMPI-2, was originally developed as an aid in clinical assessment (see Butcher, 1989; Butcher, 1987). The Minnesota Report was revised in 1989 to incorporate the new MMPI-2 norms and new clinical information. Several goals were kept in mind in developing the Minnesota Report interpretation systems:

1. The interpretive system was developed as a conservative evaluation of the client based as closely as possible on established research.
2. Several specific programs were developed to match needs according to setting or application. Reports were developed for a number of settings:
    a. Adult inpatient
    b. Adult outpatient
    c. College counseling
    d. Correctional
    e. Medical settings
    f. Chronic pain programs
3. Special demographic considerations were taken into account. Reports are tailored to certain demographic characteristics of a case, particularly age and marital status. New data on personality corre-

lates for the scales from the MMPI-2 Restandardization Project were incorporated in the reports.

4. The interpretive reports were developed in a format that would be clinically useful, with information provided to meet the clinician's informational needs concerning symptom description, diagnostic hypotheses, and treatment considerations.

5. The interpretive system was written in a format that allows for easy modification as new research findings on the MMPI-2 emerge.

ILLUSTRATION OF THE MINNESOTA REPORT—REVISED

Computer-based MMPI-2 interpretation will be illustrated with an in-depth evaluation and exploration of two individuals who were being evaluated for substance abuse treatment programs. The two people were a man, aged 23, who was being evaluated for admission into an inpatient substance abuse program, and his girlfriend, a 25-year-old woman, who was being evaluated for outpatient substance abuse treatment.[2]

▶ **Case 135**

> This 23-year-old man was evaluated in conjunction with his entry into a substance abuse program. He has been using cocaine daily for a period of at least 2 years and recently had an episode of disorientation that became very frightening to him and the woman with whom he lived. The episode lasted for several hours and, according to his girlfriend, he was alternately violent toward her (he struck her several times and threatened her with a knife) and suicidal (he apparently sat on a window ledge for about 45 minutes threatening to jump). She called his brother, who subdued him and took him to a hospital emergency room. He was admitted and sedated. The next morning, he signed himself out and returned home. His girlfriend was already packing to move out on his return. He pleaded with her to stay, and she agreed, provided he seek help. She has also used cocaine during the past 8 months while they have lived together and has agreed to enter treatment with him (see Case 136).
>
> He is the second of two sons (his brother, age 25, is a CPA). His father, age 48, is a CPA and owns his own small firm. His mother, age 48, is a college graduate and has taught elementary school for 5 years (she did not finish her college studies until S. entered college, although she had completed 2 years before her oldest son was born). There is no reported psychiatric history in the immediate family.
>
> The patient graduated from college at age 21 having majored in business. His GPA was 2.9. Since graduation he has been employed as an industrial salesman for a chemical manufacturing firm (solvents). His work history is

2. This case was provided by John Exner. The Rorschach protocols were processed by Rorschach Workshops, Asheville, North Carolina; the scoring summaries are reproduced in the book's Appendix with the permission of John Exner.

reported to be good, and he has received four salary increases during 27 months, as well as a bonus during the past year. He indicated that he enjoys his work and expects to become an assistant sales manager in the near future. He has asked for and received a 3-week leave of absence. He reported an unremarkable developmental history with no serious injuries or illnesses. He reported that he was close to both parents and especially close to his brother, with whom he shared a bedroom until age 9. He and his brother both played little league baseball and were in Boy Scouts until he was 15.

The patient claims many high school and college friends, and was in a fraternity in college. He reportedly first had sex at age 15. He denied any homosexual experiences. He dated one girl regularly during his sophomore year in college, but she broke up with him. He met his current girlfriend about 18 months ago, and they began living together in his apartment about 9 months ago. They have discussed marriage, but he is reluctant until he feels more secure in his work. He admits that their sexual relationship is "not always good," but he now attributes this to his cocaine addiction (she has reported that he has a high frequency of impotence or premature ejaculation; she also notes that he frequently asks her to dress in unusual ways to provoke him).

S. reported that he became involved with cocaine casually during his senior year in college (he had been using marijuana since high school) and that he found it helpful to him in dealing with the pressures of his job. Ultimately, he began using it daily (he gets it through a co-worker). S. claims that he usually would not use it during the day, except during the past month, but that he did use it each evening at home. He drinks wine daily (one or two glasses). He is 5 feet, 11 inches, 175 pounds, athletic looking, blonde, quite attractive, and neatly dressed. During the interview he was often guarded and asked that questions be repeated, but in responding he seemed open and willing to be cooperative. He was especially cautious in describing his feelings for his girlfriend: "She's just great, I don't know how she's put up with me. She really deserves better. I hope everything works out for her, I owe her a lot."

The treatment program that he is entering requires 14 days (minimum) of inpatient routine followed by a minimum of 6 weeks of outpatient treatment (twice per week—once individual and once group). His girlfriend will not go through the inpatient routine but instead will begin an 8-week outpatient routine (individual and group). Drug screening prior to the evaluation is positive but not toxic. The neuropsychological screening was essentially negative.

▶ Case 136

This 25-year-old woman was evaluated because she applied for outpatient treatment in a substance abuse program. She admits to the frequent use of cocaine (in the evenings) with her boyfriend (see Case 135). He has become disabled because of cocaine addiction and is entering an inpatient program. She says that she wants to enter treatment to (1) help with his rehabilitation, and (2) because she feels unable to "say no" when drugs are offered to her.

She does not want to go through the inpatient program for fear of losing her job. If accepted into the outpatient program, she will be seen twice a week—once individually and once in a group—for a minimum of 8 weeks.

She is the only child of a couple who divorced when she was 9. She lived with her mother, who is now 47, and an aunt, now age 51, until age 22. Her mother works as an assistant manager in a bookstore, and her aunt is a secretary. She has had no contact with her father, age 50, for 6 years except for occasional letters or cards. He remarried and moved to a distant state shortly after her high school graduation. Prior to that time he visited five to eight times per year, usually on special occasions (Christmas, birthday, etc.). He was apparently treated for alcoholism when she was in junior high school, and to the best of her knowledge he has remained dry. He works for an oil company in a blue-collar position. She is vague about the reasons for her parents' divorce but suspects that her father was unfaithful to his wife and was alcoholic.

She reported that a series of urinary infections caused her to be bedridden quite often when she was between the ages of 3 and 6 and that she entered school a year late. She had problems with skin rashes in grades 6 through 8 that were apparently caused by allergies, and for that reason was exempt from gym classes. That problem cleared up by the time she entered high school, although she continued with allergy shots until age 16. She graduated from high school at age 19 (C+, B− average). She worked 1 year in the bookstore where her mother works and then began training as a dental technician. She completed that course, was certified at age 22, and obtained a position as dental assistant with a group practice, where she still works. She says that she likes her work and anticipates staying in her present position indefinitely.

She says that because she was "frail" she often did not join in the games of other children during elementary school, and because of her allergy problems she did not have many friends in junior high or in her first 2 years of high school. She began menstruation at age 13 and had serious cramping problems for the next 2 years. She went to her first school dance at age 16. Not long after, at another dance, a boy kissed and fondled her. She had her first experience of intercourse with him about 4 months later, which she says was not very pleasant for her. She abstained from further sex until she was in dental training. After completing her training she began sharing an apartment with two other girls (a secretary, age 27, and an airline agent, age 25). Since that time she has "slept with 8 or 10 guys," but did not experience orgasm until she met her current boyfriend at a party about 18 months ago. They have been living together for the past 9 months. She says, "I love him and he loves me. If we didn't do all the coke we'd get along a lot better, but when we get high, things just don't go right and he loses his temper a lot when that happens." She says that sex with him is "really good except when he has trouble and then he makes me do a lot of weird things." Apparently he buys exotic underwear for her and asks her to dance in it. He has also bought her a vibrator. If she is reluctant he loses his temper, although he has not been assaultive to her until his recent episode of disorientation. She is clearly concerned about his treatment and implies that she is quite apprehensive about their future relationship.

She was described as 5 feet, 5 inches, 126 pounds, long brown hair, and though not striking, somewhat attractive. She was cooperative and smiled a great deal while talking about herself. The drug screening was negative although some trace activity was noted. Neuropsychological screening was negative.

PSYCHOLOGICAL TEST RESULTS: MINNESOTA REPORTS FOR THE MMPI-2

The Minnesota Report narrative interpretations for Cases 135 and 136 are shown in the Chapter Appendix as Figures 6-2 and 6-3. The computer-based interpretation of the MMPI-2 profiles provided a clear description of the two individuals described in the case histories.

Minnesota Report Narrative for Case 135

The client's approach to the MMPI-2 was oriented toward presenting himself as having considerable problems and low resources for dealing with them at this time. As noted in the narrative report (see Figure 6-2), he perceived his problems as mostly centering on poor health. He attempted to convey that his present problems were largely somatic in origin. As described in the computer report, the symptom pattern he presented often follows a period of intense stress or trauma. In addition, the narrative report, attempting to account for the excitability, sense of frustration, and anger in his response pattern, suggests that these problems might reflect some organic impairment in his case.

The client seems to be viewing his physical problems as his most important treatment need at this time; however, this self-presentation (as viewed largely through the MMPI-2 clinical scales) is highly exaggerated. The content scales provide a somewhat different and perhaps a more pathological view of his personality functioning. His performance on the content scales suggest a severe personality disorder that requires careful consideration in any treatment plan. A number of statements in the narrative report address clear antisocial personality features and anger control problems that require consideration in his case. His psychological adjustment was considered to be unstable, and the possibility of erratic, unpredictable, and aggressive behavior was noted in the report.

The narrative report also addresses the client's somewhat negative view of women. He appears to be rather intolerant and insensitive in relationships with women and may easily become frustrated and lose his temper with them.

The computer report presents a somewhat cautious picture concerning his treatment amenability, noting that individuals with this pattern tend not to be very insightful or reflective in viewing their problems and may resist psychological interpretation. Insight-oriented treatment may be inappropriate for him because of his cynical attitudes about life and his tendency to exaggerate physical problems in dealing with conflict. Since he apparently has a problem with anger control, treatment relationship difficulties may be encountered. The computer report suggests the possibility that a cognitive–behavioral treatment approach to anger control might result in a reduction of his aggressiveness and loss of control.

Another situation that needs to be considered in any rehabilitative effort with him is that he presents some negative work attitudes that could hamper future adjustment to life. These negative work attitudes should be addressed in treatment if he remains in therapy.

Minnesota Report Narrative for Case 136

The Minnesota Report narrative for Case 136, shown in Figure 6-3, addressed many of the problems this woman was experiencing, and described several important personality features she appears to possess.

First, the validity paragraph pointed out an interesting aspect of her self-report that requires some discussion. Even though she reported a number of problems and acknowledged several chronic personality problems, she had a very high L score, which suggests caution in interpreting her clinical profile. The nature of her scale elevations on the clinical scales (D and Pt) probably confirms the interpretation of scale L as rigidity of her personal adjustment.

The symptomatic pattern in her narrative report addressed her depressed mood and intense psychological distress. Moreover, her self-report also focused on a prominent pattern of somatization that could prove resistant to treatment. Her personal history offers some suggestion of complicating somatic predisposition (she was described as being "frail" and having had numerous medical problems in the past). A therapist attempting to engage her in psychological treatment should be aware that she may tend to somatize psychological conflict rather than deal with it on a psychological level.

Central to her adjustment problems appears to be her passive-dependent personality style, low self-esteem, and poor self-concept. The Minnesota Report narrative, drawing both from the clinical scales configuration and the MMPI-2 content scales, particularly Low Self-Esteem, points to the pervasive, chronic nature of her problems. These self-esteem problems are salient in her inability to "resist" drugs when they are offered to her. Her MMPI profile and LSE scores are quite consistent with that of a long-suffering, codependent behavior pattern often found in spouses of alcoholics.

Two problematic features, noted in the narrative, were drawn from the

MMPI-2 content scales WRK and TRT. She appears to endorse many symptoms and attitudes suggestive of an inability to change her behaviors toward more productive work attitudes and positive self-change in therapy. It is likely that, early in her treatment, a therapist would need to address these possibly negative indicators that could signal both treatment and work failures.

PSYCHOLOGICAL TEST RESULTS: RORSCHACH INTERPRETATION

The Rorschach scoring summaries for Cases 135 and 136 are included, in full, in the Appendix at the end of the book. The Rorschach protocols have also been interpreted by John Exner, using the Exner Comprehensive Rorschach Interpretation System, and are included in the following summaries.

▶ Interpretive Summary—Case 135

Although this 23-year-old man usually has about as much capacity for control and tolerance for stress as do most adults, those features have now become more limited because of some situationally related stress. This experience has created a form of stimulus overload that has had an impact on both his thinking and his feelings. As a consequence, he has become more vulnerable to impulsive behavior, both ideational and emotional. He tends to feel much more helpless and unable to form meaningful responses than is usually the case, and his psychological functioning has become much more complex because of this. He tends to be confused about his feelings and uncertain about his ability to contend with this situation.

He is an extremely self-centered person who exaggerates his own personal worth considerably. In effect, he harbors a narcissisticlike feature that he usually expects those around him to reinforce. He prefers to be dependent upon others who become crucial in allowing him to form and maintain deep and mature interpersonal relationships. In reality, he is less interested in others than are most people, perceiving them mainly as a source on which he can depend. He is quite defensive about his self-image and often takes a more authoritarian approach to those who pose challenges for him.

He is the type of person who invests feelings into most of his decision-making operations and is less concerned with the modulation of his own emotional displays than are most adults. In other words, when he discharges his feelings, they tend to be overly intense and possibly overly influential in his decisions.

He is quite aware of acceptable and conventional behaviors; however, his exquisite self-centeredness often causes him to disregard them in favor of more idiographic patterns of behavior that are in concert with his own needs and wants. He tends to look on the environment negatively and often attempts to deal with it in a pseudointellectual manner that permits him to justify his own activities. He is usually very unwilling to accept responsibility for any behavioral errors, preferring instead to rationalize the causes of problems as being the responsibility of the external world.

Overall, he is the type of person who has a strong need to be in control of his environment. It is unlikely that he would seek out any form of psychological intervention unless he could feel assured that it was directly beneficial to him and in a model over which he had control. He is not very insightful and has no strong interest in changing.

▶ Interpretive Summary—Case 136

The test data suggests that this 25-year-old woman is quite immature. She does not have good capacities for control or tolerance for stress, and those limitations have become reduced even further by the presence of situationally related stress. As such, she is extremely vulnerable to impulsiveness, both ideational and emotional, and will have considerable difficulty functioning in all but the most highly structured situations.

Basically, she is a very passive and dependent kind of person who probably finds the demands of adulthood to be much more hectic and complex than she is able to deal with easily. She has learned to be very cautious in processing information and works hard to avoid processing errors. When she translates information that she has processed, however, she is often prone to be more individualistic than conventional in her interpretation of it. It seems reasonable to speculate that she is the type of person who would prefer more mature interactions, but has been unable to establish them, and as a result has settled on a more peripheral coexistence with her world.

Her self-image is much more negative than positive. She often perceives others as having more assets and capacities than she, and tends to feel quite inadequate. She often ruminates about her own negative characteristics, and this ruminative tendency will frequently give rise to experiences of depression.

She is the type of person who prefers to think things through before forming or implementing a decision, but much of her thinking is unfortunately more detached from reality than focused on it. In fact, flights into fantasy have become a major defensive tactic for her. In other words, whenever the world becomes too harsh or ungiving, she is prone to replace it with a fantasy existence that is more easily managed. She dislikes responsibility and tries to avoid making major decisions whenever possible, relying instead on those around her for that task. She sets very low goals for herself and has come to view the future much more pessimistically than do most adults.

Overall, she is the type of person who seems to have resigned herself to roles in life in which she can be passively dependent on those around her. Her expectations are low, and she seems to anticipate that life will be a series of crises in which she will become the victim. She would like to experience more positive interactions with others but does not expect that this will evolve. She is the sort of person who can benefit considerably from long-term developmental forms of intervention.

LIMITATIONS OF COMPUTER-BASED MMPI-2 INTERPRETATION

In spite of their acceptability, ease of use, and relative accuracy, computer-based reports should not be used as the sole source of clinical information. The Minnesota Report should be used with appropriate cautions. Several factors need to be considered: the limited range of available correlates; the prototypal match of the particular patient being evaluated; and the degree of accuracy in predicting and describing personality.

The Limited Range of Available Test Correlates

Over the past 35 or so years, investigators have attempted to catalog empirical correlates for the various MMPI scales and indexes. Unfortunately, the actuarial base for the MMPI does not, at present, provide for interpretation of the full range of possible profile configurations. Given this fact, it is likely that the clinical experience of the program developer will determine the makeup of many of the reports generated. The decisions concerning which component to employ in the development of a computer-interpretation program clearly influences the accuracy and generalizability of the report. As Fowler (1987) noted, it is therefore important in choosing a computer-based interpretation program to evaluate carefully the expertise of the system developer. Most MMPI computer-interpretation programs, in order to be comprehensive and interpret all cases, must extrapolate from the available research information base. For example, solid actuarial data do not exist for a 1-9-6 MMPI profile code; consequently, the interpretation needs to be based on the component scales. The computer program developer might follow a scale-by-scale interpretation strategy or one that involves extracting elements from the component codes, 1-9, 9-6, or 1-6. Whichever approach is taken will result in somewhat different narrative reports.

Determining the Prototypal Match

Does the report fit the patient? This decision rests with the system user. At present, computerized MMPI reports are not designed to stand alone in a clinical psychological assessment. They are designed to be used by a trained psychologist or psychiatrist in conjunction with other sources of clinical assessment information. As resource material the automated MMPI report can provide a useful summary of hypotheses, descriptions, and test inferences about patients in a rapid and efficient manner. Narrative reports, since they are based on modal or typical descriptions of the profile type, should be verified for goodness of fit by the clinician through other sources of information.

An interesting paradox presents itself. We are most comfortable with a computer-based report (or a clinician-derived report) when it meets the expectations we have developed about the patient from our clinical interview. We usually then consider the computer narrative "a good match" because it confirmed our expectations; however, we tend to consider suspect reports that do *not* match our expectations and that seem to be presenting disparate information.

There is, of course, the possibility that the report contains information that is correct, but the clinician was unaware of it. Thus, even seemingly inaccurate reports might provide the clinician with leads to potentially fruitful material. A relatively common situation that occurs in clinical settings is the incorrect impressions generated by high Pd or 4-9 clients. These people commonly present well, make favorable impressions, and are generally adept at influencing others in interpersonal interaction. In such cases, the MMPI may actually be more accurate (less vulnerable to interpersonal influence) than the practitioner's early impressions.

Control Over Access to Computerized Narrative Reports

Patients are typically fascinated with computer-based MMPI reports. Many patients will ask for a copy of their computerized report for their own records. For many reasons this is not a good idea. The most important reason for not providing reports to clients is that the computerized report is typically written for professionals and employs language not usually understandable by laypersons. Consequently, reports are easily misinterpreted unless the user is trained in the MMPI-2.

SUMMARY

Computer-based MMPI interpretation has gained considerable acceptance over the past few decades. Clinicians are finding that computer-generated personality reports are valuable additions to the pretreatment psychological assessment study. This chapter has discussed a number of issues concerning computer-based MMPI interpretation and provided a detailed description of one MMPI-2 system, the Minnesota Report. Two illustrations of computerized reports were given. Possible limitations or special considerations in using computer-based MMPI-2 reports were discussed.

CHAPTER 6 APPENDIX

FIGURE 6–2
Case 135

THE MINNESOTA REPORT:™
ADULT CLINICAL SYSTEM
INTERPRETIVE REPORT

By James N. Butcher

Minnesota Multiphasic
Personality Inventory~2™
S.R. Hathaway and J.C. McKinley

```
           Client ID:  0026135
         Report Date:  03-AUG-89
                Age:   23
                Sex:   Male
            Setting:   Outpatient Mental Health
          Education:   12
     Marital Status:   Never Married
```

PROFILE VALIDITY

This is a valid MMPI-2 profile. The client has cooperated in the
evaluation, admitting to a number of psychological problems in a frank and
open manner. Individuals with this profile tend to be blunt and may openly
complain to others about their psychological problems. The client tends to
be quite self-critical and may appear to have low self-esteem and inadequate
psychological defense mechanisms. He may be seeking psychological help at
this time since he feels that things are out of control and unmanageable.

SYMPTOMATIC PATTERNS

The client is exhibiting a pattern of physical problems which has reduced
his level of psychological functioning. These symptoms may be vague and may
have appeared suddenly after a period of stress or trauma. The pattern of
pain, physical symptoms, irritability, low frustration tolerance, and anger
outbursts suggests that the possibility of an organic brain dysfunction
should be evaluated.

The client seems to have a rather limited range of interests and tends to
prefer stereotyped masculine activities over literary and artistic pursuits
or introspective experiences. He tends to be somewhat competitive and needs
to see himself as masculine. He probably prefers to view women in
subservient roles. Interpersonally, he is likely to be intolerant and
insensitive, and others may find him rather crude, coarse, or narrow-minded.

In addition, the following description is suggested by the content of this
client's responses. He complains about feeling quite uncomfortable and in
poor health. The symptoms he reports reflect vague weakness, fatigue, and
difficulties in concentration. In addition, he feels that others are
unsympathetic toward his perceived health problems. He seems to be highly
manipulative and self-indulgent. He seems to have had much past conflict
with authority and is quite resentful of societal standards of conduct.

INTERPERSONAL RELATIONS

He is probably experiencing difficulty with interpersonal relationships.
He may have an overly critical, perfectionistic, and rigid interpersonal
style, and may be prone to losing his temper.

His social interests appear to be high and he seems to enjoy social
participation. However, his interpersonal behavior may be problematic at
times in the sense that he may lose his temper in frustrating situations.

```
          TM                                                      page 2
MMPI-2                  TM
THE MINNESOTA REPORT:                  ID: 0026135    REPORT DATE: 03-AUG-89
ADULT CLINICAL SYSTEM
INTERPRETIVE REPORT
```

The content of this client's MMPI-2 responses suggests the following
additional information concerning his interpersonal relations. He appears
to be an individual who holds rather cynical views about life. Any efforts
to initiate new behaviors may be colored by his negativism. He may view
relationships with others as threatening and harmful. He feels some family
conflict at this time. However, this does not appear to him to be a major
problem in his life. He feels like leaving home to escape a quarrelsome,
critical situation, and to be free of family domination. He feels intensely
angry, hostile, and resentful of others, and would like to get back at them.
He is competitive and uncooperative, tending to be very critical of others.

BEHAVIORAL STABILITY

Apparently rather unstable, he may behave in erratic, unpredictable, and
possibly aggressive ways. Social introversion-extraversion tends to be a
very stable personality characteristic over time. The client's typically
outgoing and sociable behavior is likely to remain similar if retested at a
later time.

DIAGNOSTIC CONSIDERATIONS

The possibility of an organic illness should be evaluated. If organic
problems are ruled out, the most characteristic diagnosis would be
Conversion Disorder or Somatization Disorder. His behavioral
characteristics can also be exhibited by individuals with a Post-Traumatic
Stress Syndrome.

TREATMENT CONSIDERATIONS

If physical findings are negative, there is a strong possibility that his
problems are based on psychological factors. Discussing the possible
psychological basis to his disorder with him may be somewhat problematic,
since he tends to resist psychological interpretation.

Insight-oriented treatment approaches tend not to be very appropriate for
individuals with this personality makeup. They are not very insightful and
may resist actively entering into a therapeutic relationship. Individuals
with this MMPI-2 profile tend to have problems establishing a
psychotherapeutic alliance, since they view their problems as organically
based.

The strong hostility component in his personality pattern may militate
against his developing a positive therapeutic relationship. Behavior
modification procedures may be valuable in reducing his agitation and
anxiety. Cognitive-behavioral anger control procedures may be employed to
reduce his aggressiveness and potential for loss of control. He harbors

```
        TM                                                      page 3
MMPI-2                  TM
THE MINNESOTA REPORT:                ID: 0026135    REPORT DATE: 03-AUG-89
ADULT CLINICAL SYSTEM
INTERPRETIVE REPORT
```

some negative work attitudes which could limit his adaptability in the work place. His low morale and disinterest in work could impair future adjustment to employment, a factor which should be taken into consideration in treatment.

NOTE: This MMPI-2 interpretation can serve as a useful source of hypotheses about clients. This report is based on objectively derived scale indexes and scale interpretations that have been developed in diverse groups of patients. The personality descriptions, inferences and recommendations contained herein need to be verified by other sources of clinical information since individual clients may not fully match the prototype. The information in this report should most appropriately be used by a trained, qualified test interpreter. The information contained in this report should be considered confidential.

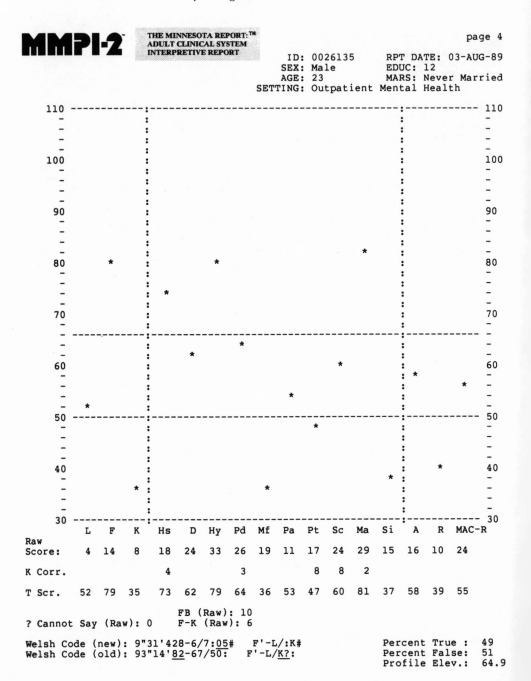

ID: 0026135   RPT DATE: 03-AUG-89
SEX: Male   EDUC: 12
AGE: 23   MARS: Never Married
SETTING: Outpatient Mental Health

	L	F	K	Hs	D	Hy	Pd	Mf	Pa	Pt	Sc	Ma	Si	A	R	MAC-R
Raw Score:	4	14	8	18	24	33	26	19	11	17	24	29	15	16	10	24
K Corr.				4			3			8	8	2				
T Scr.	52	79	35	73	62	79	64	36	53	47	60	81	37	58	39	55

? Cannot Say (Raw): 0

FB (Raw): 10
F-K (Raw): 6

Welsh Code (new): 9"31'428-6/7:05#   F'-L/:K#
Welsh Code (old): 93"14'82-67/50:   F'-L/K?:

Percent True : 49
Percent False: 51
Profile Elev.: 64.9

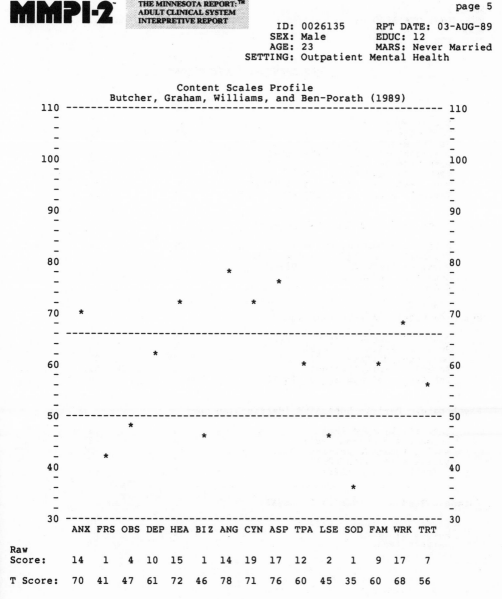

MMPI-2

THE MINNESOTA REPORT:™
ADULT CLINICAL SYSTEM
INTERPRETIVE REPORT

page 5

ID: 0026135   RPT DATE: 03-AUG-89
SEX: Male   EDUC: 12
AGE: 23   MARS: Never Married
SETTING: Outpatient Mental Health

Content Scales Profile
Butcher, Graham, Williams, and Ben-Porath (1989)

	ANX	FRS	OBS	DEP	HEA	BIZ	ANG	CYN	ASP	TPA	LSE	SOD	FAM	WRK	TRT
Raw Score:	14	1	4	10	15	1	14	19	17	12	2	1	9	17	7
T Score:	70	41	47	61	72	46	78	71	76	60	45	35	60	68	56

```
     TM                                                         page 6
MMPI-2                 TM
THE MINNESOTA REPORT:                ID: 0026135    REPORT DATE: 03-AUG-89
ADULT CLINICAL SYSTEM
INTERPRETIVE REPORT
```

SUPPLEMENTARY SCORE REPORT

	Raw Score	T Score
Ego Strength (Es)	35	45
Dominance (Do)	17	51
Social Responsibility (Re)	17	42
Overcontrolled Hostility (O-H)	10	41
PTSD - Keane (PK)	24	77
PTSD - Schlenger (PS)	30	74
True Response Inconsistency (TRIN)	8	57F
Variable Response Inconsistency (VRIN)	7	57

Depression Subscales (Harris-Lingoes):

	Raw Score	T Score
Subjective Depression (D1)	12	64
Psychomotor Retardation (D2)	4	43
Physical Malfunctioning (D3)	5	67
Mental Dullness (D4)	6	67
Brooding (D5)	3	57

Hysteria Subscales (Harris-Lingoes):

	Raw Score	T Score
Denial of Social Anxiety (Hy1)	5	56
Need for Affection (Hy2)	3	36
Lassitude-Malaise (Hy3)	11	88
Somatic Complaints (Hy4)	9	82
Inhibition of Aggression (Hy5)	3	48

Psychopathic Deviate Subscales (Harris-Lingoes):

	Raw Score	T Score
Familial Discord (Pd1)	5	71
Authority Problems (Pd2)	3	48
Social Imperturbability (Pd3)	5	58
Social Alienation (Pd4)	7	67
Self-Alienation (Pd5)	6	63

Paranoia Subscales (Harris-Lingoes):

	Raw Score	T Score
Persecutory Ideas (Pa1)	5	70
Poignancy (Pa2)	4	62
Naivete (Pa3)	2	36

```
        TM                                                          page 7
MMPI-2                  TM
THE MINNESOTA REPORT:              ID: 0026135     REPORT DATE: 03-AUG-89
ADULT CLINICAL SYSTEM
INTERPRETIVE REPORT


                                        Raw Score      T Score

Schizophrenia Subscales (Harris-Lingoes):

        Social Alienation (Sc1)             7             68
        Emotional Alienation (Sc2)          2             59
        Lack of Ego Mastery, Cognitive (Sc3) 2            54
        Lack of Ego Mastery, Conative (Sc4)  5            65
        Lack of Ego Mastery, Def. Inhib. (Sc5) 5          75
        Bizarre Sensory Experiences (Sc6)    6            70


Hypomania Subscales (Harris-Lingoes):

        Amorality (Ma1)                      6             81
        Psychomotor Acceleration (Ma2)       9             68
        Imperturbability (Ma3)               4             53
        Ego Inflation (Ma4)                  4             56


Social Introversion Subscales (Ben-Porath, Hostetler, Butcher, & Graham):

        Shyness / Self-Consciousness (Si1)   0             39
        Social Avoidance (Si2)               0             41
        Alienation--Self and Others (Si3)   10             65


Uniform T scores are used for Hs, D, Hy, Pd, Pa, Pt, Sc, Ma, and the Content
Scales; all other MMPI-2 scales use linear T scores.
```

```
        TM                                                              page 8
MMPI-2              TM
THE MINNESOTA REPORT:                   ID: 0026135    REPORT DATE: 03-AUG-89
ADULT CLINICAL SYSTEM
INTERPRETIVE REPORT
```

CRITICAL ITEMS

The following critical items have been found to have possible significance in
analyzing a client's problem situation. Although these items may serve as a
source of hypotheses for further investigation, caution should be taken in
interpreting individual items because they may have been inadvertently
checked.

Acute Anxiety State (Koss-Butcher Critical Items)

    2. I have a good appetite. (F)
    3. I wake up fresh and rested most mornings. (F)
    5. I am easily awakened by noise. (T)
   10. I am about as able to work as I ever was. (F)
   15. I work under a great deal of tension. (T)
   28. I am bothered by an upset stomach several times a week. (T)
   39. My sleep is fitful and disturbed. (T)
  140. Most nights I go to sleep without thoughts or ideas bothering me. (F)
  218. I have periods of such great restlessness that I cannot sit long in a
       chair. (T)
  444. I am a high-strung person. (T)
  463. Several times a week I feel as if something dreadful is about to
       happen. (T)
  469. I sometimes feel that I am about to go to pieces. (T)

Depressed Suicidal Ideation (Koss-Butcher Critical Items)

    9. My daily life is full of things that keep me interested. (F)
   38. I have had periods of days, weeks, or months when I couldn't take care
       of things because I couldn't "get going." (T)
  273. Life is a strain for me much of the time. (T)
  388. I very seldom have spells of the blues. (F)
  506. I have recently considered killing myself. (T)
  518. I have made lots of bad mistakes in my life. (T)

Threatened Assault (Koss-Butcher Critical Items)

   37. At times I feel like smashing things. (T)
   85. At times I have a strong urge to do something harmful or shocking. (T)
  134. At times I feel like picking a fist fight with someone. (T)
  213. I get mad easily and then get over it soon. (T)
  389. I am often said to be hotheaded. (T)

Situational Stress Due to Alcoholism (Koss-Butcher Critical Items)

```
        TM                                                        page 9
MMPI-2                  TM
THE MINNESOTA REPORT:                ID: 0026135      REPORT DATE: 03-AUG-89
ADULT CLINICAL SYSTEM
INTERPRETIVE REPORT
```

125. I believe that my home life is as pleasant as that of most people I
     know. (F)
264. I have used alcohol excessively. (T)
487. I have enjoyed using marijuana. (T)
489. I have a drug or alcohol problem. (T)
502. I have some habits that are really harmful. (T)
511. Once a week or more I get high or drunk. (T)
518. I have made lots of bad mistakes in my life. (T)

Mental Confusion (Koss-Butcher Critical Items)

 31. I find it hard to keep my mind on a task or job. (T)
 32. I have had very peculiar and strange experiences. (T)

Persecutory Ideas (Koss-Butcher Critical Items)

 17. I am sure I get a raw deal from life. (T)
 42. If people had not had it in for me, I would have been much more
     successful. (T)
124. I often wonder what hidden reason another person may have for doing
     something nice for me. (T)
145. I feel that I have often been punished without cause. (T)

Antisocial Attitude (Lachar-Wrobel Critical Items)

 27. When people do me a wrong, I feel I should pay them back if I can, just
     for the principle of the thing. (T)
 35. Sometimes when I was young I stole things. (T)
227. I don't blame people for trying to grab everything they can get in this
     world. (T)
254. Most people make friends because friends are likely to be useful to
     them. (T)

Family Conflict (Lachar-Wrobel Critical Items)

 21. At times I have very much wanted to leave home. (T)
 83. I have very few quarrels with members of my family. (F)
125. I believe that my home life is as pleasant as that of most people I
     know. (F)
288. My parents and family find more fault with me than they should. (T)

Somatic Symptoms (Lachar-Wrobel Critical Items)

 28. I am bothered by an upset stomach several times a week. (T)
 33. I seldom worry about my health. (F)

                    TM   page 10
MMPI-2   TM
THE MINNESOTA REPORT: ID: 0026135   REPORT DATE: 03-AUG-89
ADULT CLINICAL SYSTEM
INTERPRETIVE REPORT

40. Much of the time my head seems to hurt all over. (T)
44. Once a week or oftener I suddenly feel hot all over, for no real
    reason. (T)
53. Parts of my body often have feelings like burning, tingling, crawling,
    or like "going to sleep." (T)
57. I hardly ever feel pain in the back of my neck. (F)
101. Often I feel as if there is a tight band around my head. (T)
111. I have a great deal of stomach trouble. (T)
159. I have never had a fainting spell. (F)
164. I seldom or never have dizzy spells. (F)
176. I have very few headaches. (F)
182. I have had attacks in which I could not control my movements or speech
     but in which I knew what was going on around me. (T)
224. I have few or no pains. (F)
229. I have had blank spells in which my activities were interrupted and I
     did not know what was going on around me. (T)

Sexual Concern and Deviation (Lachar-Wrobel Critical Items)

121. I have never indulged in any unusual sex practices. (F)

Anxiety and Tension (Lachar-Wrobel Critical Items)

15. I work under a great deal of tension. (T)
17. I am sure I get a raw deal from life. (T)
218. I have periods of such great restlessness that I cannot sit long in a
     chair. (T)
405. I am usually calm and not easily upset. (F)
463. Several times a week I feel as if something dreadful is about to
     happen. (T)

Sleep Disturbance (Lachar-Wrobel Critical Items)

5. I am easily awakened by noise. (T)
39. My sleep is fitful and disturbed. (T)
140. Most nights I go to sleep without thoughts or ideas bothering me. (F)

Deviant Thinking and Experience (Lachar-Wrobel Critical Items)

32. I have had very peculiar and strange experiences. (T)
122. At times my thoughts have raced ahead faster than I could speak
     them. (T)

Depression and Worry (Lachar-Wrobel Critical Items)

2. I have a good appetite. (F)

3. I wake up fresh and rested most mornings. (F)
10. I am about as able to work as I ever was. (F)
150. Sometimes I feel as if I must injure either myself or someone
     else. (T)
273. Life is a strain for me much of the time. (T)
339. I have sometimes felt that difficulties were piling up so high that I
     could not overcome them. (T)
415. I worry quite a bit over possible misfortunes. (T)

Deviant Beliefs (Lachar-Wrobel Critical Items)

42. If people had not had it in for me, I would have been much more
    successful. (T)

Substance Abuse (Lachar-Wrobel Critical Items)

168. I have had periods in which I carried on activities without knowing
     later what I had been doing. (T)
264. I have used alcohol excessively. (T)
429. Except by doctor's orders I never take drugs or sleeping pills. (F)

Problematic Anger (Lachar-Wrobel Critical Items)

85. At times I have a strong urge to do something harmful or shocking. (T)
134. At times I feel like picking a fist fight with someone. (T)
213. I get mad easily and then get over it soon. (T)
389. I am often said to be hotheaded. (T)

FIGURE 6–3
Case 136

000262

THE MINNESOTA REPORT:™
ADULT CLINICAL SYSTEM
INTERPRETIVE REPORT

By James N. Butcher

*Minnesota Multiphasic
Personality Inventory -2*™

S.R. Hathaway and J.C. McKinley

```
          Client ID:  26136
        Report Date:  03-AUG-89
               Age:   25
               Sex:   Female
           Setting:   Outpatient Mental Health
         Education:   12
    Marital Status:   Never Married
```

PROFILE VALIDITY

The client has responded to the MMPI-2 items by claiming to be
unrealistically virtuous. This test-taking attitude weakens the validity of
the test and shows an unwillingness or inability on the part of the client
to disclose personal information. The resulting MMPI-2 profile is unlikely
to provide much useful information about the client since she was too
guarded to cooperate in the self-appraisal. Despite this extreme
defensiveness, she has responded to items reflecting some unusual symptoms
or beliefs. Many reasons may be found for this pattern of
uncooperativeness: conscious distortion to present herself in a favorable
light; limited intelligence or lack of psychological sophistication; or
rigid neurotic adjustment.

The client's efforts to thwart the evaluation and project an overly positive
self-image produced an MMPI-2 profile that substantially underestimates her
psychological maladjustment. The test interpretation should proceed with
the caution that the clinical picture reflected in the profile is probably
an overly positive one and may not provide sufficient information for
evaluation.

SYMPTOMATIC PATTERNS

This client's profile presents a broad and mixed picture in which physical
complaints and depressed affect are salient elements. The client is
exhibiting much somatic distress and may be experiencing a problem with her
psychological adjustment. Her physical complaints are probably extreme,
possibly reflecting a general lack of effectiveness in life. She is
probably feeling quite tense and nervous, and may be feeling that she cannot
get by without help for her physical problems. She is likely to be
reporting a great deal of pain, and feels that others do not understand how
sick she is feeling. She may be quite irritable and may become hostile if
her symptoms are not given "proper" attention.

Many individuals with this profile have a history of psychophysiological
disorders. They tend to overreact to minor problems with physical symptoms.
Ulcers and gastrointestinal distress are common. The possibility of actual
organic problems, therefore, should be carefully evaluated. Individuals
with this profile report a great deal of tension and a depressed mood. They
tend to be pessimistic and gloomy in their outlook toward life.

In addition, the following description is suggested by the content of this
client's responses. She is preoccupied with feeling guilty and unworthy.
She feels that she deserves to be punished for wrongs she has committed.
She feels regretful and unhappy about life, and seems plagued by anxiety and
worry about the future. She feels hopeless at times and feels that she is a
condemned person. She has difficulty managing routine affairs, and the item

content she endorsed suggests a poor memory, concentration problems, and an
inability to make decisions. She appears to be immobilized and withdrawn
and has no energy for life. According to her self-report, there is a strong
possibility that she has seriously contemplated suicide. She feels somewhat
self-alienated and expresses some personal misgivings or a vague sense of
remorse about past acts. She feels that life is unrewarding and dull, and
finds it hard to settle down.

INTERPERSONAL RELATIONS

She appears to be somewhat passive-dependent in relationships. She may
manipulate others through her physical symptoms, and become hostile if
sufficient attention is not paid to her complaints.

She appears to be rather shy and inhibited in social situations, and may
avoid others for fear of being hurt. She has very few friends, and is
considered by others as "hard to get to know." She is quiet, submissive,
conventional, and lacks self-confidence in dealing with other people.
Individuals with this passive and withdrawing lifestyle are often unable to
assert themselves appropriately, and find that they are frequently taken
advantage of by others.

BEHAVIORAL STABILITY

There are likely to be long-standing personality problems predisposing her
to develop physical symptoms under stress. Her present disorder could
reflect, in part, an exaggerated response to environmental stress. Social
introversion tends to be a very stable personality characteristic. Her
generally reclusive interpersonal behavior, introverted life style, and
tendency toward interpersonal avoidance would likely be evident in any
future test results.

DIAGNOSTIC CONSIDERATIONS

Individuals with this profile type are often seen as neurotic, and may
receive a diagnosis of Somatoform Disorder. Actual organic problems such as
ulcers and hypertension might be part of the clinical picture. Some
individuals with this profile have problems with abuse of pain medication or
other prescription drugs.

TREATMENT CONSIDERATIONS

Her view of herself as physically disabled needs to be considered in any
treatment planning. She tends to somatize her difficulties and to seek
medical solutions rather than to deal with them psychologically. She seems
to tolerate a high level of psychological conflict and may not be motivated
to deal with her problems directly. She is not a strong candidate for

insight-oriented psychotherapy. Psychological treatment may progress more
rapidly if her symptoms are dealt with through behavior modification
techniques. However, with her generally pessimistic attitude and low energy
resources, she seems to have little hope of getting better.

The item content she endorsed indicates attitudes and feelings that suggest
a low capacity for self-change. Her potentially high resistance to change
might need to be discussed with her early in treatment in order to promote a
more treatment-expectant attitude. In any intervention or psychological
evaluation program involving occupational adjustment, her negative work
attitudes could become an important problem to overcome. She holds a number
of attitudes and feelings that could interfere with work adjustment.

NOTE: This MMPI-2 interpretation can serve as a useful source of hypotheses
about clients. This report is based on objectively derived scale indexes
and scale interpretations that have been developed in diverse groups of
patients. The personality descriptions, inferences and recommendations
contained herein need to be verified by other sources of clinical
information since individual clients may not fully match the prototype. The
information in this report should most appropriately be used by a trained,
qualified test interpreter. The information contained in this report should
be considered confidential.

MMPI-2

THE MINNESOTA REPORT:™
ADULT CLINICAL SYSTEM
INTERPRETIVE REPORT

page 4

```
              ID: 26136        RPT DATE: 03-AUG-89
             SEX: Female       EDUC: 12
             AGE: 25           MARS: Never Married
         SETTING: Outpatient Mental Health
```

```
110 -------------:---------------------------------------------:------------ 110
  -             :                                               :            -
  -             :                                               :            -
  -             :            *                                  :            -
100             :                                               :          100
  -             :                                               :            -
  -             :                                               :            -
  -             :                                               :            -
 90             :                                               :           90
  -             :                                               :            -
  -             :                                               :            -
  -             :    *                                          :            -
 80             :        *                      *               :           80
  -             :                                               :            -
  -     *       :              *                                :            -
  -             :                                        *      :            -
  - *           :                                               :            -
 70             :                                     * : *                  70
  -             :                                               :            -
  - ------------:--------------------------------*------------:------------ -
  -             :                                               :            -
  -             :                                               :            -
 60             :                                               :           60
  -             :                      *                        :            -
  -             :                                               :            -
  -             :                                               :            -
 50 ------------:-----------------------------------------------:------------ 50
  -             :                                               :            -
  -         *   :                                 *             :            -
  -             :                                               :   *        -
 40             :                                               :           40
  -             :                                               :            -
  -             :                                               :            -
  -             :              *                                :            -
 30 ------------:-----------------------------------------------:------------ 30
        L   F   K   Hs  D   Hy  Pd  Mf  Pa  Pt  Sc  Ma  Si  A   R  MAC-R
```

```
Raw
Score:    8  11  13  21  43  35  28  43  12  30  22  14  46  27  25  17

K Corr.            7       5           13  13   3

T Scr.   71  75  46  82  99  80  76  33  56  79  65  45  70  69  73  42
```

```
                         FB (Raw): 4
? Cannot Say (Raw): 0    F-K (Raw): -2

Welsh Code (new): 2*13"740'8-6/9:5#    FL'-/K:           Percent True : 41
Welsh Code (old): 2*41"370'86-9/:5#    FL-K/?:           Percent False: 59
                                                         Profile Elev.: 72.8
```

MMPI-2™ THE MINNESOTA REPORT:™
ADULT CLINICAL SYSTEM
INTERPRETIVE REPORT

page 5

ID: 26136   RPT DATE: 03-AUG-89
SEX: Female   EDUC: 12
AGE: 25   MARS: Never Married
SETTING: Outpatient Mental Health

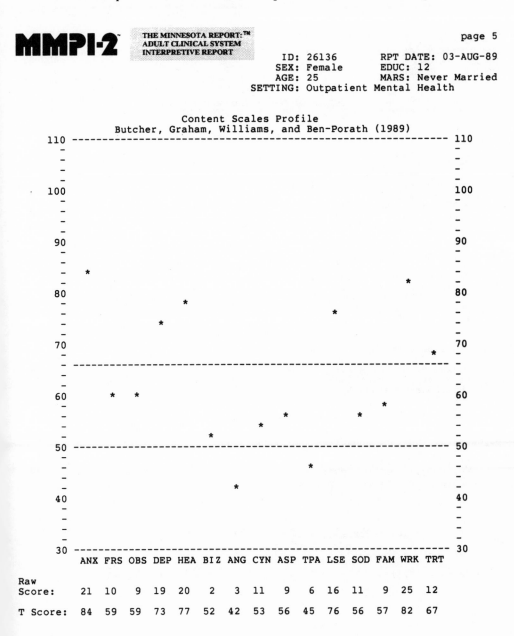

Content Scales Profile
Butcher, Graham, Williams, and Ben-Porath (1989)

	ANX	FRS	OBS	DEP	HEA	BIZ	ANG	CYN	ASP	TPA	LSE	SOD	FAM	WRK	TRT
Raw Score:	21	10	9	19	20	2	3	11	9	6	16	11	9	25	12
T Score:	84	59	59	73	77	52	42	53	56	45	76	56	57	82	67

SUPPLEMENTARY SCORE REPORT

	Raw Score	T Score
Ego Strength (Es)	22	30
Dominance (Do)	8	30
Social Responsibility (Re)	22	53
Overcontrolled Hostility (O-H)	15	55
PTSD - Keane (PK)	27	78
PTSD - Schlenger (PS)	32	73
True Response Inconsistency (TRIN)	7	65F
Variable Response Inconsistency (VRIN)	7	58

Depression Subscales (Harris-Lingoes):

Subjective Depression (D1)	26	94
Psychomotor Retardation (D2)	9	68
Physical Malfunctioning (D3)	5	63
Mental Dullness (D4)	13	97
Brooding (D5)	9	83

Hysteria Subscales (Harris-Lingoes):

Denial of Social Anxiety (Hy1)	0	30
Need for Affection (Hy2)	7	50
Lassitude-Malaise (Hy3)	12	87
Somatic Complaints (Hy4)	9	73
Inhibition of Aggression (Hy5)	4	54

Psychopathic Deviate Subscales (Harris-Lingoes):

Familial Discord (Pd1)	6	74
Authority Problems (Pd2)	2	47
Social Imperturbability (Pd3)	0	31
Social Alienation (Pd4)	5	55
Self-Alienation (Pd5)	11	87

Paranoia Subscales (Harris-Lingoes):

Persecutory Ideas (Pa1)	1	45
Poignancy (Pa2)	4	59
Naivete (Pa3)	5	50

```
                                              Raw Score      T Score

Schizophrenia Subscales (Harris-Lingoes):

    Social Alienation (Sc1)                       3             50
    Emotional Alienation (Sc2)                    4             76
    Lack of Ego Mastery, Cognitive (Sc3)          5             74
    Lack of Ego Mastery, Conative (Sc4)           8             80
    Lack of Ego Mastery, Def. Inhib. (Sc5)        3             59
    Bizarre Sensory Experiences (Sc6)             5             63


Hypomania Subscales (Harris-Lingoes):

    Amorality (Ma1)                               2             54
    Psychomotor Acceleration (Ma2)                3             40
    Imperturbability (Ma3)                        2             43
    Ego Inflation (Ma4)                           3             49


Social Introversion Subscales (Ben-Porath, Hostetler, Butcher, & Graham):

    Shyness / Self-Consciousness (Si1)           12             68
    Social Avoidance (Si2)                        2             47
    Alienation--Self and Others (Si3)            12             69
```

Uniform T scores are used for Hs, D, Hy, Pd, Pa, Pt, Sc, Ma, and the Content
Scales; all other MMPI-2 scales use linear T scores.

                            CRITICAL ITEMS

The following critical items have been found to have possible significance in
analyzing a client's problem situation. Although these items may serve as a
source of hypotheses for further investigation, caution should be taken in
interpreting individual items because they may have been inadvertently
checked.

Acute Anxiety State (Koss-Butcher Critical Items)

    3. I wake up fresh and rested most mornings. (F)
    5. I am easily awakened by noise. (T)
   10. I am about as able to work as I ever was. (F)
   15. I work under a great deal of tension. (T)
   28. I am bothered by an upset stomach several times a week. (T)
   39. My sleep is fitful and disturbed. (T)
   59. I am troubled by discomfort in the pit of my stomach every few days or
       oftener. (T)
  140. Most nights I go to sleep without thoughts or ideas bothering me. (F)
  208. I hardly ever notice my heart pounding and I am seldom short of
       breath. (F)
  223. I believe I am no more nervous than most others. (F)
  301. I feel anxiety about something or someone almost all the time. (T)
  444. I am a high-strung person. (T)
  463. Several times a week I feel as if something dreadful is about to
       happen. (T)
  469. I sometimes feel that I am about to go to pieces. (T)

Depressed Suicidal Ideation (Koss-Butcher Critical Items)

    9. My daily life is full of things that keep me interested. (F)
   38. I have had periods of days, weeks, or months when I couldn't take care
       of things because I couldn't "get going." (T)
   65. Most of the time I feel blue. (T)
   71. These days I find it hard not to give up hope of amounting to
       something. (T)
   75. I usually feel that life is worthwhile. (F)
   95. I am happy most of the time. (F)
  130. I certainly feel useless at times. (T)
  146. I cry easily. (T)
  215. I brood a great deal. (T)
  233. I have difficulty in starting to do things. (T)
  273. Life is a strain for me much of the time. (T)
  388. I very seldom have spells of the blues. (F)
  411. At times I think I am no good at all. (T)
  485. I often feel that I'm not as good as other people. (T)

Threatened Assault   (Koss-Butcher Critical Items)

   37. At times I feel like smashing things.   (T)

Situational Stress Due to Alcoholism   (Koss-Butcher Critical Items)

  125. I believe that my home life is as pleasant as that of most people I
       know.   (F)
  264. I have used alcohol excessively.   (T)
  487. I have enjoyed using marijuana.   (T)
  489. I have a drug or alcohol problem.   (T)
  502. I have some habits that are really harmful.   (T)
  511. Once a week or more I get high or drunk.   (T)

Mental Confusion   (Koss-Butcher Critical Items)

   31. I find it hard to keep my mind on a task or job.   (T)
   32. I have had very peculiar and strange experiences.   (T)
  325. I have more trouble concentrating than others seem to have.   (T)

Antisocial Attitude   (Lachar-Wrobel Critical Items)

   35. Sometimes when I was young I stole things.   (T)

Family Conflict   (Lachar-Wrobel Critical Items)

   21. At times I have very much wanted to leave home.   (T)
   83. I have very few quarrels with members of my family.   (F)
  125. I believe that my home life is as pleasant as that of most people I
       know.   (F)

Somatic Symptoms   (Lachar-Wrobel Critical Items)

   28. I am bothered by an upset stomach several times a week.   (T)
   33. I seldom worry about my health.   (F)
   44. Once a week or oftener I suddenly feel hot all over, for no real
       reason.   (T)
   53. Parts of my body often have feelings like burning, tingling, crawling,
       or like "going to sleep."   (T)
   57. I hardly ever feel pain in the back of my neck.   (F)
   59. I am troubled by discomfort in the pit of my stomach every few days or
       oftener.   (T)
  101. Often I feel as if there is a tight band around my head.   (T)
  111. I have a great deal of stomach trouble.   (T)

159. I have never had a fainting spell. (F)
164. I seldom or never have dizzy spells. (F)
176. I have very few headaches. (F)
182. I have had attacks in which I could not control my movements or speech
     but in which I knew what was going on around me. (T)
224. I have few or no pains. (F)

Sexual Concern and Deviation (Lachar-Wrobel Critical Items)

 12. My sex life is satisfactory. (F)
121. I have never indulged in any unusual sex practices. (F)
166. I am worried about sex. (T)

Anxiety and Tension (Lachar-Wrobel Critical Items)

 15. I work under a great deal of tension. (T)
223. I believe I am no more nervous than most others. (F)
261. I have very few fears compared to my friends. (F)
301. I feel anxiety about something or someone almost all the time. (T)
320. I have been afraid of things or people that I knew could not hurt
     me. (T)
405. I am usually calm and not easily upset. (F)
463. Several times a week I feel as if something dreadful is about to
     happen. (T)

Sleep Disturbance (Lachar-Wrobel Critical Items)

  5. I am easily awakened by noise. (T)
 30. I have nightmares every few nights. (T)
 39. My sleep is fitful and disturbed. (T)
140. Most nights I go to sleep without thoughts or ideas bothering me. (F)
328. Sometimes some unimportant thought will run through my mind and bother
     me for days. (T)

Deviant Thinking and Experience (Lachar-Wrobel Critical Items)

 32. I have had very peculiar and strange experiences. (T)
122. At times my thoughts have raced ahead faster than I could speak
     them. (T)

Depression and Worry (Lachar-Wrobel Critical Items)

  3. I wake up fresh and rested most mornings. (F)
 10. I am about as able to work as I ever was. (F)
 65. Most of the time I feel blue. (T)
 73. I am certainly lacking in self-confidence. (T)

 75. I usually feel that life is worthwhile. (F)
130. I certainly feel useless at times. (T)
273. Life is a strain for me much of the time. (T)
339. I have sometimes felt that difficulties were piling up so high that I
     could not overcome them. (T)
411. At times I think I am no good at all. (T)
415. I worry quite a bit over possible misfortunes. (T)

Deviant Beliefs (Lachar-Wrobel Critical Items)

466. Sometimes I am sure that other people can tell what I am thinking. (T)

Substance Abuse (Lachar-Wrobel Critical Items)

168. I have had periods in which I carried on activities without knowing
     later what I had been doing. (T)
264. I have used alcohol excessively. (T)
429. Except by doctor's orders I never take drugs or sleeping pills. (F)

7
Providing the Patient Feedback
with the MMPI-2

This chapter addresses the interrelated topics of the patient's "need to know" and the therapist's "need to provide" pertinent personality information to the client in the early stages of treatment. A number of topics are addressed, beginning with the patient's need to have objectively based information about himself or herself. Second, a viewpoint detailing the therapist's duty to provide psychological test feedback to potential or ongoing therapy patients is covered. Next, a description and illustration of a method for conducting test feedback sessions using the MMPI-2 with patients will be described. And, finally, some of the pitfalls and limitations in the feedback process of which the therapist-diagnostician needs to be aware will be detailed.

FEEDBACK AS THE THERAPIST'S DUTY

People in psychological distress who seek professional help make a number of assumptions about the qualities and the qualifications of their potential therapist. They assume that their therapists, in order to be "eligible" for the title they hold, and the function they fulfill, possess knowledge of psychology and psychological problems, are savvy about life generally, have experience working with individuals with similar problems, and are ethical and devoted to helping others. Prospective patients further assume that the "knowledge base" of the therapist involves training and the use of some professional skills that could aid them in their troubles. In fact, therapists, whether they attempt to project it or not, are usually viewed with considerable respect and regard. Indeed, much of the "curative powers" of a psychotherapist, at least in the early stages of treatment, are inherent in the a priori beliefs and assumptions held by the patient. The patient may or may not be aware that the specific training and academic background of different professions that engage in psychological treatment qualify them to apply some procedures but not others.

For example, having a medical background enables a psychiatrist to prescribe medications for a patient but may not prepare him or her well in psychological assessment. A background in clinical or counseling psychology may lead the therapist to use different techniques, such as psychological tests, to help understand the problem situation, but it does not enable them to prescribe medications. Whatever the background of the therapist, as far as the patient is concerned, they all have in common the ability and capability to understand personal problems and to relate to them a systematic and consistent view of *what is the matter with them* and *how they might proceed to remedy the problem(s)*. In short, patients expect the therapist to give them direct feedback about their problems that will assist them in their recovery. This expectation translates into an important duty on the part of the therapist—the necessity to provide detailed information about the client's personality and problems at appropriate times in the treatment process. Yet, many therapists and psychotherapeutic schools do not meet this basic need.

The therapist's requirement to provide feedback is variously interpreted by different schools of psychotherapy. Some approaches to treatment give extensive, in-depth psychological feedback to the client early in the therapy; others may only indirectly address the task of providing personality and interpersonal data for the patient to incorporate into his or her treatment plan. Perhaps the most extreme viewpoint is the psychoanalytic view, which follows the strategy of providing limited feedback and limited direction early in the therapy; interpretations often do not enter into treatment directly until it is rather far along. Other theoretical views, such as the client-centered approach, provide minimal feedback and operate on the assumption that individuals will, under the conditions of unconditional positive regard and assurance of the therapist, eventually develop a consistent view of themselves without much directive feedback from the therapist.

FEEDBACK AS A CLINICAL APPROACH

One of the most important and clinically useful applications of the MMPI-2 involves its use in providing personality and symptom information to individual clients. An MMPI-2 profile interpretation or computerized clinical report, since it is usually based on established empirical correlates, provides objective, "external" information for appraising the client. Providing the patient feedback on his or her problems early in treatment or in the pretreatment diagnostic assessment can provide very valuable clues to (1) the extent and nature of the problems the individual is currently experiencing in comparison with those of other patients, (2) whether the individual is likely to be experiencing problems that require psychological intervention, and (3) the direction therapy needs to take in order to ameliorate the problems. Discussing the MMPI-2 test results with potential clients provides valuable entry into the treatment process. In presenting MMPI-2 feedback to clients several factors, such as those that follow, need to be taken into account.

Timeliness of the Feedback

The psychological status or mood of the client receiving the feedback needs to be gauged to determine how and when the feedback should be presented. Providing test information to patients requires that the patient be in sufficient contact with reality and have a "receptive" attitude toward the session in order to perceive the test information accurately. Patients who are angry over the referral or are uncooperative with the evaluation may be particularly antagonistic toward test feedback. Patients who are extremely depressed may be unable to attend to or process information accurately in a single session early in treatment. It might be advisable to present feedback over several sessions "in manageable bits" or defer feedback until later in treatment, when the patient has acquired sufficient energy to deal with it. There is not necessarily a standard time or point in the treatment to provide test feedback. The earlier in the sessions feedback is provided, the better it is in enabling the patient to utilize test findings in treatment. The clinician needs to judge the patient's readiness to attend to and incorporate test results.

Patient Expectation

The setting in which the test was given is important to consider; for example, if the test was administered as part of a court-ordered evaluation, the test feedback is likely to be viewed differently by the client than if it was given at the person's request. Consequently, the amount of detail and the level of the test inference need to be adapted to fit various situations. In providing feedback to bright normal individuals in adoption counseling, the clinician would select different adjective descriptors from those used with disturbed patients in an inpatient treatment context. Published sources such as Graham (1979; 1987) or Greene (1980) contain information about relevant MMPI-2 scale descriptors for varied groups. The clinician needs to decide on the appropriate reference group for the subject and select the test correlates accordingly. For example, it may be more relevant for the assessment of some groups, such as college students in a counseling setting, to refer to Drake and Oetting's (1959) code book or Graham's (1987) correlates rather than using Gil-

berstadt and Duker's (1965) correlates developed on an inpatient population in a Veterans' Administration hospital.

Ability of the Patient to Incorporate Personal Feedback

The patient's level of intellectual functioning should be taken into account in deciding the amount and type of feedback to provide. For example, if the patient is a well-educated person, more specific and detailed information as to the test findings and implications can be given;
however, most people have neither the background nor the interest in
technical factors about the test to dwell on psychometric properties. The
presentation should be varied to suit each individual's general fund of
information and psychological sophistication.

Likely Length of Treatment

There is a more pressing need to provide test feedback early in therapy
if treatment is to be brief (8–10 sessions) than if the therapy is to be of
several months duration; however, since most therapies are brief—less
than 25 sessions—(Koss & Butcher, 1986) feedback should not be de-
layed too long lest treatment terminate before the patient has been able
to learn about his or her test results.

PROCEDURES FOR PROVIDING MMPI-2 FEEDBACK TO THE PATIENT ENTERING TREATMENT

The following guidelines might be useful in conducting a test-feedback
session.

Step 1. Explain why the test was administered. Patients may not know the
reason they have been given the MMPI-2, so it is a good idea to explain
why this was recommended. In this introduction, the therapist can explain that he or she would like to use every means available to try to
understand the patient fully (patients actually like this!). The therapist
may then indicate that the use of a test like the MMPI-2 can provide a
valuable external source of information about their problems.

Step 2. Describe what the MMPI-2 is and how widely it is used. Most people
are not going to know much about psychological testing or the MMPI-2.
In some communities where the MMPI-2 is widely used there may be
preconceived ideas about the test or misconceptions about its use. It is
important to establish the credibility and objectivity of the MMPI-2 for
the patient by providing some background on the instrument, such as its
length of service to the mental health profession (about 50 years), its

extensive usage (it is the most widely used psychological test; see Lubin, Larsen & Matarazzo, 1984), its respected status as the major personality–clinical test in the majority of clinical settings in the United States and, for emphasis, the fact that the test is the most widely used personality instrument in the world, with more than 115 separate translations and broad use in over 46 other countries.

Step 3. Describe how the MMPI-2 works. In a few words, describe how the scales were developed and highlight the extent of empirical scale development and validation. Beginning with the clinical and validity scale profile:

1. Point out what an "average" or typical performance on each scale is.
2. Point out where the elevated score range is on the clinical profile (i.e., above a score of T = 65). Explain that this means that 92 percent of people fall below that score. Next, show the diagram presented in Figure 7-1. The two lines in this graph show how clinically depressed patients compare to nonpatients in terms of symptoms of depression. One line represents the nondepressed individual whose scores fall in the diagram that peaks at the left side of the chart. The second line represents the depressed patients' scores—these range quite a bit higher (toward the right). Comparison of the two groups' scores shows that a T-score of 65 classifies most of the depressed patients as depressed while most "normals" fall well below a T-score of 65.

Next, point out that the profile patterns have been widely studied for diverse groups of patients. It is helpful to use the client's own profile as an illustration of the scale score average range, elevation differences, their meaning, and so on.

Step 4. Describe how the validity scales work. Briefly describe the validity indicators and discuss the strategies the patient used in approaching the test content. Focus on areas of self-presentation and on how the patient is viewing the problem situation at this time. Discussion of the validity pattern is one of the most important facets of test feedback since it provides the therapist with an opportunity to explore the patient's motivation for treatment and his or her initial accessibility to treatment. Patients with elevated L or K (T > 60) and greater than F would be viewed, for example, as defensive, self-protective, and not entering into the treatment process with the goal of a self-revelation. In cases of high initial treatment resistance the therapist can explore possible factors influencing this reluctance and can discuss the potentially negative outcomes from such resistance with the patient.

Step 5. Point out the most significant departures from the norms on the clinical scales. It is important to give the patient a clear understanding that his

D

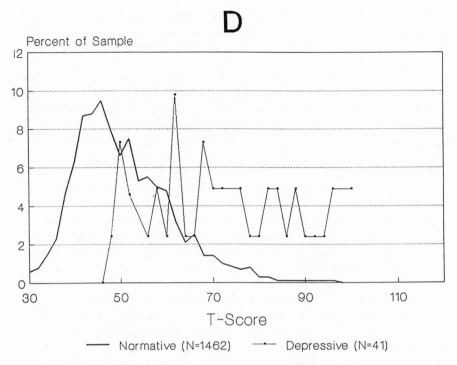

Figure 7–1. Comparison of depressed patients with Minnesota normative subjects on the Depression scale.

or her responses have been compared with thousands of other individuals who have taken the MMPI-2 under different conditions. Describe the patient's highest ranging clinical scores in terms of prevailing attitudes, symptoms, problem areas, and the like. It is also valuable to discuss the individual's low points on the profile to provide a contrast with other personality areas in which he or she does not seem to be having problems. Avoid low base rate predictions. MMPI-2 correlates or descriptions that are low in occurrence should not be included in feedback. It is often useful and desirable in treatment feedback sessions to use the psychological test indexes as a basis for predictions about future behavior of the patient. In providing personality feedback it is important to avoid using psychological jargon by translating clinical words into language the patient can understand. The personality descriptions and symptoms presented by the patient through the item responses are important concepts to communicate. The therapist, however, should not try to communicate everything at once; be selective and choose the most pertinent features.

It is possible that the client, having little insight into his or her behavior at this point, will have problems "seeing" or accepting feedback on some issues or characteristics. In this case, the therapist should avoid getting into a shouting match with the individual in order to "ram home" the results. The goal here is to present tentative findings from the test that have high validity and generalizability and that might prove useful in the individual's treatment.

Step 6. Seek responses from the client during the feedback session. Give the client an opportunity to ask questions about his or her scores and clear up any points of concern. A person will sometimes become fixed on an irrelevant or inconsequential point or an incorrect interpretation. It is important to ensure that the misconceptions are cleared up and that the individual becomes aware of the most salient elements of his or her test performance. Providing an active interchange over issues raised by the test can promote a treatment-oriented atmosphere that encourages self-knowledge on the part of the client.

Step 7. Appraise client acceptance of the test feedback. It is a good idea to obtain a closing summary from the client to show how each one feels the test characterized his or her problems. The clinician can evaluate whether there were aspects of the test results that were particularly sur-prising or distressing and whether there were aspects of the interpreta-tion to which the patient objected. (This does not mean that the test was necessarily wrong, only that there is a point at which test indexes dis-agree with the individual's self-perception.) The information exchange occurring in the feedback session may actually provide excellent material and focuses from which to proceed directly in the treatment process.

With some clients it is a good idea to schedule more than one test feedback session to get an idea of how the person has incorporated, re-jected, or elaborated upon the feedback. I have often been amazed with the "hearing loss" associated with high elevations on the Pd scale. High Pd individuals do not take feedback to heart; they do not incorporate outside opinion well and tend to distort the information to minimize their problems. In the second feedback session the therapist might begin by having the client summarize conclusions drawn from the previous session. This provides the therapist with an opportunity to reiterate points that have been ignored or forgotten and to correct inaccurate per-ceptions. Many people, after a few days' consideration, will raise ques-tions they were hesitant to ask before.

An outline of the suggested steps for providing client feedback on the MMPI-2 is provided in Table 7-1. This outline is provided as a Reference Guide for use as an outline in test feedback sessions.

AN APPROACH FOR PROVIDING FEEDBACK

The case example that follows may be useful in illustrating how test feed-back sessions can provide helpful information to clients and help them to gain insight into problems or issues they might address in psycholog-ical treatment. (See the profiles in Figures 7-2 and 7-3.)

Table 7–1. An Approach to Providing MMPI-2 Feedback

Step 1. Explain why the test was administered.
- Explain the rationale behind your giving test feedback to the client.
- Indicate that you want to provide information about the problem situation that is based on how the client responds to various questions. Explain that personality characteristics and potential problems revealed in the test scores are compared to those of other people who have taken the test, and that feedback gives the client perspective on his or her problems that can be used as a starting point in therapy.

Step 2. Describe what the MMPI-2 is and how widely it is used.
- Describe the MMPI-2 and provide the patient with an understanding of how valid and accurate the test is for clinical problem description. Explain that the MMPI-2 was originally developed as a means of obtaining objective information about patients' problems and personality characteristics.
- Indicate that the MMPI-2 is the most widely used clinical test in the United States, which has been translated into many languages and which is used in many other countries for evaluating patient problems.
- Explain that it has been developed and used with many different patient problems and provides accurate descriptive information about problems and issues the client is dealing with at this time.

Step 3. Describe how the MMPI-2 works.
Begin this step in the feedback process by providing a description of several elements of the MMPI-2. Use the patient's own clinical and content scale profiles to provide a basis for visualizing the information you are going to provide.
- Explain that a scale is a group of items or statements that measure certain characteristics or problems such as depression or anxiousness.
- Describe what an "average" score is on the profile. Show how scores are compared on the profile, and indicate that higher scores reflect "more" of the characteristics involved and problems the patient is experiencing.
- Point out where the elevated score range is and what a score at T = 65 or T = 80 means in terms of the number of people obtaining scores in this range.
- If available, use an average profile from a relevant clinical group from the published literature to illustrate how people with particular problems score on the MMPI-2. For example, if the patient has significant depression, showing a group mean profile of depressed clients provides a good comparison group.

Step 4. Describe how the validity scales work.
Discuss the strategies the patient used in approaching the test content. Focus on the person's self-presentation and on how he or she is viewing the problem situation at this time. Discussion of the client's validity pattern is one of the most important facets of test feedback because it provides the therapist with an opportunity to explore the patient's motivation for and accessibility to treatment.

Step 5. Point out the client's most significant departures from the norm on the clinical scales.
Indicate that the client's responses have been compared with those of thousands of other individuals who have taken the MMPI-2 under different conditions. Describe your patient's highest ranging clinical scores in terms of prevailing attitudes, symptoms, or problem areas. It is also valuable to discuss the individual's low points on the profile to provide a contrast with other personality areas in which he or she does not seem to be having problems. But avoid descriptions that are low in occurrence, and avoid using psychological jargon.
- Emphasize the individual's highest point(s) on the clinical and content scale profiles.

Table 7–1. Continued

- Point out where the scores fall in relation to the "average" scores.
- Provide understandable descriptions of the personality characteristics revealed by the prominent scale elevations.

Step 6.   Seek responses from the client during the feedback session.
Encourage the client to ask questions about the scores and clear up any points of concern.

Step 7.   Appraise client acceptance of the test feedback.
Ask the client to summarize how he or she feels the test characterized personal problems to evaluate whether there were aspects of the test results that were particularly surprising or distressing, and whether there were aspects of the interpretation to which the patient objected.

▶ Case Example: Interpretation of Feedback in Couple Counseling

Patients' Names: Charles V. and Betty S.

Referral
The patients were referred by Dr. R. for an evaluation with the MMPI-2. His patient of 3 years, Betty S. and her friend, Charles V., were seeking information about their personality adjustment, with specific interest in obtaining test results that might address possible personality differences and "congruences" between them. Ms. S. was employed as an executive in a large corporation, and Mr. V. was vice president of a bank. They have been dating for a brief period of time and have recently moved in together with the possibility of establishing a more permanent relationship.

Testing
Mr. V. and Ms. S. were administered the MMPI-2 and scheduled for their first (individual) feedback session on separate days a week later. His MMPI-2 profiles are given in Figures 7-2 and 7-3; her profiles are shown in Figures 7-4 and 7-5.

Observations
Mr. V. and Ms. S. were seen individually for their initial feedback session for approximately an hour and a half. They were both highly motivated to learn about their test results and to discuss the findings. Each session began by encouraging the patient to discuss the reasons for referral and to provide a description of his or her present situation. Both were very open and cooperative. After completion of the individual sessions, a joint feedback session was scheduled.

Psychological Evaluation
Mr. V.'s approach to the psychological evaluation was open and cooperative. He responded in a manner characteristic of individuals entering into a treatment-oriented evaluation. He reported a number of problems that he was

Figure 7-2. MMPI-2 clinical profile for Mr. V.

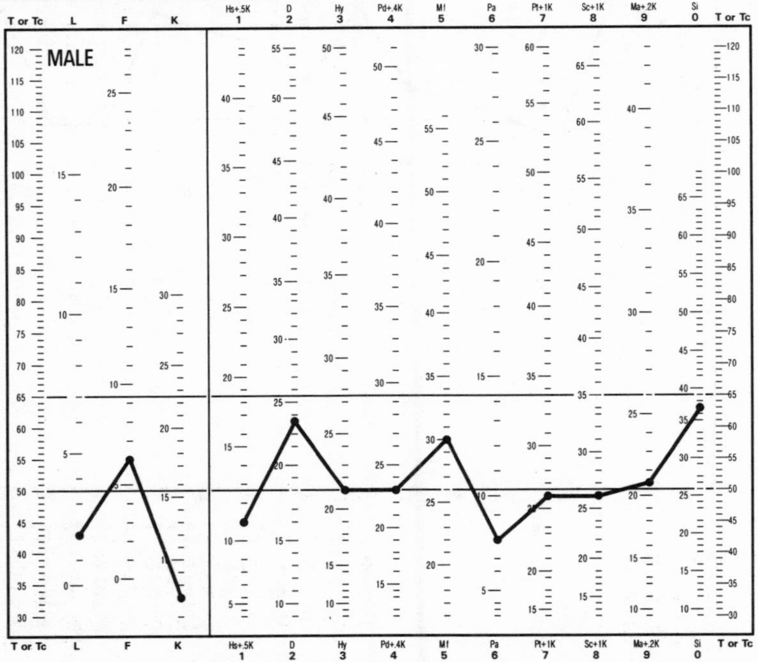

Name **Mr. V.**

Address _____

Occupation **Vice President - Bank** Date Tested ___/___/___

Education **16** Age **57** Marital Status **Divorced**

Referred By _____

Scorer's Initials _____

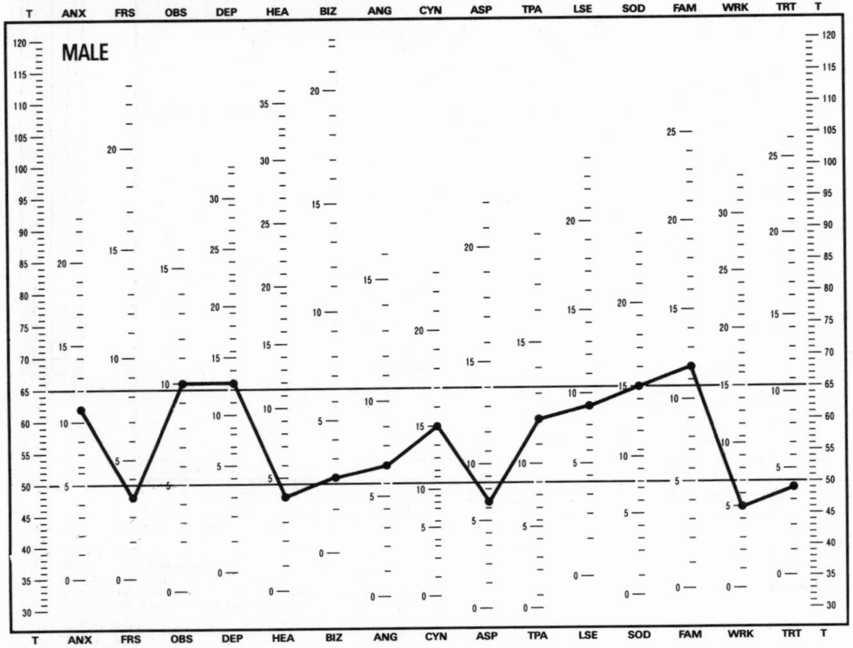

MMPI-2™
S.R. Hathaway and J.C. McKinley
Minnesota Multiphasic Personality Inventory-2™

Profile for Content Scales
Butcher, Graham, Williams and Ben-Porath (1989)

Minnesota Multiphasic Personality Inventory-2
Copyright © by THE REGENTS OF THE UNIVERSITY OF MINNESOTA
1942, 1943 (renewed 1970), 1989. This Profile Form 1989.
All rights reserved. Distributed exclusively by NATIONAL COMPUTER SYSTEMS, INC.
under license from The University of Minnesota.
"MMPI-2" and "Minnesota Multiphasic Personality Inventory-2" are trademarks owned by
The University of Minnesota. Printed in the United States of America.

MALE

	ANX	FRS	OBS	DEP	HEA	BIZ	ANG	CYN	ASP	TPA	LSE	SOD	FAM	WRK	TRT
Raw Score	11	3	10	12	4	2	7	15	7	12	9	15	12	5	4

Figure 7–3. MMPI-2 contest scale profile for Mr. V.

156

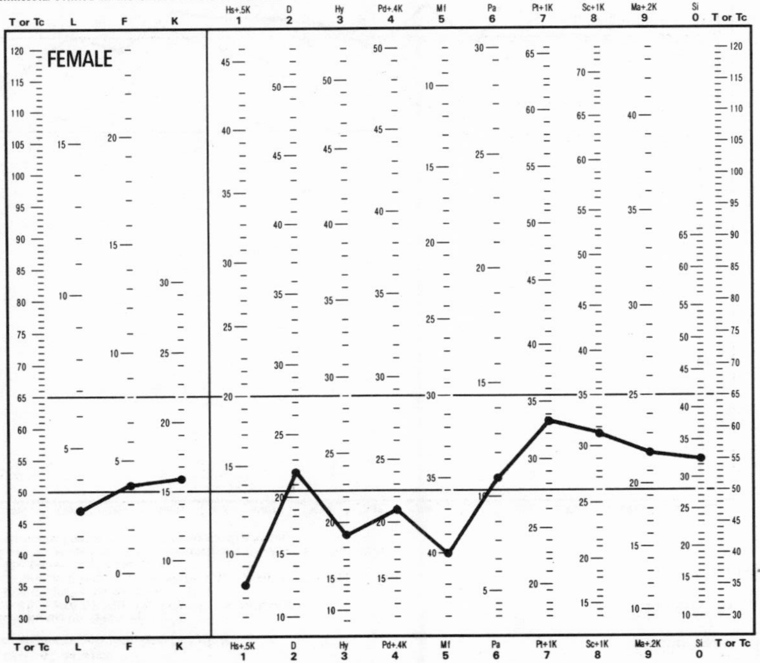

Figure 7–4. MMPI-2 clinical profile for Ms. S.

Name _____ Ms. S.

Profile for Basic Scales

Address _____
Occupation __Manager__ Date Tested __/__
Education __16__ Age __53__ Marital Status __Divorced__
Referred By _____
MMPI-2 Code _____

Scorer's Initials _____

FEMALE

	L	F	K	Hs+.5K	D	Hy	Pd+.4K	Mf	Pa	Pt+1K	Sc+1K	Ma+.2K	Si
Raw Score	3	4	16	0	22	19	15	40	11	17	15	19	33
K to be Added				8			6			16	16	3	
Raw Score with K				8			21			33	31	22	

? Raw Score _____

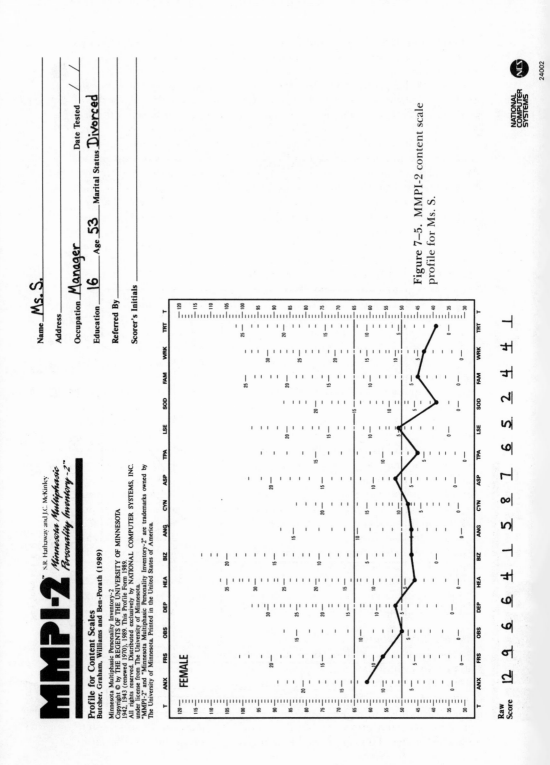

Figure 7-5. MMPI-2 content scale profile for Ms. S.

158

experiencing, largely the result of what he views as present-day stressors with his family and career. He appeared to be interested in reporting accurate information about himself.

The MMPI-2 profile appears to be a very accurate representation of his present problems. He reports difficulties centering on feelings of low mood and indecisiveness; he seems to be depressed and has negative self-attitudes. His depression can be characterized as greater than most people's. He reported problems with the physical symptoms of depression, such as sleep and appetite problems, as well as the social manifestations of depression. While many of these symptoms may represent a response to some stressors he is experiencing, there are indications that he has personality characteristics of a long-standing nature that predispose him to negative evaluations and low moods. Individuals with MMPI-2 patterns like this tend to be passive and nonassertive in relationships, and highly conventional. He dislikes taking risks and resists change. He is quite shy and prefers a few friends rather than large crowds. His high elevations on the MMPI-2 content scales (DEP, OBS, and SOC) further confirm his tendencies toward low mood, obsessive thinking, and social maladjustment.

Ms. S's MMPI-2 was valid. She approached the testing in a frank and open manner, although she may have had some concerns about being evaluated. She viewed herself as "under the gun" since Mr. V. had strongly pressed her to participate in the evaluation. This concern did not, however, result in a distorted profile. The testing appears to be a valid representation of her current psychological functioning.

In the interview and on the MMPI-2, Ms. S. reported few psychological problems. Her overall performance was well within the normal range and did not reflect significant adjustment problems at this time. She appears to be a generally happy, self-satisfied woman who enjoys sufficient self-esteem. Although her adjustment at this time appears good, there is some suggestion that she may be predisposed to transitory problems. Two trends are suggested. First, she appears to be a somewhat rigid and perfectionistic person who is prone to guilt and self-punishment. She may be somewhat prone to developing anxious states when under outside pressure. There is some suggestion that she becomes easily bored and needs to seek stimulation and activity more than most people. The second area in which she might create problems for herself lies in a tendency to be impulsive and to act before she contemplates her actions. She is likely to experience guilt and remorse in response to actual acting-out behavior she might engage in. She may be prone to irritable moods at times. Her high score on the MMPI-2 content scale, ANX, supports the view that she is at times prone to anxiety.

Interpersonal Relations

Interpersonally, Mr. V. and Ms. S. appear to have rather different styles of interacting with others. Mr. V. is shy, inhibited, and concerned with social interactions. Mr. V. appears to be overly concerned, even hypersensitive, about what others think of him. Ms. S., on the other hand, appears to meet people easily and enjoys social interaction; she seems adept at interpersonal relationships. They appear to be "polar opposites" in terms of social interests and abilities. This might lead to some periods of conflict and result in their placing different strains on the relationship. If they maintain their security and trust in the relationship, however, this set of differences need not be a point of difficulty.

Trust

There seems to be a strong element of mistrust in Mr. V.'s current thinking. He is an insecure, uncertain man who appears to need a great deal of re-assurance, especially about what others think of him. Some of the depression and low self-esteem may result from his being insecure and feeling inadequate. He appears to become threatened easily. It is possible that Ms. S.'s social confidence and "impulsivity" actually threaten Mr. V.

Summary and Recommendations

The relationship between Ms. S. and Mr. V. appears to have some points of difficulty that may need to be addressed. Their different modes of interacting and the tendency for Mr. V. to become threatened, alienated, and mistrustful are likely points of conflict. Mr. V.'s proneness to feeling inadequate and his low self-esteem make him vulnerable to negative mood states such as suspicion, mistrust, and depressed affect. He appears not to have much confidence in himself or in the future. It is likely that he could benefit from psychological treatment that would help to alleviate his low moods and engender more self-efficacy.

No recommendations are made with regard to Ms. S.'s treatment. She appears to have gained substantially from her present therapy and plans to continue her treatment in the coming months. All things considered, she appears to be functioning well in her present situation.

Feedback Sessions

Test feedback with Mr. V. Mr. V. was seen first in an initial session. He was very motivated to receive the test feedback. The session was structured so that he would secure feedback on his MMPI-2 *only* in the individual session and that Ms. S's profile would not be discussed. Later, a joint session was scheduled to discuss their profiles together since they both requested a session where the information concerning their personality testing could be shared.

Mr. V. is a bright, well-educated man who was quite interested in how the MMPI-2 was originally developed and how the test correlates were researched. He asked a number of questions about the profile, such as "What percentage of average people score in the 'critical' range?" When the personality descriptions based on the MMPI-2 were shared with him, he appeared to painfully accept the characteristics, such as depressed, shy, and socially withdrawn, by quiet acknowledgment. He also thought that the feeling of inadequacy and insecurity that the test-based hypotheses addressed were mostly appropriate for his social–personal life and did not apply to his professional behavior. He indicated that he was quite successful and prided himself in his work competence (which is supported by his WRK Content Scale score). He did acknowledge the tendencies toward perfectionism and self-critical behavior that appear to cause him some problems at times.

He also acknowledged that the test was accurate with regard to his feeling low and felt that the recommendations for his treatment were possibly very useful. He agreed to accept a referral for a therapist to explore some sources of his low mood and personal discomfort.

Test feedback with Ms. S. Ms. S. was quite enthusiastic about receiving feedback on her test profile, although she seemed very nervous about "what was going to be revealed." She admitted that she was somewhat concerned about the testing because Mr. V. had (possibly because she *was* in therapy she thought) pushed for the evaluation. She clearly felt that there was "a lot riding" on the results because she loved him and wanted to reassure him.

She did not show initial inquisitiveness about the test itself but wanted to quickly get to the results. When she was told that her test scores were generally within normal limits and reflected a generally good adjustment with no serious psychological problems, she appeared to be pleasantly surprised and said, "It certainly wouldn't have been like that a couple of years ago!"

She also acknowledged that she does have a tendency to "lose it" now and then, and become extremely anxious and self-doubting on those occasions. She also felt that the test finding that she is somewhat rigid and set in her ways was "right on."

The treatment recommended in the report reflected the view that she was probably sufficiently improved and did not need much further therapy. She, too, had thought that her treatment was reaching an end, but she was still working on some issues and did not foresee a time for termination in the near future.

Joint feedback session. The couple arrived arm in arm for the joint feedback session and both seemed to be looking forward to discussing the tests together. The session actually began in a somewhat anticlimactic atmosphere since they had both already shared the test information in great detail. The session was started with each summarizing their conclusions from the individualized sessions, she with her notebook in hand since she had taken careful notes on the feedback. In sum, most of the points were correctly reiterated and seemingly digested, especially by Ms. S. since she was a practiced hand at interpretation after having been in treatment for 3 years. Mr. V. plodded through his points, showing some clear indecisiveness with regard to his "feelings of insecurity and inadequacy."

A large portion of the time was devoted to the issue of alienation and mistrust in interpersonal relationships. The differences between their abilities to trust were discussed. This seemed to be a persistent personality problem for Mr. V. In fact, his lack of trust was one important reason he had been insistent upon her having a psychological evaluation in the first place. He appeared to show both insight and acceptance of this problem and acknowledged that it may have had some bearing in previous relationships since he had always been somewhat wary and suspicious of anyone with whom he was intimately involved. This was the first time they had objectively discussed this problem even though it had clearly had an impact on their relationship in the past. Much of the remaining time in the test feedback was spent exploring ways he might appropriately seek reassurance from her when he feels threatened and possible ways she might try to alleviate or circumvent his developing "feelings of uncertainty."

It is interesting that the feedback sessions that were initiated as a part of the diagnostic assessment evaluation, in which the assessment psychologist was not planning to be involved in the treatment, ended with a clear "blending" of the diagnostic study into therapy-oriented content. At the end of the joint session, Mr. V.'s need to initiate a therapeutic contact was reiterated. He was clearly motivated to obtain treatment and did follow up on the referral.

CAUTIONS, LIMITATIONS, AND PITFALLS IN PROVIDING FEEDBACK

There are possible negative effects of providing test feedback to patients at the beginning of treatment, which we now examine.

1. *Prematurely setting the therapist's "switches" and foreclosing on other possibilities in treatment.* Test data should be presented as "provisional" information rather than as revelations of how the client has always been or will "always be." Psychological tests can provide hypotheses about the person's problems, symptoms, and behavior that the therapist and client can further explore in the sessions ahead.

2. *More intense, more detailed, or more divergent information than the patient can incorporate.* The therapist should gauge how much feedback or how detailed the information for this client can be, and so avoid overwhelming the client. The therapist may choose to spread the test findings over more than one session or defer some aspects of the test information until a stronger treatment relationship is established. Before providing feedback the therapist should determine the extent of symptom exaggeration and the severity of the client's plea for help as reflected in the profile. Careful appraisal of the validity scales, especially the F score, will provide clues to symptom exaggeration that may accompany many initial test administrations. The possibility that the patient has presented a large number of problems in an effort to "tell it all" should be considered. The amount of information to provide needs to be carefully appraised before test feedback is given. Symptom "extremity" may need to be soft-pedalled or carefully explained so that the patient does not get demoralized by too much input too early in the treatment.

3. *Selective perception of information.* Patients often seize on descriptions of characteristics that are of lesser relevance to the treatment and ignore points, possibly those that are less favorable or more emotionally painful, that the therapist wishes to make. It is important to order the hypotheses by levels of importance to the treatment to assure that the important themes do not get lost in the session. Patients sometimes sit passively in

the sessions while the "oracle" reads the descriptions—not really absorbing important points because their attention gets fixed on one point, but not asking questions. In this way, the individual may selectively attend to minutiae and miss major points.

4. *Selective remembering.* One interesting strategy for providing patient feedback involves providing the test information over two sessions. In the first session the material is discussed, providing the patient with opportunity to absorb information. In the second scheduled session the therapist begins by asking the client to recall the main themes he or she remembers from the previous feedback session. Afterward, the therapist has the opportunity to follow up and correct any misconceptions the patient might have or to reiterate important points that were "lost" in the interim period. As noted earlier, this technique is particularly valuable with some types of individuals (i.e., the high Pd or Ma person, who tends to gloss over or ignore problems).

5. *Control over test materials and protocols.* Patients will frequently ask for copies of their profiles or other test results. For most therapists, test materials such as the MMPI-2 profiles and computer-based reports are working materials or notes the psychologist employs in developing hypotheses about patient problems. They are not readily understandable by laypersons and should not be made available to them to keep. Patients not trained in the use of psychological tests, who gain copies of these materials, can, in the quiet of their homes, make grand misinterpretations of this type of data. Requests for copies of test protocols by the patient can usually be handled by telling them "I can't release profiles or computer-generated narratives, but any time you would like to discuss them further we can."

6. *Perception of confrontation.* When providing MMPI-2 test feedback, there is the danger that a confrontational style will be employed. In this type of clinical interaction the "expert" is providing secret and inaccessible information to the client, who has the role of a passive and probably defensive listener. It is easy for a feedback session to gravitate to a "tell all, tell it like it is" format, in which the patient quickly becomes as defended as a trapped animal. In a self-protective mode the besieged patient fights back against the therapist's assault. An extreme example of this confrontational style, and one with an extremely unprofessional thrust, was reported to the author. A psychiatrist was using computerized MMPI-2 reports as a confrontation technique in group treatment sessions with disturbed, acting-out adolescents. He typically gave the computer-generated output to patients and had them read them aloud in group sessions. Not only is this technique likely to be unproductive, in that few adolescents would accept such interpretations even if correct, but the clinician is flirting with malpractice litigation if such aggressive confrontations produce negative outcomes, such as acting-out behavior or suicide.

7. *The implication of specific medication or dosage levels from MMPI-2 profiles.* The MMPI-2 has been used as a pre–post measure in numerous drug treatment studies; however, there is insufficient research to use scale scores or elevation levels to guide medication prescriptions. For example, high elevations on D reflect the presence of significant depressive symptoms. It is also correct to say that many patients with this profile respond to antidepressant medication. It is not possible to say, with any degree of certainty, however, that an antidepressant medication should be administered. It is also possible that lithium would be the treatment of choice for some patients with high D scores because depressive-phase bipolar manic-depressive patients can produce a spike D profile. The MMPI-2 profile can provide some clues to symptoms, but the clinician needs to apply other criteria on which appropriate medication prescriptions will be based.

SUMMARY

This chapter addressed the importance of providing feedback on personality characteristics and psychological symptoms to clients early in the treatment process. Factors important to the feedback process such as timeliness, receptivity of the client, and ability of the individual to incorporate information were discussed. A suggested approach for providing MMPI-2 feedback was outlined. The process of providing test feedback was illustrated and described with a diagnostic case of a couple seeking information about their compatibility and possible need for treatment. Finally, several cautions or limitations to the patient feedback process were described in order to sensitize the clinician to potential problems that may emerge in the course of interpreting MMPI-2 profiles to clients.

8

Postscript: Treatment Planning and the MMPI-2

Patients in psychological treatment usually expect a high level of expertise and understanding from their therapist—not simply a sympathetic listener. They anticipate that the therapist will be competent to evaluate their problems in a nonjudgmental way and will employ objective, scientific means of helping them resolve their problems. Furthermore, when people go to a psychotherapist, they anticipate that the therapist will provide them with more information and insight into their problems than they can get from a friend or relative.

For therapy to proceed as clients actually expect, the therapist must have a good understanding of the client's problems, personality characteristics, needs, motivations, aspirations, and social relationships. Without a sound psychological assessment, the treatment situation is likely to be superficial and disjointed and may drift aimlessly toward an unsuccessful outcome. One thesis of this book is that psychological treatment works best when it proceeds from a clear understanding of the patient's contribution to his or her personality problems, symptomatic behavior, and familial and social conflicts. The use of the MMPI-2 introduces new, relevant material into the treatment sessions in an objective way.

This book addresses the processes and strategies for employing one important method of understanding the individual's perception of his or her problems—responses to the MMPI-2. I have presented the view that many important aspects of the patient's behavior can become incorporated into the treatment process by using objective personality information available through the MMPI-2.

ASSESSMENT OF TREATMENT READINESS AND PSYCHOLOGICAL ACCESSIBILITY

The MMPI-2 can provide the therapist with clues to whether the individual is ready for treatment and is willing to approach the task of self-discovery with honesty. Test indicators that are helpful in assessing client reluctance or inability to cooperate with treatment are described in Chapters 2 and 3. As described earlier, the MMPI-2 validity indicators are among the most useful means available to the clinician for determining treatment readiness. The way in which the client approaches the task of self-disclosure in response to the test items provides valuable information about treatment readiness.

Clues to the individual's motivation for treatment can be obtained from the MMPI-2, as well as possible negative factors that could interfere with treatment, such as a tendency to feel threatened and to form hasty conclusions about people in authority. It may be valuable to discuss possible negative factors with the client early in treatment to head off beliefs or behaviors that can threaten treatment before they become fatal issues in therapy.

Amenability to change is also measurable with the MMPI-2. The prospects of a failed outcome to the therapy might be shared with the client early in therapy, perhaps to provoke a better outcome by challenging the patient and forewarning the therapist of potential perils ahead.

BUILDING RAPPORT IN THERAPY

Clinicians find that sensitive, tactful test interpretation can be shared with clients early in therapy and can actually improve the treatment relationship because it reassures the patients that they are not going to be embarrassed or harmed by the process of self-discovery with the therapist. Many patients approach treatment with the fear that even the therapist, when he or she "finds out about them," will despise or reject them. The evaluation stage of treatment, if properly and sensitively handled by the therapist, can serve to teach clients that disclosing "secrets" about themselves is important and that the treatment situation is a safe place in which to discuss their private thoughts. Finn and Butcher (in press) describe the value of the MMPI-2 in building rapport with the client.

THE NEED FOR TREATMENT

One of the most important functions of the MMPI-2 in treatment planning is that it provides the therapist with a perspective on the extent and nature of the patient's symptom pattern. It provides the clinician with an objective "outside opinion" concerning the nature of the problems the individual is experiencing and gives important information about the person's contribution to his or her problems. An important facet of the MMPI-2 evaluation is that the scale scores provide summaries of symptoms and attitudes that indicate the relative strength or magnitude of the problems experienced. The clinical and supplementary scales can assist the therapist in uncovering feelings or problems of which the patient might be unaware. For example, the extent of manifest depression might not be evident in initial interviews since many individuals, even in a therapist's office, attempt to "put on a good face" and not acknowledge the full extent of their problems. Many people are able to admit to problems through their response to personality questionnaires that they would not voluntarily report in a face-to-face context.

The hypotheses and descriptions generated from MMPI-2 scores provide information about how the client compares with numerous other clinical groups and patient problem types. Information on the relative importance of the various problems the individual is experiencing in the overall clinical picture is valuable in charting the course of treatment and provides clues in the initial session to possible hidden or unseen problems. For example, if significant elevations on the Pa scale are prominent in the client's profile, the clinician and patient need to be aware of the possibility that the treatment can be threatened by early and intense problems in their relationship.

The MMPI-2 can provide information about the general quality of the individual's adjustment as well as the prevalence of long-term problems versus more situationally based difficulties, which would be beneficial for the therapist to assess early in treatment. Are the problems long-standing and chronic? Or are the individual's problems situational in scope? The tasks of setting treatment goals and attempting to project a course of therapy are made easier if the therapist and patient have a clear idea of the overall "shape" of the problems for which the patient is seeking help. What has been the past "course" of similar problems in the patient's experience is also very helpful to client and therapist. In some cases, more realistic, obtainable treatment goals can be developed if both therapist and client are fully aware that there are unresolvable issues or personality factors that are not going to be manageable in the treatment plan or in the time available for therapy.

The MMPI has been shown to be valuable in treatment planning since different MMPI-based profile types appear to respond to treatments differently (Sheppard, Smith, & Rosenbaum, 1988).

THE ROLE OF PERSONALITY IN TREATMENT SUCCESS

The hypotheses and descriptions about the client's social relationships reflected in the MMPI-2 can be of value in forewarning the therapist that the patient's social perceptions and typical styles of interacting with other people may be problematic. Particularly valuable to the therapist in the early stages of therapy are clues to the presence of such detrimental factors as a debilitating lack of confidence in social relationships and feelings of isolation or alienation from others. Such feelings of social distance may be particularly difficult to overcome in relationship-oriented psychotherapy. The advance knowledge that one's client possesses such beliefs or attitudes can warn the therapist that problems can occur in the development of a treatment relationship and need to be averted. The therapist might be able to structure the treatment situation in such a way as to prevent the client from feeling isolated, which would cause further withdrawal or premature termination of treatment.

Another factor that can negatively affect treatment is the possibility that the client possesses an unrecognized substance abuse problem. The growing problem of substance abuse in contemporary society makes it likely that addictive disorder will occur in situations where it is least expected—in your client who was referred to you for a very different problem! Addictive disorders are difficult enough to deal with in settings where they are expected. When they occur in settings or clients for which the base rate expectancy is low, they can have a highly detrimental effect on the treatment situation. Clinicians who see a broad variety of clients in their practice usually discover early in their careers that not all people with addictive disorders recognize their problems and promptly check in at the local alcohol or drug program. Most of us have had the unfortunate situation of discovering, perhaps well into the treatment, that our client's real problem was not the initial referral issue but actually a matter of substance abuse. The MMPI-2 at initial assessment can provide the clinician with clues to whether the individual is likely to have a problem with alcohol or drugs. Regardless of setting or the particular reason for referral, the clinician is well advised, given the pervasiveness of substance abuse in society, to view addictive disorder routinely as a potential problem and to evaluate this possibility in pretreatment assessment.

Other forms of acting-out behavior can be quite disruptive to psychological treatment as well. Several MMPI-2 profile types (i.e., the high Pd, the high Ma, or the 49 profile type) manifest a high potential for acting out in impulsive, destructive ways—for example, by violence toward family members or engaging in reckless sexual behavior. Such characteristics need to be carefully monitored and addressed in treatment to head off calamity.

Other character traits that can result in difficulties in treatment can also be appraised by the MMPI-2. For example, pathological distrust, which is illustrated in Chapter 1, can deter the development of a treatment relationship in initial stages of therapy and result in early termination if not dealt with adroitly. Another factor, assessed by prominent Pt scale elevations, is unproductive rumination. Individuals with very high elevations on Pt are likely to be overly ideational, obsessive, and possess a seemingly unrelenting rigidity that is difficult to "re-route" in insight-oriented treatment because they have problems implementing new behaviors or viewing themselves in different ways.

COMMUNICATION OF INFORMATION TO THE CLIENT

The MMPI-2 is an excellent vehicle for providing personality information in a feedback session to clients because the information provided represents a summary of the broad range of problems the client has in comparison with many other patient groups. In addition, because the information is from an "outside" source, the therapist can present the findings in a comfortable, perhaps even provisional and provocative, manner in order to challenge the patient or raise issues that the patient has not felt comfortable addressing. The MMPI profile sheet and the computer-generated narrative are good didactic materials for presenting test feedback. Information about how insightful the client is, and whether he or she is able to incorporate test feedback information, is also often available from the test profile. For example, a person with a very high Hs scale score may be engaging in a flight into physical symptoms and may be unable to absorb information about personality problems.

Clients can usually grasp the meaning and significance of their prominent MMPI-2 scores. As noted earlier, the patient expects to obtain this type of information from the therapist and usually appreciates the feedback when it is appropriately given.

MMPI-2 personality descriptors are valuable in therapy since they provide names for relevant and powerful emotions the patient may be feeling. Finn and Butcher (in press) describe the *naming* function of MMPI-2 interpretation with clients and illustrate the process by which the client can learn to describe feelings in the relatively safe interpersonal context of therapy.

TRACKING PROGRESS IN TREATMENT

The MMPI-2 can be a very valuable tool for documenting how a person can change over time in treatment. Administering the instrument at the beginning of treatment to establish a baseline of self-reported problems and personality characteristics and retesting at a later date can provide valuable information for the treatment. The initial testing can serve as an interesting backdrop for evaluating changes in personality and problem "hang-ups" over the course of treatment. Patients appreciate feedback and are usually reassured when the therapist conducts progress evaluations by readministering the MMPI-2 during the course of therapy or as it ends.

LIMITATIONS OF THE APPROACH

The MMPI-2 is approximately the same length (567 items) as the original instrument. This length does not present much of a problem for most applications because many clinical settings make it a routine practice of administering the full MMPI to all patients at intake. In some clinical practices, however, it may be viewed as problematic to administer a questionnaire of this length on several occasions, or even in an initial assessment, because of a lack of space or inexperience in testing. Sometimes, the therapist is employed in a setting that is simply not conducive to testing. It has been my experience that if the therapist explains the purpose of the test and indicates the importance of the results for treatment planning, most clients cooperate well with the evaluation. Concerning the question of office space for test administration or time to take the test, it is important not to fall into the practice of allowing clients to take the test home to complete it. This is not a recommended practice because professional ethics call for a tight control of psychological test materials. More problematic, however, is the fact that if the test is administered away from the office setting you can never be sure that the inventory was completed by the client.

In the event that the client is unable to respond to the full 567-item version of the MMPI-2 because of time restrictions, it is still possible to obtain the full MMPI-2 clinical and validity scales by having the client complete the first 370 items in the booklet. The abbreviated form, however, does not allow for scoring of the MMPI-2 content scales and many supplementary scales.

Another issue of concern to therapists using the MMPI-2 in treatment planning is the possibility that the instrument does not address all questions for which we seek answers. Even the revised and broadened MMPI-2 will not address some important areas of interest in treatment evaluation and planning. The highly structured nature of the MMPI-2 dictates that there are areas of personality, environment, or treatment dynamics that remain untouched by the personality assessment. The clinician must be alert to the need for verification of test-based impressions and scores, as well as the need to look beyond the particular profile for other possible relevant treatment variables.

The issue that psychological tests possibly bias the therapist against the client was raised earlier. The argument that tests should not be used in treatment planning because they provide information that could close the therapist's mind to the client and prejudice the therapist against the person was not considered relevant. The benefits that accrue from the appropriate use of the test far outweigh any possible negative "mind sealing" effects of test usage. The view described here that MMPI-2–based descriptors are used as hypotheses or provisional interpretations to be introduced, discussed, and verified in therapy sessions reduces the likelihood that particular test findings will be given the significance of "revealed truths" and will become fruitful treatment topics.

The MMPI has become the most widely used objective personality instrument for assessing individuals in clinical settings. The original MMPI enjoyed considerable success in guiding clinicians through difficult assessment situations and in providing psychotherapy researchers with a valuable, objective outcome measure. The MMPI-2 promises to be an even more relevant and valuable instrument for treatment evaluation because the nonworking items in the original instrument have been deleted and broader, more therapy-relevant content and scales have been included.

References

Altman, H., Gynther, M.D., Warbin, R.W., & Sletten, I.W. (1973). Replicated empirical correlates of the MMPI 8–9/9–8 code type. *Journal of Personality Assessment, 37,* 369–371.

American Psychological Association (1986). *American Psychological Association Guidelines for Computer-Based Tests and Interpretations.* Washington, D.C.: American Psychological Association.

Apfeldorf, M., & Huntley, P.J. (1975). Application of MMPI alcoholism scales to older alcoholics and problem drinkers. *Journal of Studies on Alcohol, 37,* 645–653.

Archer, R.P., Gordon, R.A., Zillmer, E.A., & McClure, S. (1985). Characteristics and correlates of MMPI change within an adult psychiatric inpatient setting. *Journal of Clinical Psychology, 41* (6), 739–746.

Arnold, P.D. (1970). Recurring MMPI two-point codes of marriage counselors and "normal" couples with implications for interpreting marital interaction behavior. Unpublished doctoral dissertation. University of Minnesota.

Barron, F. (1953). An ego strength scale which predicts response to psychotherapy. *Journal of Consulting Psychology, 17,* 327–333.

Ben-Porath, Y., Hostetler, K., Butcher, J.N., & Graham, J.R. (1989). New subscales for the MMPI-2 Social Introversion (Si) Scale. *Psychological Assessment: A Journal of Consulting and Clinical Psychology, 1,* 169–174.

Ben-Porath, Y., Slutsky, W., & Butcher, J.N. (1989). A real-data simulation of computerized adaptive administration of the MMPI. *Psychological Assessment: A Journal of Consulting and Clinical Psychology, 1,* 18–22.

Ben-Porath, Y., Waller, N.G., Slutsky, W., & Butcher, J.N. (1988). A comparison of two methods for adaptive administration of MMPI-2 Content Scales. Paper presented at the 96th Annual meeting of the American Psychological Association. August, 1988, Atlanta, Georgia.

Boerger, A.R., Graham, J.R., & Lilly, R.S. (1974). Behavioral correlates of single scale MMPI code types. *Journal of Consulting and Clinical Psychology, 42,* 398–402.

Brandwin, M.A., & Kewman, D.G. (1982). MMPI indicators of treatment response to spinal epidural stimulation in patients with chronic pain and patients with movement disorders. *Psychological Reports, 51* (3, Pt. 2), 1059–1064.

Burisch, M. (1984). Approaches to personality inventory construction. *American Psychologist, 39,* 214–227.

Butcher, J.N. (ed.), (1972). *Objective personality assessment: changing perspectives.* New York: Academic Press.

Butcher, J.N. (1985). Current developments in MMPI use: an international perspective. In J.N. Butcher and C.D. Spielberger (eds.). *Advances in personality assessment.* Volume 4. Hillsdale, N.J.: Lawrence Erlbaum Press.

Butcher, J.N. (1987). Computerized clinical and personality assessment using the MMPI. In J.N. Butcher (ed.). *Computerized psychological assessment.* New York: Basic Books.

Butcher, J.N. (ed.). (1987). *Computerized psychological assessment.* New York: Basic Books.

Butcher, J.N. (1989, August). *MMPI-2: Issues of continuity and change.* Paper presented at the 97th Annual Convention of the American Psychological Association, New Orleans, La.

Butcher, J.N. (1989). *User's guide for the Minnesota Personnel Report.* Minneapolis, MN: National Computer Systems.

Butcher, J.N., Dahlstrom, W.G., Graham, J.R., Tellegen, A., & Kaemmer, B. (1989). *Manual for the restandardized Minnesota Multiphasic Personality Inventory: MMPI-2. An administrative and interpretive guide.* Minneapolis, MN: University of Minnesota Press.

Butcher, J.N., & Finn, S. (1983). Objective personality assessment in clinical settings. In M. Hersen, A.E. Kazdin, & A.S. Bellack (eds.). *The clinical psychology handbook.* New York: Pergamon Press.

Butcher, J.N., Graham, J.R., Williams, C.L., & Ben-Porath, Y. (1990). *Development and use of the MMPI-2 Content Scales.* Minneapolis, MN: University of Minnesota Press.

Butcher, J.N., Keller, L.S., & Bacon, S. (1989). Current developments and future directions in computerized personality assessment. *Journal of Consulting and Clinical Psychology, 53,* 803–815.

Butcher, J.N., & Owen, P. (1978). Survey of personality inventories: recent research developments and contemporary issues. In B. Wolman (ed.), *Handbook of clinical diagnosis.* New York: Plenum.

Butcher, J.N., & Pancheri, P. (1976). *Handbook of cross-national MMPI research.* Minneapolis, MN: University of Minnesota Press.

Carson, R.C. (1969). Interpretive manual to the MMPI. In J.N. Butcher (ed.). *MMPI: Research developments and clinical applications.* New York: McGraw-Hill.

Cernovsky, Z. (1984). ES scale level and correlates of MMPI elevation: Alcohol abuse vs. MMPI scores in treated alcoholics. *Journal of Clinical Psychology, 40* (6), 1502–1509.

Chodzko-Zajko, W.J., & Ismail, A.H. (1984). MMPI interscale relationships in middle-aged males before and after an 8-month fitness program. *Journal of Clinical Psychology, 40* (1), 163–169.

Clavelle, P., & Butcher, J.N. (1977). An adaptive typological approach to psychological screening. *Journal of Consulting and Clinical Psychology, 45,* 851–859.

Clayton, M.R., & Graham, J.R. (1979). Predictive validity of Barron's ES scale:

The role of symptom acknowledgement. *Journal of Consulting and Clinical Psychology, 47* (2), 424–425.

Colligan, R.C., Osborne, D., Swenson, W.M., & Offord, K.P. (1983). *The MMPI: A contemporary normative study.* New York: Praeger.

Cuadra, C.A. (1953). A scale for control in psychological adjustment (Cn). In G.S. Welsh & W.G. Dahlstrom (eds.). *Basic readings in the MMPI in psychology and medicine.* Minneapolis, MN: University of Minnesota Press.

Dahlstrom, W.G. (1972). Whither the MMPI? In J.N. Butcher (ed.). *Objective personality assessment: changing perspectives.* New York: Academic Press.

Dahlstrom, W.G., Welsh, G.S., & Dahlstrom, L.E. (1972). *A MMPI handbook.* Volume 1. Minneapolis: University of Minnesota Press.

Dahlstrom, W.G., Welsh, G.S., & Dahlstrom, L.E. (1975). *An MMPI handbook.* Volume 2. Minneapolis: University of Minnesota Press.

Deiker, T.E. (1974). A cross-validation of MMPI scales of aggression on male criminal criterion groups. *Journal of Consulting and Clinical Psychology, 42,* 196–202.

Drake, L.E., and Oetting, E.R. (1959). *An MMPI codebook for counselors.* Minneapolis, MN: University of Minnesota Press.

Elliott, T.R., Anderson, W.P., & Adams, N.A. (1987). MMPI indicators of long-term therapy in a college counseling center. *Psychological Reports, 60* (1), 79–84.

Eyde, L., Kowal, D., & Fishburne, J. (1987). Clinical implications of validity research on computer based test interpretations of the MMPI. Paper given at the Annual Meeting of the American Psychological Association, New York, New York.

Finn, S., & Butcher, J.N. (in press). Clinical objective personality assessment. In Hersen, M., Kazdin, A.E., & Bellack, A.S. *The clinical psychology handbook* (Second Edition). New York: Pergamon Press.

Fishburne, J., Eyde, L., & Kowal, D. (1988). Paper given at the Annual Meeting of the American Psychological Association, Atlanta, Georgia.

Fordyce, W. (1987). Use of the MMPI with chronic pain patients. Paper given at the Ninth International Conference on Personality Assessment, Brussels, Belgium.

Fowler, R.D. (1985). Landmarks in computer-assisted psychological test interpretation. *Journal of Consulting and Clinical Psychology, 53,* 748–759.

Fowler, R.D. (1987). Developing a computer based interpretation system. In J.N. Butcher (ed.). *Computerized psychological assessment.* New York: Basic Books.

Fowler, R.D., Jr., & Athey, E.B. (1971). A cross-validation of Gilberstadt and Duker's 1–2–3–4 profile type. *Journal of Clinical Psychology, 27,* 238–240.

Gilberstadt, H., & Duker, J. (1965). *A handbook for clinical and actuarial MMPI interpretation.* Philadelphia: Saunders.

Gocka, E. (1965). American Lake norms for 200 MMPI scales. Unpublished materials. Veteran's Administration.

Goldberg, L.R., & Jones, R.R. (1969). The reliability of reliability; the generality and correlates of intra-individual consistency in response to structured personality inventories. Oregon Research Monograph, *9,* No. 2.

Gough, H.G., McClosky, H., & Meehl, P.E. (1952). A personality scale for social responsibility. *Journal of Abnormal and Social Psychology, 47,* 73–80.

Graham, J.R. (1973). Behavioral correlates of simple MMPI code types. Paper given at the Eighth Annual Symposium on Recent Developments in the Use of the MMPI, New Orleans, La.

Graham, J.R. (1979). Using the MMPI in counseling and psychotherapy. *Clinical notes on the MMPI*. Minneapolis, MN: National Computer Systems.

Graham, J.R. (1987). *The MMPI: a practical guide*. (Second Edition). New York: Oxford University Press.

Graham, J.R. (1990). *MMPI-2: Assessing personality and psychopathology*. New York: Oxford University Press.

Graham, J.R., & McCord, G. (1985). Interpretation of moderately elevated MMPI scores for normal subjects. *Journal of Personality Assessment, 49* (5), 477–484.

Grayson, H.M. (1951). *Psychological admission testing program and manual*. Los Angeles: Veterans Administration Center, Neuropsychiatric Hospital.

Greene, R. (1980). *The MMPI: An interpretive manual*. New York: Grune & Stratton.

Gynther, M.D. (1972). A new replicated actuarial program for interpreting MMPIs of state hospital inpatients. Paper given at the Seventh Annual Symposium on Recent Developments in the Use of the MMPI, Mexico, 1972.

Gynther, M.D., Altman, H., & Sletten, I.W. (1973). Development of an empirical interpretive system for the MMPI: Some after-the-fact observations. *Journal of Clinical Psychology, 29*, 232–234.

Gynther, M.D., Altman, H., & Warbin, R.W. (1972). A new empirical automated MMPI interpretive program: the 2–4/4–2 code type. *Journal of Clinical Psychology, 28*, 498–501.

Gynther, M.D., Altman, H., & Warbin, R.W. (1973a). A new actuarial-empirical automated MMPI interpretive program: the 4–3/3–4 code type. *Journal of Clinical Psychology, 29*, 229–231.

Gynther, M.D., Altman, H., & Warbin, R.W. (1973b). A new empirical automated MMPI interpretive program: The 2–7/7–2 code type. *Journal of Clinical Psychology, 29*, 58–59.

Gynther, M.D., Altman, H., & Warbin, R.W. (1973c). A new empirical automated MMPI interpretive program: The 6–9/9–6 code type. *Journal of Clinical Psychology, 29*, 60–61.

Gynther, M.D., Altman, H., Warbin, R.W., & Sletten, I.W. (1972). A new actuarial system for MMPI interpretation: rationale and methodology. *Journal of Clinical Psychology, 28*, 173–179.

Gynther, M.D., Altman, H., Warbin, R.W., & Sletten, I.W. (1973). A new empirical automated MMPI interpretive program: the 1–2/2–1 code type. *Journal of Clinical Psychology, 29*, 54–57.

Halbower, C.C. (1955). A comparison of actuarial versus clinical prediction to classes discriminated by MMPI. Unpublished doctoral dissertation, University of Minnesota.

Harris, R.E., & Lingoes, J.C. (1955, 1968). Subscales for the MMPI: an aid to profile interpretation. Unpublished manuscript. The Langley Porter Neuropsychiatric Institute.

Hathaway, S.R. (1940). A multiphasic personality schedule (Minnesota): I. Construction of the schedule. *Journal of Psychology, 10*, 249–254.

Hathaway, S.R. (1980). Scales 5 (Masculinity–Femininity) 6 (Paranoia), and 8 (Schizophrenia). In W.G. Dahlstrom & L.E. Dahlstrom (1980). *Basic readings on the MMPI*. Minneapolis: University of Minnesota Press.

Hathaway, S.R., & McKinley, J.C. (1943). *The Minnesota Multiphasic Personality Schedule*. Minneapolis, Minnesota: University of Minnesota Press.

Henrichs, T.F. (1987). MMPI profiles of chronic pain patients: some methodological considerations that concern clusters and descriptors. *Journal of Clinical Psychology, 43*, 650–660.

Hollon, S., & Mandell, M. (1979). Use of the MMPI in the evaluation of treatment effects. In J.N. Butcher (ed.). *New developments in the use of the MMPI*. Minneapolis: University of Minnesota Press.

Hostetler, K., Ben-Porath, Y., Butcher, J.N., & Graham, J.R. (1989). New subscales for the MMPI-2 Social Introversion scale. Paper presented at the Society for Personality Assessment, New York.

Johnson, J.H., Butcher, J.N., Null, C., & Johnson, K. (1984). Replicated item level factor analysis of the full MMPI. *Journal of Personality and Social Psychology, 47*, 105–114.

Jung, K. (1933). *Psychological types*. New York: Harcourt, Brace & World.

Kelly, C.K., & King, G.D. (1978). Behavioral correlates for within-normal limit MMPI profiles with and without elevated K in students at a University mental health center. *Journal of Clinical Psychology, 34*, 695–699.

Kleinmuntz, B. (1961). The College Maladjustment Scale (MT): norms and predictive validity. *Educational and Psychological Measurement, 21*, 1029–1033.

Klinge, V., Lachar, D., Grissell, J., & Berman, W. (1978). The effects of scoring norms on adolescent psychiatric drug users and non users' MMPI profiles. *Adolescence, 13*, 1–11.

Koss, M.P. (1979). MMPI item content: recurring issues. In J.N. Butcher (ed.). *New developments in the use of the MMPI*. (pp. 3–38). Minneapolis: University of Minnesota Press.

Koss, M.P., & Butcher, J.N. (1973). A comparison of psychiatric patients' self report with other sources of clinical information. *Journal of Research in Personality, 7*, 225–236.

Koss, M.P., & Butcher, J.N. (1986). Research on brief and crisis oriented psychotherapy. In S.L. Garfield & A.E. Bergin (eds.). *Handbook of psychotherapy and behavior change*. Third Edition. New York: Wiley.

Koss, M.P., Butcher, J.N., & Hoffman, N.G. (1976). The MMPI critical items: how well do they work? *Journal of Consulting and Clinical Psychology, 44*, 921–928.

Lachar, D., & Wrobel, T.A. (1979). Validating clinicians' hunches: construction of a new MMPI critical item set. *Journal of Consulting and Clinical Psychology, 47*, 277–284.

Lane, P.J., & Kling, J.S. (1979). Construct validation of the Overcontrolled-Hostility scale of the MMPI. *Journal of Consulting and Clinical Psychology, 47*, 781–782.

Leon, G., Gillum, B., Gillum, R., & Gouze, M. (1979). Personality stability and change over a thirty-year-period—middle age to old age. *Journal of Consulting and Clinical Psychology, 47*, 517–524.

Lewandowski, D., & Graham, J.R. (1972). Empirical correlates of frequently occurring two-point MMPI code types: a replicated study. *Journal of Consulting and Clinical Psychology, 39*, 467–472.

Long, C.J. (1981). The relationship between surgical outcome and MMPI profiles in chronic pain patients. *Journal of Clinical Psychology, 37* (4), 744–749.

Lubin, B., Larsen, R.M., & Matarazzo, J. (1984). Patterns of psychological test usage in the United States 1935–1982. *American Psychologist, 39*, 451–454.

MacAndrew, C. (1965). The differentiation of male alcoholic outpatients from nonalcoholic psychiatric outpatients by means of the MMPI. *Quarterly Journal of Studies on Alcohol, 26*, 238–246.

Malec, J.F. (1983). Relationship of the MMPI-168 to outcome of a pain management program at long-term follow-up. *Rehabilitation Psychology, 28* (2), 115–119.

Marks, P.A., & Seeman, W. (1963). *The actuarial description of abnormal personality.* Baltimore: Williams and Wilkins.

Marks, P.A., Seeman, W., & Haller, D.L. (1974). *The actuarial use of the MMPI with adolescents and adults.* Baltimore: Williams and Wilkins.

Meehl, P.E. (1954). *Clinical versus statistical prediction: a theoretical analysis and a review of the evidence.* Minneapolis: University of Minnesota Press.

Meehl, P.E., & Hathaway, S.R. (1946). The K factor as a suppressor variable in the MMPI. *Journal of Applied Psychology, 30*, 525–564.

Megargee, E.I., Cook, P.E., & Mendelsohn, G.A. (1967). Development and validation of an MMPI scale of assaultiveness in overcontrolled individuals. *Journal of Abnormal Psychology, 72*, 519–528.

Meikle, S., & Gerritse, R. (1970). MMPI "cookbook" pattern frequencies in a psychiatric unit. *Journal of Clinical Psychology, 26*, 82–84.

Moore, J.E., Armentrout, D.P., Parker, J.D., & Kivlahan, D.R. (1986). Empirically derived pain-patient MMPI subgroups: prediction of treatment outcome. *Journal of Behavioral Medicine, 9* (1), 51–63.

Moras, K., & Strupp, H.H. (1982). Pretherapy interpersonal relations, patients' alliance, and outcome in brief therapy. *Archives of General Psychiatry, 39*, 405–409.

Moreland, K. (1985). *Test–retest reliability of 80 MMPI scales.* Unpublished materials (Available from National Computer Systems; 5605 Green Circle Drive, Minnetonka, Mn. 55343).

Moreland, K.L., & Onstad, J. (1985, March). *Validity of the Minnesota Clinical Report I: mental health outpatients.* Paper presented at the 20th Annual Symposium on Recent Developments in the Use of the MMPI, Honolulu.

Oostdam, E.M., Duivenvoorden, H.J., & Pondaag, W. (1981). Predictive value of some psychological tests on the outcome of surgical intervention in low back pain patients. *Journal of Psychosomatic Research, 25* (3), 227–235.

Ottomanelli, G., Wilson, P., & Whyte, R. (1978). MMPI evaluation of 5-year methadone treatment status. *Journal of Consulting and Clinical Psychology, 46* (3), 579–582.

Pearson, J.S., & Swenson, W.M. (1967). *A users guide to the Mayo Clinic automated MMPI program.* New York: The Psychological Corporation.

Persons, R.W., & Marks, P.A. (1971). The violent 4–3 MMPI personality type. *Journal of Consulting and Clinical Psychology, 36*, 189–196.

Pettinati, H.M., Sugerman, A.A., & Maurer, H.S. (1982). Four year MMPI changes in abstinent and drinking alcoholics. *Alcoholism: Clinical & Experimental Research, 6* (4), 487–494.

Rathus, S.A., Fox, J.A., & Ortins, J.B. (1980). The MacAndrew scale as a measure of substance abuse and delinquency among adolescents. *Journal of Clinical Psychology, 36,* 579–583.

Rhodes, R.J. (1969). The MacAndrews alcoholism scale: a replication. *Journal of Clinical Psychology, 25,* 189–191.

Rich, C.C., & Davis, H.G. (1969). Concurrent validity of MMPI alcoholism scales. *Journal of Clinical Psychology, 25,* 425–426.

Schofield, W. (1950). Changes in response to the Minnesota Multiphasic Personality Inventory following certain therapies. *Psychological Monographs, 64,* whole Number 311.

Schwartz, M.F., & Graham, J.R. (1979). Construct validity of the MacAndrew alcoholism scale. *Journal of Consulting and Clinical Psychology, 47,* 1090–1095.

Serkownek, K. (1975). Subscales for scales 5 and 0 of the Minnesota Multiphasic Personality Inventory. Unpublished Manuscript.

Sheppard, D., Smith, G.T., & Rosenbaum, G. (1988). Use of MMPI subtypes in predicting completion of a residential alcoholism treatment program. *Journal of Consulting and Clinical Psychology, 56,* 590–596.

Sines, J.O. (1966). Actuarial methods in personality assessment. In B.A. Maher (ed.). *Progress in experimental personality research.* New York: Academic Press.

Skoog, D.K., Andersen, A.E., & Laufer, W.S. (1984). Personality and treatment effectiveness in anorexia nervosa. *Journal of Clinical Psychology, 40* (4), 955–961.

Strassberg, D.S., Reimherr, F., Ward, M., Russell, S., & Cole, A. (1981). The MMPI and chronic pain. *Journal of Consulting and Clinical Psychology, 49* (2), 220–226.

Sweet, J.J., Breuer, S.R., Hazlewood, L.A., Toye, R., & Pawl, R.P. (1985). The Millon Behavioral Health Inventory: concurrent and predictive validity in a pain treatment center. *Journal of Behavioral Medicine, 8* (3), 215–226.

Terman, L.M., & Miles, C.C. (1936). *Sex and personality: studies in masculinity and femininity.* New York: Russell and Russell.

Thurstin, A.H., Alfano, A.M., & Sherer, M. (1986). Pretreatment MMPI profiles of A.A. members and nonmembers. *Journal of Studies on Alcohol, 47* (6), 468–471.

Turner, J.A., Herron, L., & Weiner, P. (1986). Utility of the MMPI pain assessment index in predicting outcome after lumbar surgery. *Journal of Clinical Psychology, 42* (5), 764–769.

Uomoto, J.M., Turner, J.A., & Herron, L.D. (1988). Use of the MMPI and MCMI in predicting outcome of lumbar laminectomy. *Journal of Clinical Psychology, 44* (2), 191–197.

Walker, D.E., Blankenship, V., Ditty, J.A., & Lynch, K.P. (1987). Prediction of recovery for closed-head-injured adults: an evaluation of the MMPI, the Adaptive Behavior Scale, and a "quality of life" rating scale. *Journal of Clinical Psychology, 43* (6), 699–707.

Walters, G.D., & Greene, R.L. (1983). Factor structure of the Overcontrolled-Hostility scale of the MMPI. *Journal of Clinical Psychology, 39,* 560–562.

Walters, G.D., Greene, R.L., & Jeffrey, T.B. (1984). Discriminating between alcoholic and nonalcoholic blacks and whites on the MMPI. *Journal of Personality Assessment, 48,* 486–488.

Walters, G.D., Greene, R.L., Jeffrey, T.B., Kruzich, D.J., & Haskin, J.J. (1983). Racial variations on the MacAndrew alcoholism scale of the MMPI. *Journal of Consulting and Clinical Psychology, 51,* 947–948.

Walters, G.D., Greene, R., & Solomon, G.S. (1982). Empirical correlates of the Overcontrolled-Hostility scale and the 4–3 high point pair. *Journal of Consulting and Clinical Psychology, 50,* 213–218.

Walters, G.D., Solomon, G.S., & Walden, V.R. (1982). Use of the MMPI in predicting psychotherapeutic persistence in groups of male and female outpatients. *Journal of Clinical Psychology, 38* (1), 80–83.

Warbin, R.W., Altman, H., Gynther, M.D., & Sletten, I.W. (1972). A new empirical automated MMPI interpretive program: 2–8 and 8–2 code types. *Journal of Personality Assessment, 36,* 581–584.

Wiggins, J.S. (1966). Substantive dimensions of self-report in the MMPI item pool. *Psychological Monographs, 80,* (22 Whole No. 630).

Wilderman, J.E. (1984). *An investigation of the clinical utility of the College Maladjustment Scale.* Unpublished Master's Thesis, Kent State University, Kent, Ohio.

Wisniewski, N.M., Glenwick, D.S., & Graham, J.R. (1985). MacAndrew scale and sociodemographic correlates of adolescent drug use. *Addictive Behaviors, 10,* 55–67.

Wolfson, K.T., & Erbaugh, S.E. (1984). Adolescent responses to MacAndrew Alcoholism scale. *Journal of Consulting and Clinical Psychology, 52,* 625–630.

Woodworth, R.S. (1920). *The personal data sheet.* Chicago: Stoelting.

Young, R.C., Gould, E., Glick, I.D., & Hargreaves, W.A. (1980). Personality inventory correlates of outcome in a follow-up study of psychiatric hospitalization. *Psychological Reports, 46* (3, pt. 1), 903–906.

Appendix

```
==============================================================================
                          STRUCTURAL SUMMARY
==============================================================================

  R = 20      Zf = 14      ZSum = 43.0      P = 4      (2) = 5     Fr+rF = 2

  LOCATION              DETERMINANTS            CONTENTS      S-CONSTELLATION
  FEATURES          BLENDS        SINGLE                         (ADULT)
                                              H  =  2, 0    NO..FV+VF+V+FD>2
  W  = 12         M.FC           M  = 1     (H)  =  1, 1    YES..Col-Shd Bl>0
  (Wv  =  1)      M.Fr           FM = 3     Hd   =  0, 0    YES..Ego<.31,>.44
  D  =  8         m.rF.TF        m  = 0     (Hd) =  0, 0    NO..MOR > 3
  Dd =  0         CF.C'F         C  = 0     Hx   =  0, 0    NO..Zd > +- 3.5
  S  =  4         CF.YF          Cn = 0     A    =  4, 0    YES..es > EA
                  M.FC.FV        CF = 0     (A)  =  0, 1    YES..CF+C+Cn > FC
     DQ           m.CF           FC = 1     Ad   =  0, 0    YES..X+ < .70
  .........(FQ-)  CF.YF.m        C' = 0     (Ad) =  0, 0    YES..S > 3
                  CF.m           C'F= 0     Al   =  0, 0    NO..P < 3 or > 8
   +  =  6 ( 1)                  FC'= 1     An   =  0, 0    NO..Pure H < 2
   o  = 12 ( 0)                  T  = 0     Art  =  4, 0    NO..R < 17
  v/+ =  1 ( 0)                  TF = 0     Ay   =  2, 0      6.....TOTAL
   v  =  1 ( 0)                  FT = 1     Bl   =  0, 0
                                 V  = 0     Bt   =  1, 1
                                 VF = 0     Cg   =  1, 1   SPECIAL SCORINGS
                                 FV = 0     Cl   =  0, 1               L1   L2
                                 Y  = 0     Ex   =  1, 0   DV    = 0x1  0x2
                                 YF = 0     Fi   =  0, 0   INCOM = 0x2  0x4
                FORM QUALITY      FY = 0     Fd   =  1, 0   DR    = 0x3  0x6
                                 rF = 0     Ge   =  0, 0   FABCOM = 0x4 0x7
    FQx       FQf      M Qual.   Fr = 0     Hh   =  1, 0   ALOG  = 0x5
                                 FD = 0     Ls   =  0, 0   CONTAM = 0x7
   +  =  0    + =  0    + =  0    F  = 4     Na   =  1, 0      -- WSUM6 =  0
   o  = 11    o =  1    o =  4               Sc   =  0, 0   AB = 1    CP = 0
   u  =  8    u =  3    u =  0               Sx   =  0, 1   AG = 0    MOR= 0
   -  =  1    - =  0    - =  0               Xy   =  0, 0   CFB= 0    PER= 6
  none=  0             none= 0               Idio =  1, 1   COP= 2    PSV= 0
==============================================================================

                  RATIOS, PERCENTAGES, AND DERIVATIONS

  ZSum-Zest = 43.0 - 45.5        FC:CF+C  =  3: 5    W:M      = 12: 4
                                   (Pure C =  0)
  Zd         =  -2.5                                 W:D      = 12: 8
                                 Afr      = 0.82
  .------------------------------.                   Isolate:R  =  6:20
  :EB  =   4: 6.5   EA = 10.5:    3r+(2)/R =  0.55
  :                    >D= -1                        2Ab+Art+Ay =  8
  :eb  =   7:   7   es = 14 :     L        =  0.25
  '------------------------------'                   An+Xy      =  0
  (FM= 3 : C'= 2 T= 2) (Adj D=  0)  Blends:R =  9:20
  (m  = 4 : V = 1 Y= 2)                              H(H):Hd(Hd)=  4: 0
                                 X+%      =  0.55        (Pure H =   2)
  a:p     =  5: 6                 (F+%    =  0.25)    (HHd):(AAd)=  2: 1
                                 X-%      =  0.05
  Ma:Mp   =  2: 2                 (Xu%    =  0.40)    H+A:Hd+Ad  =  9: 0
  --------------------------------------------------------------------------
     SCZI2(1) = 1(1)      DEPI = 2      S-CON = 6            HVI = 0+2
==============================================================================
```

SUBJECT NAME:PROTOCOL.135   AGE:23   SEX:M   RACE:W   MS:Liv   ED:16

SEQUENCE OF SCORES

===
CARD NO   LOC   #   DETERMINANT(S)   (2)   CONTENT(S)   POP Z   SPECIAL SCORES
===

CARD	NO	LOC	#	DETERMINANT(S)	(2)	CONTENT(S)	POP	Z	SPECIAL SCORES
I	1	Wo	1	FMao		A	P	1.0	
	2	WSo	1	Fu		Ay		3.5	PER
II	3	W+	1	Ma.FCo	2	H,Cg		4.5	
	4	Do	3	FTo		A			
III	5	D+	9	Mp.Fro		H	P	4.0	
IV	6	Wo	1	FC'o		Bt		2.0	PER
V	7	Wo	1	FMpo		A	P	1.0	
	8	Wo	1	FMao		A		1.0	PER
VI	9	D/	4	mp.rF.TFo		Na		2.5	
VII	10	W+	1	Mpo	2	Art,(H)	P	2.5	
	11	WS+	1	Fu		Id,Bt		4.0	PER
VIII	12	WS+	1	CF.C'F-		Fd,Id		4.5	
	13	Wo	1	CF.YFu	2	Art,(A)		4.5	PER
IX	14	DS+	3	Ma.FC.FVo	2	(H),Ab,Cl		2.5	
	15	Do	9	Fu		Hh			
X	16	Wv	1	ma.CFu		Ex,Ab			
	17	Do	11	Fo		Ay			PER
	18	Do	1	CF.YF.mpu	2	Art			
	19	Do	6	FCu		Cg,Sx			
	20	Wo	1	CF.mpu		Art,Ab		5.5	

===

(c)1976, 1985 by John E. Exner, Jr.

Abbreviations Used Above:
DQ:	CONTENTS:		SPECIAL SCORES:	
"/" = v/+	"Id" = Idiographic	"CFB" = CONFAB	"FAB" = FABCOM
	Content	"CON" = CONTAM	"INC" = INCOM

SUBJECT NAME:PROTOCOL.135   AGE:23   SEX:M   RACE:W   MS:Liv   ED:16

INTERPRETIVE HYPOTHESES FOR THE RORSCHACH
PROTOCOL UTILIZING THE COMPREHENSIVE SYSTEM
(COPYRIGHT 1976, 1985 BY JOHN E. EXNER, JR.)

THE FOLLOWING COMPUTER-BASED INTERPRETATION IS DERIVED ** EXCLUSIVELY **
FROM THE STRUCTURAL DATA OF THE RECORD AND DOES NOT INCLUDE CONSIDERATION OF
THE SEQUENCE OF SCORES OR THE VERBAL MATERIAL. IT IS INTENDED AS A GUIDE FROM
WHICH THE INTERPRETER OF THE TOTAL PROTOCOL CAN PROCEED TO STUDY AND REFINE
THE HYPOTHESES GENERATED FROM THESE ACTUARIAL FINDINGS.

* * * * *

1. THE RECORD APPEARS TO BE VALID AND INTERPRETIVELY USEFUL.

2. THE DATA INDICATE THAT THE SUBJECT IS CURRENTLY EXPERIENCING
    CONSIDERABLE SITUATIONALLY RELATED STRESS THAT HAS CREATED AN
    IMPORTANT STIMULUS OVERLOAD CONDITION. CAPACITY FOR CONTROL AND STRESS
    TOLERANCE ARE BOTH LOWERED SUBSTANTIALLY AND IT IS LIKELY THAT THE
    OVERLOAD WILL CAUSE THE SUBJECT TO BE MORE NEGLIGENT IN PROCESSING
    INFORMATION THAN IS USUALLY THE CASE. SOME BEHAVIORS MAY NOT BE WELL
    FORMULATED AND/OR IMPLEMENTED, AND A VULNERABILITY TO IMPULSIVE-LIKE
    BEHAVIORS IS CLEARLY PRESENT.

3. THIS IS THE TYPE OF PERSON WHO IS PRONE TO INVOLVE FEELINGS IN
    THINKING, DECISION OPERATIONS, AND MOST OF THEIR BEHAVIORS. SUCH
    PEOPLE PREFER A TRIAL-AND-ERROR APPROACH TO PROBLEM-SOLVING

4. THIS SUBJECT DOES NOT MODULATE EMOTIONAL DISPLAYS AS MUCH AS MOST
    ADULTS AND, BECAUSE OF THIS, IS PRONE TO BECOME VERY INFLUENCED BY
    FEELINGS IN MOST THINKING, DECISIONS, AND BEHAVIORS. THIS IS AN
    ESPECIALLY IMPORTANT PROBLEM BECAUSE IT RELATES TO THE EFFECTIVENESS
    OF THE BASIC COPING STYLE.

5. THIS PERSON IS MUCH MORE NEGATIVE THAN MOST. SUCH EXTREME NEGATIVISM
    OFTEN TAKES THE FORM OF ANGER WHICH CAN DETRACT SIGNIFICANTLY FROM THE
    FORMING AND DIRECTING OF ADAPTIVE RESPONSES.

6. THIS PERSON IS EXPERIENCING CONSIDERABLE EMOTIONAL IRRITATION BECAUSE
    OF STRONG, UNMET NEEDS FOR CLOSENESS THAT ARE USUALLY MANIFEST AS SOME
    EXPERIENCE OF LONELINESS. THIS IS MADE MORE IRRITATING BECAUSE SOME
    DATA SUGGEST A PREFERENCE FOR DEPENDENCY ON OTHERS.

7. THE SUBJECT DOES NOT HAVE AS MUCH INTEREST IN OTHERS AS DO MOST ADULTS
    AND OLDER CHILDREN.

8. THIS SUBJECT TENDS TO FOCUS MORE ON HIMSELF (HERSELF) THAN IS
    CUSTOMARY AMONG ADULTS. THIS IS TYPICAL OF THOSE WITH CONCERNS ABOUT
    THEMSELVES AND ONE CONSEQUENCE IS LESS ATTENTION TO THE EXTERNAL
    WORLD.
===

SUBJECT NAME:PROTOCOL.135   AGE:23   SEX:M   RACE:W   MS:Liv   ED:16

PAGE -2-

===

9.   THIS KIND OF PERSON TENDS TO OVERGLORIFY THEIR PERSONAL WORTH AND
     PROBABLY HARBORS MANY OF THE FEATURES THAT WOULD BE CONSIDERED
     "NARCISSISSTIC." THIS FEATURE OFTEN BECOMES A MAJOR OBSTACLE TO FORMS
     OF TREATMENT THAT INVOLVE UNCOVERING OR RECONSTRUCTIVE EFFORTS.

10. WHEN THIS PERSON ENGAGES IN SELF EXAMINATION A TENDENCY EXISTS TO
     FOCUS UPON NEGATIVE FEATURES PERCEIVED TO EXIST IN THE SELF IMAGE, AND
     THIS RESULTS IN CONSIDERABLE INTERNAL PAIN. THIS PROCESS IS OFTEN A
     PRECURSOR TO FEELINGS OF SADNESS, PESSIMISSISM OR EVEN DEPRESSION.

11. THIS SUBJECT IS VERY PRONE TO INTERPRET STIMULUS CUES IN A UNIQUE AND
     OVERPERSONALIZED MANNER. PEOPLE SUCH AS THIS OFTEN VIEW THEIR WORLD
     WITH THEIR OWN SPECIAL SET OF BIASES AND ARE LESS CONCERNED WITH BEING
     CONVENTIONAL AND/OR ACCEPTABLE TO OTHERS.

12. THIS PERSON MAKES A MARKED EFFORT TO ORGANIZE STIMULI IN A MEANINGFUL
     AND INTEGRATED WAY.

13. THIS PERSON TENDS TO SET GOALS THAT MAY BE BEYOND HIS/HER FUNCTIONAL
     CAPACITIES. THIS OFTEN LEADS TO FAILURE, DISAPPOINTMENT, AND/OR
     FRUSTRATION. ANY OR ALL OF THESE CAN CREATE A CHRONIC STATE OF
     TENSION OR APPREHENSION, AND, AS A CONSEQUENCE, THE TOLERANCE FOR
     STRESS IS LOWERED.

14. THIS PERSON IS VERY DEFENSIVE ABOUT BEING CHALLENGED. HE OR SHE OFTEN
     TRIES TO AVOID SUCH A STRESS BY AN EXCESS OF INTELLECTUALIZATION, SOME
     OF WHICH MAY BE VERY CONCRETE. PEOPLE SUCH AS THIS OFTEN TRY TO BE
     OVERLY ESOTERIC IN AN EFFORT TO NEUTRALIZE THREATS. PEOPLE LIKE THIS
     ARE OFTEN VERY RESISTIVE DURING EARLY PHASES OF INTERVENTION AS THIS
     TENDENCY TOWARD DENIAL CAUSES THEM TO AVOID ANY AFFECTIVE
     CONFRONTATIONS.

                     * * *   END OF REPORT   * * *

===

SUBJECT NAME:PROTOCOL.136   AGE:25 SEX:F RACE:W MS:Liv ED:14
==
STRUCTURAL SUMMARY
==

R = 19   Zf = 11   ZSum = 41.0   P = 3   (2) = 5   Fr+rF = 0

LOCATION FEATURES	DETERMINANTS BLENDS	SINGLE	CONTENTS	S-CONSTELLATION (ADULT)
			H = 3, 0	YES..FV+VF+V+FD>2
W = 5	M.FV	M = 1	(H) = 0, 0	NO..Col-Shd Bl>0
(Wv = 0)	FV.m	FM = 3	Hd = 2, 0	YES..Ego<.31,>.44
D = 9	M.FY	m = 0	(Hd)= 1, 1	NO..MOR > 3
Dd = 5	FM.FC'	C = 0	Hx = 0, 0	YES..Zd > +- 3.5
S = 1	m.FD	Cn = 0	A = 6, 0	YES..es > EA
	M.FC	CF = 1	(A) = 0, 0	NO..CF+C+Cn > FC
DQ		FC = 0	Ad = 1, 0	YES..X+ < .70
.........(FQ-)		C' = 0	(Ad)= 0, 0	NO..S > 3
		C'F = 0	Al = 0, 0	NO..P < 3 or > 8
+ = 8 (0)		FC' = 1	An = 1, 0	NO..Pure H < 2
o = 11 (2)		T = 0	Art = 1, 0	NO..R < 17
v/+ = 0 (0)		TF = 0	Ay = 0, 0	5.....TOTAL
v = 0 (0)		FT = 0	Bl = 0, 0	
		V = 0	Bt = 0, 1	SPECIAL SCORINGS
		VF = 0	Cg = 0, 2	L1 L2
		FV = 0	Cl = 0, 0	DV = 1x1 0x2
		Y = 0	Ex = 0, 0	INCOM = 1x2 0x4
		YF = 0	Fi = 0, 0	DR = 1x3 0x6
FORM QUALITY		FY = 1	Fd = 0, 1	FABCOM = 0x4 0x7
		rF = 0	Ge = 0, 0	ALOG = 0x5
		Fr = 0	Hh = 0, 1	CONTAM = 0x7
FQx FQf M Qual.		FD = 0	Ls = 0, 1	-- WSUM6 = 6
		F = 6	Na = 0, 0	
+ = 0 + = 0 + = 0			Sc = 1, 0	AB = 1 CP = 0
o = 11 o = 4 o = 3			Sx = 0, 0	AG = 0 MOR = 3
u = 6 u = 1 u = 1			Xy = 1, 0	CFB= 0 PER = 1
- = 2 - = 1 - = 0			Idio= 2, 0	COP = 3 PSV = 0
none= 0 none= 0				

==
RATIOS, PERCENTAGES, AND DERIVATIONS

ZSum-Zest = 41.0 - 34.5	FC:CF+C = 1: 1 (Pure C = 0)	W:M = 5: 4
Zd = +6.5		W:D = 5: 9
	Afr = 0.58	
.-------------------------.		Isolate:R = 2:19
:EB = 4: 1.5 EA = 5.5:	3r+(2)/R = 0.26	
: >D= -2		2Ab+Art+Ay = 3
:eb = 6: 6 es = 12 :	L = 0.46	
'-------------------------'		An+Xy = 2
(FM= 4 : C'= 2 T= 0) (Adj D= -1)	Blends:R = 6:19	
(m = 2 : V = 2 Y= 2)		H(H):Hd(Hd)= 3: 4
	X+% = 0.58	(Pure H = 3)
a:p = 3: 7	(F+% = 0.67)	(HHd):(AAd)= 2: 0
	X-% = 0.11	
Ma:Mp = 0: 4	(Xu% = 0.32)	H+A:Hd+Ad = 9: 5

SCZI2(1) = 1(1)   DEPI = 2   S-CON = 5   HVI = 1+2
==
(c)1976,1985 by John E. Exner, Jr.

```
SUBJECT NAME:PROTOCOL.136                AGE:25  SEX:F  RACE:W  MS:Liv  ED:14
                             SEQUENCE OF SCORES
===============================================================================
CARD NO  LOC   #    DETERMINANT(S)    (2)  CONTENT(S)  POP Z    SPECIAL SCORES
===============================================================================
  I   1 W+    1 Mp.FVo                   H,Cg           4.0
      2 Ddo  24 Fo                       Id

 II   3 D+    2 FMpu                 2  A               5.5
      4 Do    4 FC'-                    Hd                      PER,MOR

III   5 D+    1 Mpo                  2  H,Hh         P 3.0

 IV   6 Do    3 FV.mpu                  Id                      DR
      7 Ddo  33 FYo                     Xy

  V   8 Wo    1 FMao                    A            P 1.0 INC
      9 Do    1 Fo                      Hd                      MOR

 VI  10 Do    3 Fu                      A

VII  11 W+    1 FMpo                 2  A,Ls           2.5
     12 Dd+  28 Mp.FYu                  H,Cg,Ab        1.0

VIII 13 Wo    1 F-                      An             4.5 MOR
     14 Do    1 Fo                      A            P

 IX  15 Wo    1 CFu                     Art,(Hd)       5.5

  X  16 D+   11 FMa.FC'o             2  A,Bt           4.0
     17 Do    5 Fo                      Ad
     18 DdS+ 29 ma.FDu                  Sc             6.0
     19 Dd+  99 Mp.FCo              2  (Hd),Fd         4.0 DV
===============================================================================
```
(c)1976, 1985 by John E. Exner, Jr.

```
   Abbreviations Used Above:
        DQ:              CONTENTS:               SPECIAL SCORES:
     "/" = v/+      "Id" = Idiographic    "CFB" = CONFAB    "FAB" = FABCOM
                           Content         "CON" = CONTAM    "INC" = INCOM
```

SUBJECT NAME:PROTOCOL.136   AGE:25 SEX:F RACE:W MS:Liv ED:14

INTERPRETIVE HYPOTHESES FOR THE RORSCHACH
PROTOCOL UTILIZING THE COMPREHENSIVE SYSTEM
(COPYRIGHT 1976, 1985 BY JOHN E. EXNER, JR.)

THE FOLLOWING COMPUTER-BASED INTERPRETATION IS DERIVED ** EXCLUSIVELY **
FROM THE STRUCTURAL DATA OF THE RECORD AND DOES NOT INCLUDE CONSIDERATION OF
THE SEQUENCE OF SCORES OR THE VERBAL MATERIAL. IT IS INTENDED AS A GUIDE FROM
WHICH THE INTERPRETER OF THE TOTAL PROTOCOL CAN PROCEED TO STUDY AND REFINE
THE HYPOTHESES GENERATED FROM THESE ACTUARIAL FINDINGS.

* * * * *

1. THE RECORD APPEARS TO BE VALID AND INTERPRETIVELY USEFUL.

2. THE SUBJECT DOES NOT HAVE GOOD CAPACITIES FOR CONTROL AND TOLERANCE
    FOR STRESS IS SOMEWHAT LOWER THAN WOULD BE EXPECTED FOR THE
    MID-ADOLESCENT OR ADULT.

3. HOWEVER, CURRENTLY EXPERIENCED SITUATIONALLY RELATED STRESS HAS
    REDUCED THOSE CAPACITIES FOR CONTROL EVEN MORE, SO THAT THERE IS A
    CONSIDERABLE LIKELIHOOD OF IMPULSIVE-LIKE BEHAVIORS OR BEHAVIORS THAT
    ARE NOT WELL FORMULATED AND/OR IMPLEMENTED.

4. THIS IS THE TYPE OF PERSON WHO PREFERS TO DELAY MAKING RESPONSES IN
    COPING SITUATIONS UNTIL TIME HAS BEEN ALLOWED TO CONSIDER RESPONSE
    POSSIBILITIES AND THEIR POTENTIAL CONSEQUENCES. SUCH PEOPLE LIKE TO
    KEEP THEIR EMOTIONS ASIDE UNDER THESE CONDITIONS.

5. THIS PERSON TENDS TO USE DELIBERATE THINKING MORE FOR THE PURPOSE OF
    CREATING FANTASY THROUGH WHICH TO IGNORE THE WORLD THAN TO CONFRONT
    PROBLEMS DIRECTLY. THIS IS A SERIOUS PROBLEM BECAUSE THE BASIC COPING
    STYLE IS BEING USED MORE FOR FLIGHT THAN TO ADAPT TO THE EXTERNAL
    WORLD.

6. THIS TYPE OF PERSON IS NOT VERY FLEXIBLE IN THINKING, VALUES, OR
    ATTITUDES. IN EFFECT, PEOPLE SUCH AS THIS HAVE SOME DIFFICULTY IN
    SHIFTING PERSPECTIVES OR VIEWPOINTS.

7. THERE IS A STRONG POSSIBILITY THAT THIS IS A PERSON WHO PREFERS TO
    AVOID INITIATING BEHAVIORS, AND INSTEAD, TENDS TOWARDS A MORE PASSIVE
    ROLE IN PROBLEM SOLVING AND INTERPERSONAL RELATIONSHIPS.

8. THIS SUBJECT DOES NOT MODULATE EMOTIONAL DISPLAYS AS MUCH AS MOST
    ADULTS AND, BECAUSE OF THIS, IS PRONE TO BECOME VERY INFLUENCED BY
    FEELINGS IN MOST THINKING, DECISIONS, AND BEHAVIORS.

9. THIS IS AN INDIVIDUAL WHO DOES NOT EXPERIENCE NEEDS FOR CLOSENESS IN
    WAYS THAT ARE COMMON TO MOST PEOPLE. AS A RESULT, THEY ARE TYPICALLY
    LESS COMFORTABLE IN INTERPERSONAL SITUATIONS, HAVE SOME DIFFICULTIES

SUBJECT NAME:PROTOCOL.136   AGE:25 SEX:F   RACE:W MS:Liv ED:14

PAGE -2-

===

IN CREATING AND SUSTAINING DEEP RELATIONSHIPS, ARE MORE CONCERNED WITH
ISSUES OF PERSONAL SPACE, AND MAY APPEAR MUCH MORE GUARDED AND/OR
DISTANT TO OTHERS. IN SPITE OF THIS GUARDED INTERPERSONAL STANCE, SOME
OF THE DATA SUGGEST A PREFERENCE FOR DEPENDENCY ON OTHERS WHICH WOULD
SEEM TO CREATE A CONFLICT SITUATION. IN OTHER WORDS, THE SUBJECT WANTS
TO TAKE FROM OTHERS WHILE REMAINING DISTANT FROM THEM.

10.   THIS SUBJECT HAS AS MUCH INTEREST IN OTHERS AS DO MOST ADULTS AND
      CHILDREN.

11.   THIS SUBJECT HAS MORE NEGATIVE SELF ESTEEM OR SELF VALUE THAN IS
      COMMON FOR EITHER ADULTS OR CHILDREN. IT IS THE PRODUCT OF MAKING
      COMPARISONS OF ONESELF TO OTHERS, USUALLY PEERS, AND CONCLUDING THAT
      THOSE EXTERNAL MODELS ARE MORE ADEQUATE. THIS CREATES A TENDENCY TO
      DISLIKE ONESELF AND CAN BECOME THE NUCLEUS FROM WHICH FEELINGS OF
      INFERIORITY AND/OR INADEQUACY EVOLVE. IN LIGHT OF THIS FINDING, IT IS
      VERY IMPORTANT TO REVIEW THE OVERALL RECORD CAREFULLY TO OBTAIN A
      SENSE OF THE SELF IMAGE.

12.   THIS PERSON IS PRONE TO MUCH MORE INTROSPECTION THAN IS COMMON. WHEN
      THIS OCCURS, MUCH OF THE FOCUS CONCERNS NEGATIVE FEATURES PERCEIVED TO
      EXIST IN THE SELF IMAGE. THIS PROVOKES INTERNAL PAIN. SUCH A PROCESS
      IS OFTEN A PRECURSOR TO FEELINGS OF SADNESS, PESSIMISM, OR EVEN
      DEPRESSION.

13.   THIS SUBJECT IS VERY PRONE TO INTERPRET STIMULUS CUES IN A UNIQUE AND
      OVERPERSONALIZED MANNER. PEOPLE SUCH AS THIS OFTEN VIEW THEIR WORLD
      WITH THEIR OWN SPECIAL SET OF BIASES AND ARE LESS CONCERNED WITH BEING
      CONVENTIONAL AND/OR ACCEPTABLE TO OTHERS.

14.   THIS SUBJECT IS NOT AS ORIENTED AS MOST PEOPLE TO MAKING CONVENTIONAL
      AND/OR SOCIALLY ACCEPTABLE RESPONSES IN THOSE SITUATIONS WHERE THE
      CONVENTIONAL RESPONSE IS EASILY IDENTIFIED.

15.   THIS PERSON MAKES A MARKED EFFORT TO ORGANIZE STIMULI IN A MEANINGFUL
      AND INTEGRATED WAY.

16.   THIS IS A PERSON WHO TENDS TO USE MORE TIME AND ENERGY THAN IS
      NECESSARY TO ORGANIZE EACH NEW STIMULUS FIELD. SUCH PEOPLE PREFER TO
      HAVE AN ABUNDANCE OF INFORMATION AVAILABLE BEFORE DECISION MAKING AND
      TYPICALLY ARE MORE PERFECTIONISTIC IN MOST OF THEIR DAILY BEHAVIORS.
      THIS IS NOT NECESSARILY A LIABILITY. HOWEVER, THEY TEND TO
      UNDERESTIMATE TIME WHICH CAN BECOME A PROBLEM IN THOSE SITUATIONS
      WHERE TIME FACTORS ARE IMPORTANT. IN THAT THIS SUBJECT TENDS TO DELAY
      AND TO THINK THINGS THROUGH BEFORE MAKING RESPONSES, THIS
      CHARACTERISTIC COULD CREATE THE APPEARANCE OF RUMINATIVENESS.

17.   THIS PERSON PREFERS TO MINIMIZE AMBIGUITY. PEOPLE LIKE THIS OFTEN TRY
      TO MAKE A STIMULUS FIELD OVERLY PRECISE AND ARE EXCESSIVELY CONCERNED
      WITH BEING ACCURATE. THIS MAY BE A CHARACTERISTIC OF AN INDIVIDUAL
===

SUBJECT NAME:PROTOCOL.136   AGE:25   SEX:F   RACE:W   MS:Liv   ED:14

PAGE -3-

===
WHO SEEMS MORE PERFECTIONISTICALLY ORIENTED.

18.   IN SPITE OF THE FACT THAT THE SUBJECT MAKES AN EFFORT TO ORGANIZE
      STIMULI, THIS PERSON IS SOMEWHAT CONSERVATIVE IN SETTING GOALS.
      USUALLY PEOPLE LIKE THIS WANT TO COMMIT THEMSELVES ONLY TO OBJECTIVES
      WHICH OFFER A SIGNIFICANT PROBABILITY OF SUCCESS.

                    * * *   END OF REPORT   * * *

===

Author Index

Subject Index